Discovering QlikView

Tom Meers, Troy Gottfried, Joe Roberts

INFINITY
PUBLISHING

ISBN 978-0-7414-7900-6 Black and White Paperback
ISBN 978-0-7414-7901-3 Color Paperback
ISBN 978-0-7414-7902-0 eBook

Printed in the United States of America

Published October 2012

INFINITY PUBLISHING
1094 New DeHaven Street, Suite 100
West Conshohocken, PA 19428-2713
Toll-free (877) BUY BOOK
Local Phone (610) 941-9999
Fax (610) 941-9959
Info@buybooksontheweb.com
www.buybooksontheweb.com

Acknowledgements

We would like thank our friends and colleagues at QlikTech, Inc. for their assistance and input in completing this book. Special thanks go to Donald Farmer, who helped us to understand and share the fundamentals of the Business Discovery topic. We also very much appreciate the support and feedback from Cynthia Mathis without whom this book would have been much more difficult to complete. Several other friends at QlikTech continually encouraged and helped us through a process that took a lot longer than we anticipated. They have been a great group of people with whom to work and we wish them continued success. Finally, we would also like to thank the entire team at Result Data, especially Jeremy, Josh and Aaron for their passion and commitment to being the best at what they do. In many ways they're as much a part of this book as we are.

Introduction

This book has been developed by the principals at Result Data Consulting, Ltd; a Business Intelligence (BI) and data warehousing design-build firm offering BI solutions, consulting, software development and training in the BI field since 1997. Our background includes experience developing and implementing BI solutions from a variety of the leading BI vendors. Our team provides certified public and private training and consulting services to users of many of these products across a wide variety of organizations and markets.

It is the objective of this book to provide you with a foundation in how QlikView differs from other BI solutions. Additionally, and perhaps more importantly, the book is designed to provide a solid understanding of the QlikView software and how to use it at a reasonably advanced level. Although we have made an effort to ensure that beginners to QlikView and BI in general can benefit from this book, we have also included enough depth to help those interested in obtaining a deeper understanding of QlikView document creation. We have also included a limited amount of information about the QlikView server environment, which deserves its own book. The server information is aimed at helping you understand how QlikView documents are deployed and used from within a QlikView server environment so that you can incorporate considerations for how your QlikView documents will behave and look when deployed to a QlikView server.

When our BI team was introduced to QlikView a number of years ago, it took us a while to completely appreciate the doors it opens. Although we understood at a conceptual level how in-memory data allows for associations without the constraints imposed by relational database systems and OLAP based data cubes, we didn't immediately see how such features as ad hoc aggregation and load scripting completely change the way people can interact with data. QlikTech, the manufacturer of QlikView, provided and continues to provide a great deal of valuable information that helps with the paradigm shift that must occur for you to get your head around QlikView. We strongly recommend you register and participate in the online QlikView community at the QlikView Web site (community.qlikview.com), which is a free service.

Our hope is that after reading this book and using it to help in your development of QlikView documents, you will begin to see how QlikView changes the way in which you think about data. Whether your experience with data analysis and visualization prior to working with QlikView was based on using Excel or more advanced BI and query tools, we hope that this helps you see how the very innovative way in which QlikView leverages in-memory and associative data management opens doors for you and your users.

This book is structured in a manner designed to provide you with both a conceptual understanding and the specific steps for accomplishing various things in QlikView. It is not strictly a reference guide or a re-hash of the QlikView help files. Our goal is to provide insight into why certain things should be done certain ways while including the specifics of how to do them. For this reason you will find that there is substantial narrative surrounding the various steps to create QlikView content. Our approach has been developed as a result of field experience with a wide range of QlikView customers as well as from experience teaching QlikView in the classroom. We hope you find our insights valuable even if you establish different approaches to development as your QlikView skills improve.

Conventions

When describing how to use various aspects of QlikView we have employed the following conventions:

- *Italics* – Words that represent specific features and objects in QlikView, or elements of syntax will appear italicized. In some cases these items represent what you should click on or select; in others they represent what you type to create a script or expression.
- Expressions – Where expression syntax is provided as an example, it will appear in Courier 9pt font. Here's an example: `=Sum(Order Amount)`
- A plus sign (+) between two key names means that you must press those keys at the same time. For example Ctrl+Alt represent the simultaneous pressing of the CTRL and ALT keys on the keyboard.
- QlikView – When referring to the software that is QlikView, the terms "QlikView","QlikView for Windows" and "QlikView Windows client" are synonymous.

Table of Contents

Acknowledgements i

Introduction iii

Conventions v

Chapter 1: Understanding Data Analysis 1

What is Business Intelligence? 4

Business Discovery v. Business Intelligence 7

Data Structure: Transactional v. Analytical Data 10

Data Interactivity: Understanding the difference between reporting and analysis 11

Data Visualization and Dashboards: An Introduction 13

Chapter 2: What is QlikView 17

Understanding Associative Data Analysis 20

In-Memory Data Storage: Advantages and Disadvantages 21

QlikView Software and Architecture Overview 23

What is a QlikView Document? 24

How is Data Accessed and Managed in a QlikView Document? 27

What are QlikView Expressions? 27

How can a QlikView Document be shared? 29

Chapter 3: Accessing Data with QlikView 31

Data Loading Fundamentals 31

Important Data Load Terms 32

Understanding Functions, Commands, Statements and Clauses 34

The QlikView Data Load Process 35

Creating a Load Script 37

Database Sources 39

Relational Database Fundamentals 40

Accessing Databases in QlikView 41
The CONNECT Function 42
The SQL SELECT Function 45
Using the SQL Function to Access a Stored Procedure 46
The LOAD Function 47
File Based Data Sources 50
Types of File Data Sources 50
Loading Data from File Based Data Sources 52
File Data Source Considerations 54
Associating Data across Disparate Data Sources 57
Understanding the QlikView Data Model 58
How QlikView Associates Tables 58

Chapter 4: Creating a QlikView Document 61

Document Design Basics 62
Using the *Getting Started Wizard* to Create a Document 65
Creating a QlikView Document from the Ground Up 67
Loading Data 68
Using and Managing Tab Sheets 72
Creating and Using List Boxes 73
Adding Simple Charts and Gauges 76
Charting Tips 80
Navigating Selection History 81
Showing and Managing Current Selections 82
Creating and using Bookmarks 83

Chapter 5: Advanced Data Loading Techniques 87

Synthetic Keys 87
Managing and Optimizing In-Memory Tables 88
Joining Tables 88
Concatenating Tables 93
Performing Lookups with a Mapping Load 96
Addressing Complex Associations, Circular References 98
Multi-field Keys in QlikView 100
Slowly Changing Dimensions: A Common Data Challenge 101
Circular References 106

Creating Custom Date and Calendar Options....................... 108
Basic Manipulation of Date and Time Values.................. 108
Creating a Custom Calendar in the Load Script.............. 109
Translating Source Data Values into Meaningful Semantics 115
Adding Metadata to Enhance Usability........................... 116
Data Abstraction Using QlikView Data Files.................... 118

Chapter 6: Expressions and Set Analysis................................ 125
What are QlikView Expressions?.. 125
Expression Fundamentals.. 126
Expression Elements.. 129
Commenting.. 132
Understanding Functions.. 132
Performing Calculations.. 133
String Manipulation.. 134
Working with Date Values.. 138
Summarizing (Aggregating) Data....................................... 141
Basic Data Aggregation.. 141
Controlling Aggregation Scope (TOTAL, ALL)................. 143
Nesting Aggregated Values (AGGR)................................ 145
Grouping Values into Buckets.. 148
Set Analysis.. 149
Set Identifiers.. 150
Set Operators.. 152
Set Modifiers.. 152
Dollar Sign Expansion and Previous Period Comparison. 154
Conditional Calculations.. 157
Working with QlikView Variables...................................... 158
What do Variables do in QlikView?................................ 159
Variable Overview: Managing Document Variables....... 160
SET v. LET Statements.. 161
Using Variables.. 162
Expressions with Images.. 164

Chapter 7: Advanced Document Design................................. 167
List Boxes and User Selections.. 167
Changing Selection Appearance.................................... 168

Adding Columns to List Boxes 170
Spark Lines and other Mini Charts 172
Showing and Managing User Selections 175
Visualizing Data with Charts 177
Data Ink 178
Chart Usage 179
Comparisons: Showing distribution 180
Trends: Showing changes over time 187
Ratios: Showing values relative to a total 191
Correlation: Showing value proximity 195
Chart Tips and Tricks 206
Data Tables & Detail Level Data 208
Using Straight Tables 209
Using Pivot Tables 216
Creating Search Capabilities 218
Understanding Associative Searching 219
Searching from List Boxes 219
Types of Searches 221
Searching Using an Expression 222
Creating a Search Object 223
Layout and Object Management 224
Leveraging Tab Sheets 225
Container Objects 227
Object Linking 230
Comparative Analysis (Alternate States) 231
Working with Data from Users 235
Other Topics 237
Actions 237
Triggers 238

Chapter 8: Reporting, Printing and Exporting 241

Object Printing and Exporting 241
Object Printing 241
Object Exporting 242
QlikView Reporting 242
Types of Reports 243
Creating a QlikView Report 247

Editing an Existing Report 250
Previewing and Printing Reports 250
QlikView Report Best Practices 251
Managing QlikView Objects for Reporting 251
Create Report Selections Tab Sheet 252
Report Development 253
Adding Pages 253
Managing Report Data Selections 254
QlikView Possible Values 254
Showing Selections on the Report 255
Headers and Footers 256
Report Headers and Footers 256
Listing, Grouping and Sub-Totaling Data in a Report with Table Objects 258
Pivot Table Formatting 259
Managing Borders 261
Formatting Tags for Dimensions and Expressions 261
Custom Formatting of Cell Attributes in Pivot and Straight Tables 262
Report Banding and Looping 265
What does Banding do? 265
Activating Banding at the Page Level 265
Controlling Banding with Selections 266

Chapter 9: Sharing and Securing QlikView Documents 267

Sharing a QlikView Document: Two Approaches 268
QlikView Servers and Clients: An Introduction 268
QlikView Server Features 269
QlikView Clients 270
QlikView Editions and Licensing 271
QlikView Editions 272
Connecting to a QlikView Server 275
QlikView Server Deployment 277
Deploying a Document to QlikView Server 278
Securing Documents on a QlikView Server 279
Server Authentication 280
Server Authorization 281

Securing and Sharing Load Script Connection Strings..... 281
Sharing QlikView Documents without a QlikView Server 283
How to Share Documents 283
Important Considerations when Sharing Documents..... 284
Securing QlikView Documents for Distribution 285
Protecting the Load Script 287
Securing Data (Section Access) 288

Chapter 10: Best Practices 301
Load Script Best Practices 302
User Interface Design Best Practices 305
Data Model Best Practices 309
General Settings 313
User Preferences 313
Document Properties 314
Designing for Mobile Best Practices 315
iPad 315

Appendix A: Formatting Tips, Keyboard Shortcuts and Command Line Options 319
Using Formatting Attributes on Dimensions and Expressions 319
Text Color 321
Text Format 322
Background Color 323
Line Format 323
The Pie Slice Attribute for Pie Charts 324
The Show Value Attribute 324
Formatting Masks (numbers, dates etc.) 324
Chart Numbers (Format Pattern) 325
General Keyboard Shortcuts 325
Using Keyboard Shortcuts and the Mouse to Manipulate Charts 327
QlikView Command Line Options 327

Chapter 1: Understanding Data Analysis

The process of analyzing data is fundamental to how all of us perceive and interact with the world. Data analysis is arguably the single most important activity in which you participate on a daily basis, and without the ability to analyze data you would have a very difficult time surviving. You use your senses to collect data and organize it into various associated groups. These associated groups become the foundation for percepts (perceptions). When they are combined you begin to conceptualize the world around you. This process of data analysis enables you to make decisions based on complex associations and summarizations of the data available to you. As anyone will tell you, sometimes the initial collection of data (percepts) and resulting concepts are less than accurate, resulting in an unexpected experience. This causes you to observe and incorporate new data, which allows you to learn from your experiences. This process is repeated throughout your life. You likely don't think too much about it, but your very existence is fundamentally dependent on your ability to access, organize and analyze data. It is innate.

When it comes to business and organizational data analysis, your ability to organize data and draw conclusions may not be as obvious and natural as it is for other aspects of your life. Understanding and acting on business data usually proves challenging to even the most adept and experienced business people if the data or work experience is new. Even repetitive scenarios, when they require extensive analysis of data, can be difficult. This is, in part, because of the overwhelming amount of data created by organizations and the speed with which the data is changing. Organizations such as companies, governments and associations, by definition, are collections of people. When people interact they frequently create very complex scenarios. These scenarios interrelate in an infinite number of ways, resulting in a large amount of complex data. Additionally, the data you encounter within your organization is largely based on text and numbers, narrowing the number of senses and areas of your brain you can leverage to analyze and understand it. For these reasons, and others, the common experience of analyzing business data is often less than satisfactory for the decision making that is required. As a result, business decisions are often made on the basis of intuition. Intuition is great; however it is unpredictable and inconsistent, making it a poor substitute for conclusions drawn from facts and logic. Yet your ability to gather vast quantities of facts and apply complex logic to such a collection is limited. This is fundamentally why computers came into existence. Computers make it possible to deal with very large volumes of data and they give you the ability to apply logic in the form of rules to process data.

Conventionally, data analysis is based on the concept of summarizing data into one or more levels of categorization. This is commonly known as data reporting, or just "reporting." Reports, by their most common definition, represent a predetermined and consistent structure into which data is inserted. Reports are processed periodically to provide updated summarizations of processes or events and have become the foundation for many organizational decisions. While some situations are addressed in a satisfactory manor through the use of reporting, many others are not. Yet, many organizations continue to use reporting as the only means through which decision making is supported. To quote Bernard Baruch, an advisor to several U.S. presidents, "when all you have is hammer, everything looks like a nail." Yet, not everything is a nail and new ways of experiencing data are not only necessary, but inevitable. Reporting, for all of its success, does not provide you with a high degree of interactivity. Some reports can be driven by parameters that prompt you for input, such as a date range or set of regions to be used in filtering the results and affecting summarizations in the report, but this requires you to run the report repeatedly to compare results for different ranges or sets. One advantage of reports is that they can provide access to detail level data. In some cases reports can contain hundreds or even thousands of pages. However, the consensus in most organizational environments is that such output isn't necessary and is rarely useful. The more common scenario is a grouped report that shows subtotals and grand totals. Reports may also include charts which help the user conceptualize the data. However, reports carry with them a common set of problems. Often a report provides only part of the summarization and data needed to make a decision. In some cases a report may contain so much data and so many summarizations that it becomes difficult to understand, rendering it useless. This is often the case when a single report is provided to address a wide variety of information needs.

Other common approaches to data analysis include the use of spreadsheet tools such as Microsoft Excel. This approach allows you to organize and visualize the data in a variety of ways. Excel is a very popular software tool and unlikely to be completely replaced by other tools. This is true despite a desire by IT departments and software vendors to eliminate it in favor of more controllable and predictable solutions. The benefit of Excel and similar unstructured software tools is that they liberate you to interact with the data in whatever way is needed or desired. You can sort, group and subtotal data in Excel with relative ease. Yet, Excel and similar tools present a number of problems that challenge organizations in profound ways. A few of them include the following:

1. **Data Quality**: Because Excel allows users to not only import data from trusted sources but also to manually change and augment the data, the results can have questionable validity.
2. **Data Volume**: Excel is not engineered to handle large volumes of data. Even though new technology from Microsoft is seeking to address this problem, users who need to summarize hundreds of millions or billions of data records will be challenged or may not be able to accomplish what they want using Excel.

3. **User Skills**: Excel and similar tools require training and experience that is more significant than most managers realize. Many users do not possess the necessary skills to get what they want from these tools. In addition, the learning curve is often too steep for them to overcome. Users can create erroneous or inaccurate results because they lack the requisite abilities to properly leverage the tools.

For those users with the appropriate skills and a limited set of data, as well as confidence in their ability to accurately augment or change data, Excel and similar tools may fit well. Other users, most users in fact, require a more comprehensive and standardized approach to data analysis in which complex logic and the structure of summarized data is predetermined to assist them in making sense of the information provided.

What is Business Intelligence?

Business Intelligence, commonly referred to as "BI," is a term originally created in the 1950's to describe the interrelationship of facts. The term has since been accepted across industries as a reference for the collection of tools, methods and processes that support decision-making based on digital data. If something can be represented digitally, it has the potential to become part of a BI system through which it can play a role in decision-making. While BI content can include such items as digitized photos, audio or video, the vast majority of BI data is represented by text and numbers.

In its modern uses BI encapsulates a wide variety of software solutions, all of which have something to do with the organization, summarization and presentation of data. In virtually all cases BI content plays a role in some sort of decision making. To help with understanding the breadth of technologies associated with BI, our team has created "the five pillars of business intelligence," which is a concept we use to help managers and end users understand all of the things BI can do for them.

The first pillar is called "Collection." It represents the process of gathering important information from one or more systems, organizing that information into meaningful categories and storing the information either temporarily or permanently outside of the originating system structure.

The Collection pillar can be represented by several technology concepts common to BI. They include:

1. Source Systems
2. Data Warehouses, Data Marts and Data Stores
3. ETL (Extract, Transform, Load) processes
4. Data Semantics

Data collection is perhaps the most challenging and critical aspect of BI. Preparing data for specific analytical needs is difficult and usually requires special software processes to be created. QlikView is somewhat unique in that it addresses data collection as part of the same tool used to present data to users. QlikView is more comprehensive in this respect than most other BI tools.

The second pillar of BI is "Reporting." Reporting, as mentioned previously, represents the preformatted and summarized presentation of data. It allows for low levels of user interaction such as parameter prompting, which alters what data is presented in a report. QlikView includes basic reporting and report distribution capabilities, but reporting is not what QlikView is designed to do. QlikView is fundamentally targeted at data interaction and, in many cases, makes the need for conventional reporting obsolete.

The third pillar of Business Intelligence is "Analysis." This area of BI provides you with the ability to interact with the data by selecting and filtering categories of data known as dimensions. Analysis is typically associated with a category of software tools that provide Online Analytical Processing or "OLAP." OLAP makes it possible to see summaries such as counts, sums and averages at various intersections of dimensional data. For example, OLAP might enable you to see sales amounts by both *region* and *product line* at the same time, and then filter the results by either or both of those dimensions. OLAP also includes predetermined hierarchies, which provide you with the ability to drill down to more granular levels of data. For example, you might drill from region to city to see the sales amount for cities within a given region. While powerful, OLAP imposes limitations on how you analyze your data. QlikView addresses these issues by making data associative. This is a core principle in how QlikView changes BI and one of the reasons for its rapid acceptance and growth in the BI market.

The fourth pillar of BI is "Visualization." This area is typified by the concept of data dashboards, which provide charts, gauges and other visually oriented representations of your data. Visualization is aimed at combining the analytical interaction found in the third pillar (Analysis) with the charts sometimes found in the first pillar (Reporting). The result is a highly summarized view of the data that can be manipulated to answer questions at a high level. For technical reasons, dashboards rarely offer access to detail level data. They can also be difficult to create and maintain because a great deal of consideration must be given to how the data is prepared for them. QlikView makes the creation and evolution of visualizations and dashboards easy and it also allows for access to detail level data. This combination is a key value proposition for QlikView and rarely seen in other tools.

The fifth pillar of Business Intelligence is "Discovery." This is perhaps the most modern addition to the BI landscape and may represent the greatest potential for BI. Discovering data in the past was a process limited to high-level statistical tools via a process known as "data mining." Conventional BI analysis does not address this need well because of two limitations. First, OLAP based systems require very specific planning. This reduces the user's ability to interact with the data because OLAP solutions must operate on the basis of a known set of measures, dimensions and hierarchies. Second, BI solutions were originally designed to address technical problems associated with summarizing large volumes of data. This results in an architecture that forces users to analyze data based on predefined assumptions. With the advent of QlikView, these limitations have been overcome. Today, data discovery is a very real possibility for anyone interested in exploring data and it can be done in a more versatile manner than ever before.

Business Discovery v. Business Intelligence

The conventional approach to BI has proven to be effective in most cases. However, it is frequently found to be difficult, time consuming and expensive to implement. It also fails to provide a universally acceptable way to explore data. A new approach to Business Intelligence is emerging that addresses these concerns without reducing the value or reliability found in conventional BI solutions. Known as "Business Discovery," this new approach promises to be more agile by placing more power directly in the hands of business users while simultaneously revolutionizing the way in which data is accessed and organized for analysis. It is championed by QlikView and recognized by leading industry analysts such as the Gartner Group. Much of this book will focus on how QlikView facilitates new ways to discover associations in your data while making it easier and faster to access and work with complex data from a variety of sources.

Traditionally, BI has been centered on IT processes and practices. When the need for online reporting, data analysis or dashboards becomes significant, the IT department is engaged and the processes for platform implementation, content creation and data presentation follow a path not different from that of implementing other information systems. The reason for this is simple: Conventional BI requires investment in planning, technical expertise and infrastructure before any value can be realized. Failing to invest in these areas represents an increased likelihood of a failed BI implementation. This centralized approach to the implementation of BI solutions carries with it several challenges, each of which introduces the potential of lower return on investment for the organization. First, planning a

BI implementation tends to be more focused on standardizing how the organization should structure and analyze its data than on anything technical. Getting senior management to agree on terms, facts and dimensions of the data can be a daunting task. This, in turn, makes the planning process even more challenging because the skills to direct facilitated sessions, create data dictionaries and manage data semantics are rarely found within the IT department. The skills and the knowledge needed to complete these tasks are more often found within the business units and with outside consultants. Secondly, very specific technical capabilities are needed to create BI content. Skills in conventional software tools, such as Excel or software development languages, are not adequate to design and deploy BI content. This further complicates the BI implementation effort because the IT department must learn new technologies, rely on outside help or engage in both of these efforts simultaneously. Finally, after the first two challenges have been met, there is profound likelihood that the content and data management processes produced during implementation will fail to fully meet the user requirements due to the time it takes to complete them. These challenges result in a vicious scrap and rebuild cycle for BI content maintenance, which is costly but critical to realizing ongoing value from the investment.

The solution to the IT centric dilemma for BI implementation is to move the emphasis of BI content creation away from the centralized IT department and toward the edges of the organization where the users reside. People from various departments and organizational units perform the tasks associated with planning, operating and improving the organization regularly. They represent the actual users of information. By moving BI content emphasis from the center to the edges of the organization you realize the real potential of BI. The key is making it easy enough for business users to participate in BI content creation. When this is accomplished, new dynamics act on the BI content creation processes that drive value back to the organization in new ways. Part of this new dynamic is represented by the ability of users across departments to collaborate on the way in which data is structured and visualized without requiring IT expertise. In essence, the creation of BI content becomes an "ad hoc" process rather than a centralized one. Most departmental organizations already operate this way. It represents a fundamental reason for why unstructured content such as Excel and Word files remain so popular. Until BI is designed to facilitate this collaborative approach to data analysis, its value will remain limited to those situations that lend themselves to highly structured analysis and reporting.

To improve the return on a BI investment you must improve the consumption of BI content both qualitatively and quantitatively. This requires you to consider viewing BI content from a consumption perspective rather than from a production perspective. Information is consumed through its association to other information, not through its position within a hierarchy of information. In other words, users access and consume information in unpredictable ways and when you impose too many rules on how they access and use information, they stop using it. By enabling users to interact more freely with information and allowing them to collaborate on how BI content is defined and used, the idea of “Business Discovery” is realized. Business Discovery is rooted in a more established concept known as data discovery. This is the process through which users explore new and unique relationships in the data that have not been previously identified as meaningful. Business discovery might include situations where you search and select certain data elements based on a real world need and, as a result, begin to understand new things about how the associated dimensions of data interrelate. Such relationships may be independent of shared measures or facts, which further challenges the conventional approach to BI. For example, you might want to see a list of customers who ordered more than a certain amount of product this year. By finding these customers through an associative search of the data you might then select them creating a grouping. If the BI content is designed appropriately you may notice that these customers also reside in a given region. Prior to your analysis, no known association between that region and that product existed. This is business discovery, and it represents how BI is evolving to free information workers in profound ways.

QlikView is recognized by industry analysts as the leader in business discovery. This is in part because of its advances in the areas of in-memory storage and associative logic. However, QlikView also drives the business discovery concept by adding very strong capabilities in visualization, associative search and expression writing (formula creation). We hope to show you how to leverage these and other advanced features in this book.

Data Structure: Transactional v. Analytical Data

Understanding that data can be divided into different categories based on how it is created and used is critical to enabling you to produce and leverage data analysis. Originally, computer systems were engineered to address transactional data which represents the collection of small amounts of data from repeated processes (transactions). This data is grouped into structurally consistent sets representing what we call a transaction in the real world. Each transaction and its associated data set are finite. In other words, transactional data represents a potentially high number of relatively small data sets where each data set is identical in structure. Common examples of transactional data include bank deposits and withdrawals, customer orders, event registrations, etc.... Because transactional data is voluminous, it is a natural target for the data processing capabilities of computers. Collecting, organizing and managing thousands or millions of transactions and their data was, and is, a strong opportunity for improving operational efficiency across all types of organizations. Systems such as Enterprise Resource Planning (ERP) and Customer Relationship Management (CRM) have become the foundation of most business system architectures.

Inevitably, once millions of transaction records had been collected and processed it became apparent that by combining the data from these records you could better understand the associated business trends and relationships. This revelation brought about the idea that data should be organized in such a way as to support analysis. This restructuring of data is referred to as analytical data and it represents the birth of several technological concepts aimed at enabling large volumes of data to be stored and summarized. Among these technologies are data warehouses and online analytical processing (OLAP) systems. Analytical data differs from transactional data in two distinct ways:

1. Analytical data is usually de-normalized, which means that redundancy in the data is common. Transactional data is structured (normalized) to reduce redundancy. This allows data to be organized into categories known as dimensions, which enable users to analyze it in a meaningful way.
2. Analytical data use typically represents a small number of data queries that involve large amounts of data. Transactional data use represents a large number of data queries involving small amounts of data.

Data Interactivity: Understanding the difference between reporting and analysis

The way in which you interact with data directly affects your decision making processes. In some cases you are simply referencing data in order to lookup a given value. In these cases conventional BI reporting is often adequate. Yet even simple queries of structured data, as found with reporting, can be tedious when reviewing an online or printed report. This is because in most cases such reports are designed to address a multitude of needs. Your specific reference request is one of them, but there is likely much more data presented in the report than you need. For this reason reports can slow you down, but they are typically effective in providing the data you need. Traditionally, they have also been inexpensive to create and maintain. The result is a tradeoff. The organization saves money implementing a reporting solution at the expense of slowing down repetitive decision making processes. There is a point at which the cost associated with slow repetitive processes exceeds the cost to implement a more sophisticated solution. That point is usually when several users regularly need to look at several data elements in comparison to each other. To do this with reports requires you to open and run multiple reports and/or run one or more reports multiple times, entering different parameter values each time. The next step in your process is for you to write down values from each of the reports so you can compare them. This is often done in Excel, or the data is sometimes exported to Excel where the real analysis is performed.

When the need for accessing and comparing multiple data elements becomes profound, it is typically addressed through the deployment and use of an OLAP solution. In such cases, research is performed to determine which data elements are needed and dimensional hierarchies are created in conjunction with various numeric measures. This combination of dimensions and measures is materialized in the form of a data cube or semantic layer, which optimizes the data for interaction. The OLAP solution offers you an interface, commonly known as an OLAP worksheet, which allows your users to dynamically change their view of the data. It works, and in some cases it works well. Because your users are able to interact with the data without waiting for the report to be reprocessed, their time to obtain an answer is reduced. OLAP also provides the ability to change filtering of the data and a limited amount of data restructuring. This sets it apart from reporting because users are able to see the effect of their changes as they make them. There is no need to write anything down or to export the data in most cases.

The problem with OLAP solutions is that they require a very specific definition of dimensions (categories of data) and measures (numeric summaries). OLAP systems prepare the data by pre-calculating the measure values at every intersection and, in the case of dimensional hierarchies, at every level of the dimensions. This is sometimes referred to as "pre-aggregation" and it is the Achilles' heel of OLAP based systems. By determining the way in which dimensions are structured in advance and by pre-calculating measures you create a scenario in which the user has a limited set of analysis options. If the hierarchy of a dimension is not configured appropriately for your user, then the user will not be able to get what is needed from the solution. This results in two problems. First, the OLAP solution only works well for a small number of users. Second, it is often necessary to modify the OLAP design frequently to address unforeseen needs. Too much modification can result in an OLAP data cube that performs poorly.

QlikView dramatically changes the analysis landscape for both users and those developing and maintaining the BI content. Because QlikView combines two relatively new ideas in BI, it is able to offer a more comprehensive and versatile analysis experience to users while reducing the effort needed to create and maintain content. With QlikView there is no need to pre-calculate measures and there are no predefined hierarchies. While hierarchies can be defined where desired, users may calculate values based on any combination of dimensions and numeric values (facts), resulting in their own custom measures. They may also create their own intersections between any of the available dimensions and filter dimensional data at any level. This approach to analysis enhances your ability to quickly produce a solution that requires little on-going maintenance. It addresses the problems found in both reporting and conventional OLAP based solutions. As you begin to work with QlikView, these advantages will become evident.

Data Visualization and Dashboards: An Introduction

Among the fastest growing segments of the BI market is an area called "visualization," which is represented by the creation and use of dashboards. It seems most executives are either using a dashboard solution to manage at a high level or they plan to implement one. Dashboards, at their most basic level, are nothing more than a collection of summarized data which are presented in visual form. They typically include charts, gauges and scorecard indicators that help you understand the status or performance of something or someone. The visualizations found in a dashboard often include reference indicators to make it clear if a given value is good or bad. For example, a gauge may have red, yellow and green background segments so that you know what the gauge's needle (indicator) represents and if action is necessary. For a dashboard to have real value it is commonly assumed that the dashboard must include user controls that provide the user with selection and navigation options. This makes the dashboard interactive and differentiates it from a report with a chart in it. With a dashboard, the user may change values and see the effects of such changes in the charts immediately. Dashboards are sometimes viewed as a friendlier and more limited version of OLAP, which require little or no training. For this reason they have become very popular.

There are a wide variety of technologies available for producing dashboard interfaces. QlikView is one of them, and is widely recognized as one of the best. However, QlikView is much more than a dashboard tool. As you will see, it is unique in its ability to create dashboards that encompass strong analysis and detail level reporting features. To understand how QlikView is different from other tools you need to learn how most dashboard tools work. A typical approach to dashboard creation involves the creation of a database or data cube with aggregate data (data that is pre-summarized). This is similar to how OLAP solutions work. The dashboard interface is tied to the underlying data through a series of queries that retrieve that data based on selections you make while using the dashboard. In such common dashboard scenarios, you must have the appropriate architecture in place to build and use the dashboard. This includes data sources (source systems from which the data originally comes), a database for storing aggregate level data, a BI server to host the dashboard as well as a Web server to provide access. QlikView allows you to create a dashboard without the conventional architecture found in most BI solutions. All you need is a copy of QlikView on your computer and access to one or more underlying data sources. Once you complete a dashboard you can deploy it to a QlikView server where it is made available to any number of users who have Web browsers or their own copies of QlikView.

QlikView provides the charts and other visualizations common to all dashboard tools. These include such elements as bar charts, line charts, area charts, pie charts, gauges and the like. However, one of the features that set it apart is the inclusion of analysis components such as pivot tables, straight tables with drill down features, search boxes, multi-column pick lists and others. These features, combined with a very robust expression writing capability, make it possible to create sophisticated dashboards that include advanced analysis and drill-down to detail level data. Most dashboard tools do not offer this as part of the dashboard interface. They instead allow for linking to other types of BI content, such as reports, to show detail level data or OLAP interfaces for more robust analysis. While these tools work, they make the effort to create and maintain a unified interface for your users difficult and time consuming. As you will see, QlikView is more than a tool for creating dashboards.

Chapter 2: What is QlikView

QlikView is not new. It has been around since 1993 and has grown at an unprecedented rate since then. However, it has only been in the last few years that QlikView has been recognized by industry analysts such as the Aberdeen Group and Gartner Group as a top tier Business Intelligence (BI) tool set. This is in part because of changes QlikTech made to the QlikView product line, but it likely has more to do with the fact that computer hardware and operating system technology has evolved to a point where QlikView's in-memory data management can now be leveraged for very large sets of data. This, combined with an innovative approach to product design, has propelled QlikView to a leadership position and started a new era in data analysis and visualization software. We believe QlikView will continue to grow in popularity for a number of years. Other software vendors have already begun efforts to develop competing solutions. However, QlikTech, the creator of QlikView, enjoys a substantial market lead and its patented technology ensures that QlikView will remain at the forefront for some time.

At its most basic level, QlikView is best viewed as a development environment for creating analytical solutions. As you will see, QlikView provides a comprehensive set of features that allow you to design and develop intuitive yet sophisticated user interfaces for analyzing and visualizing data. Unlike many other BI tools it also provides a built-in data management capability. While it is easy to begin using QlikView, the depth and comprehensiveness of the product is substantial, and many who use it are unaware of all that it can do. QlikView's vast array of capabilities puts it in a class of its own. The content you can create with QlikView can address a wide variety of data analysis, reporting and data discovery needs. For this reason, the content created by the QlikView software is often referred to as an "application." However, QlikView content is commonly referred to as a “QlikView Document,” and in some cases it is called a “dashboard.” But referring to QlikView content as a dashboard is to sell it short, for it is much more than a dashboard development tool.

The complete QlikView solution is comprised of a few key components. Each of these components plays a part in creating, deploying and consuming QlikView documents. They include:

- **QlikView for Windows**: A Windows based software application that is used to create and maintain QlikView documents. This is the full development tool in which original QlikView documents must be created and edited. It’s worth noting that this component was called “QlikView Developer” in older versions and is sometime still referred to that way.
- **QlikView Server**: A Microsoft Windows based server that allows Web browsers and mobile users to access QlikView documents. QlikView server manages the sharing of documents and makes them available to a variety of QlikView clients including Web browsers, iPads, Smart Phones and others.
- **QlikView Publisher**: Publisher is an add on to QlikView server that automates content management tasks and makes it possible to distribute QlikView documents and associated reports on a managed basis. This module is not always needed and may be added at any time. The QlikView server includes the core components needed to deploy and manage QlikView documents independently of this module.
- **QlikView Clients**: These are various interfaces that allow users to access and work with QlikView documents. Examples include clients for Apple iPhone and iPad, a Web browser client and others.

While we will cover some information concerning QlikView server, this book is primarily focused on QlikView for Windows, the Windows based content creation tool. QlikView for Windows is available in two editions at the time of the writing of this book. They include personal edition (PE) and a licensed edition. While it is beyond the scope of this book to detail the licensing options, which may change from time to time, an explanation of the differences between these two editions in important.

Personal Edition: QlikView Personal Edition (PE) is a free, fully functional version of QlikView for Windows. You can download it from the QlikView Web site. It is provided on a free and perpetual basis, which means it won't time out. It is also unfettered. That is to say, it is fully functional and not restricted in terms of the type of content you can create or what you can do with your content from within the PE software. Its only limitation is that when you create a QlikView document using PE, you cannot share it. Nor can you open QlikView documents created by other PE users or licensed users. The document is essentially locked to the computer on which it was created. If you upgrade to the licensed edition, or share the QlikView document with a licensed user of QlikView for Windows, the document cannot be opened again in Personal Edition. This means that if you create something in PE and then purchase a license you can continue using it, but once it is opened in a licensed edition, it cannot be used in any PE version again. In some cases QlikTech will provide unlocked QlikView documents that work in PE. The purpose of these documents is to facilitate training and information from QlikTech. These are the only exceptions to the PE limitation.

Licensed Edition: The licensed edition of QlikView for Windows is no different than the Personal Edition from a features perspective. It is the same software, the same installation, the same code base. The only difference is that a key code or license lease has been applied to what otherwise would be a PE installation. You do not have to reinstall to convert from PE to a licensed edition. To complete the conversion from PE to a licensed edition, you have two options. You can purchase and install a Local Client license key code, which unlocks the sharing capabilities, but does not give you access to a QlikView server. If you have a Local Client license and attempt to access a QlikView server, you will either be rejected or (depending on the server configuration) you will consume one of the server licenses. The other option is for you to lease a Client Access License (CAL) from a QlikView Server. When you lease a license from a server you unlock your Personal Edition for sharing and you have access to the server for deploying and accessing server based QlikView documents. However, it is important to note that there are different kinds of server licenses and some of them limit your ability to create and access QlikView documents. You should check with your QlikView Solution Provider or QlikView representative to better understand these licenses.

Understanding Associative Data Analysis

QlikView manages data differently than other analysis tools. It associates data rather than relating it. This may seem like a semantic difference, but it is not. While QlikView accesses data from a variety of data sources such as relational databases, flat files, Web services, XML sources and others; once data is brought into QlikView it becomes "QlikView" data. The data loading process allows you to structure the data into tables based on your needs. You are not required to honor the table structures of the underlying data sources. The QlikView tables are then associated with each other based on common fields (columns). This allows QlikView to cross reference data in almost any way needed by the user. The result is that users no longer have to follow planned paths through the data when performing analysis. The most common example of this is when users create their own hierarchies, which may span several tables. Another feature of associated data is the ability for users to search across tables and fields for a match on a value.

Because data is associated and not related in a conventional way, you are able to work with all of the data at the same time. This means that when you select one or more values from a list box in QlikView, the associated values in other areas are highlighted, but the unassociated values or "excluded" values remain visible. They are, however, grayed out to show they are not related to the selected values. These excluded values are still accessible to you and can be selected to invert the selection scenario. This is very different from how other analysis tools work. The reason for this is that all of the data is in memory and cross associated at all times. Unlike other tools, QlikView does not query or filter the data while you interact with it. It treats all values as being in one of three states: selected, associated or excluded. Data is never removed from a QlikView document, but rather, it is hidden or visually altered to indicate its state relative to what the user has selected. Additionally, QlikView's expression feature includes a sophisticated capability called "set analysis," which allows you to programmatically create and work with sub sets of the data relative to what has been selected. These capabilities make it possible to provide very robust analytical interfaces and options for your users.

In-Memory Data Storage: Advantages and Disadvantages

It is important to understand that there are two types of computer memory. Long term, or nonvolatile memory, is represented by storage devices such as hard drives, disk arrays, optical media and similar technologies. We typically refer to this type of memory as "storage" because it allows data to be stored when the computer is powered off and then retrieved later. The second type of memory is volatile memory, which is often referred to as random access memory or "RAM." This is short term memory and operates much faster than the storage devices used to retain data when the computer is off. We simply refer to this type of memory as "memory." It is not persisted when the computer is powered off. Originally, computer memory (RAM) was very limited. As BI and other analytical software evolved it had to account for the limited amount of memory space available in most computers. This resulted in software that moved data to and from storage devices based on user needs. Because storage devices are very slow compared to computer memory it was important to minimize the amount of data that moved into memory. For this reason most BI software has a very formal structure around how data is presented to the user. The common example of this is an OLAP data cube, which imposes a predefined set of dimensions and hierarchies on the user.

As computer hardware evolved, a concept known as Moore's Law was established. Moore's Law states that the processing and memory capacity of computers is growing at an exponential rate resulting in the doubling of capacity approximately every two years. This has resulted in computers that have much more memory than ever before. Now that such memory capacity exists, analytical software has more working memory available. Unfortunately, however, most analytical software was designed for computers with limited memory. QlikView was not. QlikView was built from the ground up to store all of its data in memory. Other software vendors are now beginning to develop similar solutions, but you will find that none of them can do this as well as QlikView currently does. This is in part because QlikTech has patents on some of the methods QlikView uses to manage data in memory.

By placing all of the relevant user data in memory QlikView can allow you to interact with the data in ways that are impossible with conventional BI software. This means that you can cross relate fields of data freely and you can summarize and calculate data without restrictions. It is possible, and common, to have millions of rows of data on which you perform dozens of calculations in real-time. There's no need to re-query data to produce new summarizations or derived values. With QlikView's in-memory architecture you can also organize the data into custom hierarchies. This means that you don't have to define hierarchical levels such as geographies, product lines or organization charts when the data is loaded. You, or your users, may do this at will.

It is important to understand that having the data in memory doesn't mean that QlikView must reload the data from the original data sources every time you wish to use a QlikView document. The QlikView document will retain the data it contains by writing it to disk when the data load occurs. The data is then transferred into memory for use by you or the user. If the document is hosted on a QlikView server the in-memory data is shared across multiple users. There are obvious advantages to having the data loaded into memory. However, there are also disadvantages to an in-memory scenario. Among them is the fact that a significant amount of memory is needed if you have a large amount of data to analyze. QlikView handles this situation by compressing the data, which helps to reduce the amount of memory needed. It also includes a very robust data loading mechanism, which enables you to optimize memory use. The combination of these features is one of things that set QlikView apart from other in-memory solutions. As you begin to work with QlikView you will see how the load scripting capabilities allow you to do some very creative things to reduce the amount of memory needed to get all of your data loaded and available for analysis.

QlikView Software and Architecture Overview

Among the many things we like about QlikView is the fact that its architecture is reasonably straight forward. QlikView for Windows, the Windows application used to create and edit QlikView documents, includes both data loading and user interface tools, eliminating the need for multiple tool sets. Other BI tools separate these functions and require content developers to learn several different tools and how they integrate. With QlikView only one tool is needed to access, load, manage and present data. It is a complete solution even if you choose not to deploy a QlikView server.

From an architectural point of view it may help to think of QlikView for Windows as a software tool that is similar to Microsoft Excel. Both tools allow you import data from various data sources, even though most Excel users either key or paste data into Excel. Both tools allow you to manipulate the data and both allow you to present the data in both tabular and graphical forms. Also, both Excel and QlikView store your formatting of the data and the data itself in local files that can be accessed later. In the case of Excel, the file (based on its extension) is referred to an XLSX or XLS file (depending on the release); in QlikView the file is referred to as a QVW file. However, QlikView is profoundly different from Excel. It is designed to allow you to access, manage and work with hundreds of millions, or even billions of rows of data. Excel is limited to one million rows or less. QlikView is also more versatile in the way it allows you to present the data. It allows you to layout tab sheets in a free form manner and does not require the data to be displayed in rows and columns. QlikView also includes a variety of application development style features such as variable declaration and a built in macro and expression language. These offer more advanced control over the data and user interface than other tools. For these reasons it is important to understand that QlikView for Windows offers a deeper development capability than what you will find in most other analytical tools. It may also require more learning. Hopefully, this book will provide you with much of the necessary knowledge to begin using QlikView at a relatively advanced level.

What is a QlikView Document?

At its heart, QlikView content is comprised of a single file called a QVW. This is how the QlikView document file is stored on disk (with a .QVW file extension). A QlikView document contains all of the data, semantics and metadata needed to allow one or more users to work interactively with QlikView data. This can be done by providing each user with a copy of the file, in which case each user must have a licensed edition of QlikView for Windows. Alternatively, the file can be copied to a QlikView server and deployed for multiple users, who may consume the document from various QlikView clients such as the Web browser AJAX client on a desktop or a mobile device such as an iPad.

A QlikView document's metadata contains the information necessary to facilitate connection to the underlying data sources from which the data is loaded. It also includes a load script which controls how the source data is organized, altered and associated during a data load. Other parts of the QlikView metadata include the definitions for tab sheets, sheet objects such as charts, pick lists and tables as well as expression syntax for summaries and calculations used in sheet objects. By combining the data and associated settings, expression syntax and user interface properties, a QlikView document becomes a transportable piece of BI content that can be distributed and shared.

From a user perspective, a QlikView document is comprised of several key objects and features. The combination of these allows the user to navigate, select data elements and interact with the data. While not a complete list, the following fundamental user interface elements in a QlikView document include:

- **Tab Sheet**: A tab sheet represents a container into which various screen objects are placed to lay out the interface. There can be several tab sheets in a document and they can be hidden or shown based on user activity. Each tab sheet has a tab at the top with a title that you control. There are also various properties associated with a tab sheet to control things such as visibility and background colors or images.
- **Chart**: There is a wide variety of chart types which include all of the basics (i.e. bar, chart, line, pie, gauge etc.). It is also important to note that, in QlikView, tables are considered charts. There two types of tables: straight tables and pivot tables. Each chart object has a wide variety of properties associated with it. These properties make it possible for you to control the dimensions, values, layout and other attributes of the chart.
- **List Box**: List boxes are the primary selector control for allowing users to select data. There can be any number of them on a tab sheet. List boxes, beginning with version 10, can also include expressions as additional columns. They also have properties that affect how they behave and look. For example you can have selections show as check boxes instead of the default reverse video presentation.
- **Current Selections Box**: A special object type called a "Current Selection Box" provides users with the ability to

see what selections they have made and then change them without retracing their steps across tab sheets.

- **Bookmark**: Once a user has made certain selections, a bookmark can be created with a custom name. The bookmark makes it possible to invoke the same selection combination at a later time. Bookmarks can be accessed from the menu bar in QlikView for Windows or from within most QlikView client interfaces, but you can also add a bookmark object directly to a tab sheet. This object provides a list of the predefined bookmarks that you created within the document. It also allows users to create new bookmarks.
- **Navigation Buttons**: Common navigation buttons such as clear, previous and next buttons allow the user to traverse and reset the selections made while analyzing the QlikView document. There are also lock and unlock buttons that allow the user to temporarily lock certain selections to simplify analysis.
- **Text Object**: To display text, either dynamically using expressions or statically, a text object is used. It allows you to place text on a tab sheet where you desire and then control the text attributes such as font, color and background.
- **Search Object:** List boxes in QlikView have built-in searching capabilities. However in some cases you may wish to produce a search control on a tab sheet and control which dimensions of data are searched. The search object can be used to do this.

Each of the user interface objects have a set of properties associated with them that allow you to configure the object. The number and type of properties vary based on the object type, but they are vast and offer a great deal of flexibility over how each object looks and works. It is in the object's properties that you will find options for creating expressions to summarize data and affect layout, formatting and behavior.

How is Data Accessed and Managed in a QlikView Document?

When data is loaded into a QlikView document it typically originates from a known database or data file source. Such sources might include relational database systems such as Microsoft SQL Server, Oracle, IBM DB2, MySQL or others. These, and other data sources, are accessed via conventional ODBC or OLEDB connections. File data sources might include Excel, CSV files, flat file dumps from mainframe and midrange systems, or XML data. QlikView, beginning with version 10, also includes a custom data provider capability that allows programmers to create their own connections to data sources from which QlikView can load data. QlikView can also load data from one of several QlikView file formats. For example a QlikView document can load data from another QlikView document. This is called a "binary" load. There is also a proprietary QlikView data file format known as a QVD file that can serve as a data source. QVD files can be created and managed to implement incremental data loading scenarios.

In all cases, data is loaded into a QlikView document based on connection information and instructions you create in the QlikView load script. The load script is part of the QlikView document, but elements of it such as connection strings can be abstracted into separate files for sharing and security purposes. The QlikView load script also supports a rich set of functions that allow you to manipulate and restructure the data from the data sources as it is being loaded. This enables QlikView to access data from a wide variety of data sources and associate the data in a manner consistent with your users' needs. Data loading is something you can invoke manually or, in the case of a server deployment, it can be automated and run on a scheduled basis.

What are QlikView Expressions?

QlikView provides a robust and comprehensive expression language that allows you to summarize, calculate and manipulate data in other ways after it has been loaded. QlikView expressions are most commonly used to define values for charts and tables where aggregations such as summing, averaging or counting are needed across one or more dimensions to produce the desired presentation of the data. Expressions are quite easy to create, but they can also be very complex representing hundreds of lines of syntax. Many of the object properties in a QlikView document can be driven by expressions. For example, a list box that provides the user with the ability to select certain items might have its caption include the quantity of records for the selected items. This is done by creating an expression for the caption property of the list box.

QlikView expression syntax also includes some very advanced features. Among these is the ability to apply set analysis techniques to expressions. Through the use of set analysis syntax, QlikView expressions can dynamically create and compare subsets of data. These subsets can account for user selections on the main set of data or stand alone. This makes it possible to produce very dynamic and versatile functionality. Expressions may also leverage variables by reading their values or setting them. A variable in QlikView has a global scope, meaning it is always available to all expressions. Variables may store values such as dates, numbers or text. They may also store expression syntax, which can be used as part of an expression.

The most common example of how a QlikView expression is used occurs when you add a chart to a tab sheet in a QlikView document. Most charts require you to select at least one dimension, which defines how the chart will categorize the data. After selecting a dimension, you will have to create an expression to summarize a value in numeric form for each category in the dimension. For example if you create at bar chart where the bars represent regions, you have to create an expression to determine how tall each bar is relative to the other bars. The expression might perform a count of orders by counting the number of order descriptions in the data. The expression would look like the following:

```
=Count(order_description)
```

In this case the result of the expression drives the height of each bar, representing the order count for each region. You may note that we can count a non-numeric field, but we would not be able to sum or average it. This is only a very simple example of an expression, but if offers you an initial look at how expressions are created and used. There will be a great deal more about expressions in many of the chapters to come.

How can a QlikView Document be shared?

Once created, a QlikView document (a .QVW file) can be shared with other QlikView users in a variety of ways. The most basic mechanism for sharing a QlikView document is to simply copy it and send it to another user who has a licensed version of QlikView for Windows. This, however, is discouraged because it presumes several things, any one of which may not be true and may cause a serious problem. First, because QlikView can manage such large volumes of data, any user who opens a QlikView document must have the requisite amount of computer memory available. If such memory capacity doesn't exist, the computer may crash or at least the document will not be usable. Another potential problem is that in order to refresh the data, the recipient of the QlikView document must have access to the underlying data sources and may need credentials for them. If you embed the credentials in the document, which you can do, you may be in violation of your organization's security policy. If you don't, the user may not be able to refresh the data. Finally, the idea of sending potentially large documents via email or file copy is typically frowned upon by IT departments. QlikView does a great job of compressing data, but if your document includes a high volume of data you may still find that the file is rejected by the email system or takes a very long time to download.

A better approach, and one that is necessary in many cases, is to deploy a QlikView server. QlikView servers allow you to copy your QlikView document to one place, schedule the reloading of data on a regular basis and make it available to Windows, Web and mobile users. Server based documents open in the memory of the server, not the user's workstation. This means users with low end workstations can access and interact with your QlikView document even if it contains hundreds of millions of rows of data. The QlikView server also manages the users and memory very efficiently. For example, as multiple users access the same QlikView document the memory required by that document is used only once, with a small amount of overhead for each additional user to ensure each user's session is treated uniquely. While we will cover a little about QlikView server, the primary focus going forward will be on creating QlikView documents. For more information about QlikView server consider visiting the QlikView Web site.

Chapter 3: Accessing Data with QlikView

The foundation on which all QlikView documents are built is based on how the underlying data, the data from your source systems, is accessed, loaded and manipulated by QlikView. The accuracy and completeness of this data is paramount to the success and usability of your QlikView document. This chapter will provide, in some detail, the most common methods for loading data into your QlikView document. It is important to note that not all methods of loading data into QlikView are covered; only the most common. However, once you understand these features, you will be able to explore other options more easily. This chapter will also provide guidance on how to structure and organize your document's load script process, along with some examples of how you can manage and augment data as it is loaded.

The data you use to create your QlikView document may come from a variety data sources, each with its own unique data structure. QlikView does not require you to access data from a single type of data source; rather it makes it easy to access data from multiple disparate data sources during a single data load process. QlikView allows you to access data from relational databases using conventional ODBC and OLEDB connectivity or directly from file based data sources such as XML, Excel, text delimited (CSV etc.), HTML and even other QlikView files (.QVW, .QVD, .QVX and .QVO). When accessing data from a data file, the file may be stored on your local workstation, your corporate network, the Internet or an extranet.

Data Loading Fundamentals

Before diving into the process of loading data into QlikView there are some fundamentals you should understand. This includes learning a few important terms and how they are used, as well as understanding the basics of the QlikView data load process and how to create and manage it. Learning these fundamentals will help you better leverage the QlikView help files and other documentation as you develop your QlikView skills.

Important Data Load Terms

There are few key terms you should know and understand when working with QlikView data. Knowing these terms will streamline your learning and help you communicate with other QlikView developers in a consistent and correct manner. The following list provides definitions for key terms associated with QlikView data loading:

- Load Script: This is the part of a QlikView document that houses the instructions you create to connect to data sources and retrieve data. It is the most important part of your QlikView document because without it, no data can be presented to your users.
- Load Script Editor: The *load script editor* is the interface in QlikView for Windows that allows you to create and maintain the load script. It is a dialog that pops up from within QlikView.
- Tables: In QlikView a *table* is a set of data. It might represent data from a sheet in an Excel file or data that is returned by a SQL query against a relational database. Once data is loaded into QlikView, it is organized into a group of tables that you define in the load script. Each table is a distinct in-memory data set. These tables can be, and usually are, associated with each other in a predefined manner.
- Fields: A field in QlikView is an element of a table. A QlikView field may represent a column from a database query (SQL query) or a column in an Excel file. It may also represent a delimited value from a text file such as CSV file or a hard coded (constant) value. However, a field in QlikView can also be the result of instructions in the load

script that combine and manipulate data from the underlying data source using QlikView functions. This means a QlikView field is not necessary the same as a database field or column. Field names are very important in QlikView and you can control them independently of the data source structures.

- Script Syntax: The term *syntax* represents the statements in the load script. In some cases these statements may be manually typed; in other cases they may be generated by a wizard or screen object in the load script editor.
- Script Function: A script function is a predefined QlikView instruction that becomes part of the script syntax. Script functions are used to create statements in the load script that instruct QlikView on what must happen when data is loaded. Functions are combined with other syntax.
- Script Statement: A statement is comprised of script syntax that usually includes one or more script functions. Statements in QlikView are usually terminated by a semicolon (;). The semicolon indicates that one statement is completed and allows for a subsequent statement to be created.
- Reload: The reload feature causes the load script to execute. It can be invoked using the *Reload* button in the script editor. Reloading can also be invoked from the QlikView pull down menu and by a QlikView server when the document is deployed to a server environment.
- ODBC/OLEDB: These terms are not specific to QlikView. They represent conventional data connectivity features found in MS-Windows. Many software tools use these features to establish connectivity to a variety of databases and data sources such as Oracle, MS-SQL Server, DB2, etc.
- Table Files: *Table files* in QlikView are connections to a variety of data files such as Excel files, CSV files and XML data files. *Table files* may be used as data sources for QlikView and can be combined with other data sources such as relational databases.

- Data Model: A QlikView *data model* is comprised of all of the tables, fields and associations that result from the load script being executed. Taken together, all of the instructions for accessing, loading and manipulating data result in the QlikView *data model*.

Understanding Functions, Commands, Statements and Clauses

The terms function, command and statement are often used synonymously by developers. While most developers understand that within the correct context these terms are often interchangeable, in many cases they mean different things. It is important for you to know the differences between them when you begin your learning process with QlikView. Each of these terms may mean something different when referencing various technologies, but within QlikView they are best used in specific ways. For the purpose of clarity the following pertains to how these terms are used as they relate to a QlikView load script.

- Functions: A QlikView function is a predefined instruction that you include in your QlikView load script. If you have experience developing in other technologies, then this concept should be familiar to you. Functions receive and return data values. This is often referred to as *operating* on data. The data value returned by a function is modified by it. This is done by manually typing load script syntax or using a built-in wizard to generate syntax. You might think of functions as the language you use to communicate with QlikView when creating a load script or a QlikView expression. QlikView expressions use the same syntax and many of the same functions are used in load scripts. It is possible to create expressions within the load script to automatically produce calculation results at the document level. For example a field may be the result of complex expression syntax. However, in most cases, when referring to expressions, we are referring to script syntax in the user interface, not the load script. If the term “expression” is used to refer to logic in the load script it is usually prefixed with the words "load script" and reads something like "load script expression." Some functions can be used in both the load script and in QlikView expressions, but others may only pertain to one or the other. It is worth reiterating that the syntax is the same in UI expressions and the load script for the most part. The QlikView online help refers to all syntax as "Script Syntax."

- Commands: Many developers interchange the term *function* with the term *command*. In QlikView the term command is not normally used. However, if you see it, it typically means "*function*."
- Statement: The term *statement* is commonly used when describing load script syntax in QlikView. A statement is a combination of one or more QlikView functions and other syntax. A statement in QlikView is usually terminated with a semicolon (;), which allows the load script to contain a series of statements. You will see this in the examples used in this and other chapters of this book. It is important to keep in mind that a statement may span several rows. Look for the semicolon to determine where a statement ends and where the next statement begins.
- Clause: As with SQL and other data related languages, QlikView load script syntax can be described in part with the word "clause." A clause is a portion of a statement. It can be helpful to refer to more complex statements by clauses, which represent segments of a statement. For example, in SQL (and QlikView) it is common to refer to the *FROM* clause as part of a SQL statement.

The QlikView Data Load Process

Because of QlikView's unique associative database you are able to associate data across all of your document's data sources without concern for such things as consistency in data types or standardized data sourcing. The way data associations are established in QlikView is simple. They are created and maintained by controlling the field names within your load script. While some consideration for data types is always important, once data becomes available in a QlikView load process, data typing is automatic. That means that if one data source stores customer numbers in a character field and another stores them in a numeric field, the two data source tables can still be associated. This, of course, presumes there are matches in the data between the two source tables. Otherwise, the association would serve no purpose. However, what's interesting about QlikView is that it doesn't care about the difference in data types from the sources. As it loads data into memory and ultimately stores it within the QlikView document's file (.QVW file), the data becomes "QlikView data."

Users interact with your QlikView documents in a disconnected state from the original data sources. While QlikView servers can be set up to access and use real-time data, in most cases data is loaded periodically. Another way of understanding this is to consider the data "materialized" within the QlikView document structure. Each time you reload the data into the document, the load script executes and QlikView's associative database is rebuilt in memory. When the document is distributed and accessed by users for data analysis its data is loaded either manually or by a process on a QlikView Server. All of the tables, as defined by the load script, are loaded into memory. The accuracy and completeness of the data in your document is controlled entirely by the load script. It is worth noting that when QlikView loads and stores data in memory, and on disk when the document is saved, the data is highly compressed. This is one of the features that set QlikView apart from other tools. The compression ratios for in-memory and on-disk storage are exceptional with QlikView. This results in the ability for QlikView to load and access very large amounts of data for analysis. In our experience it is common for our customers to have QlikView documents that load hundreds of millions of rows across dozens or even hundreds of columns.

The way in which the load script in your QlikView document structures and associates the data from the original data sources represents what is known as the QlikView Data Model. The data model can be viewed graphically in the QlikView script editor by clicking on the *Table Viewer* icon on the right side of the script editor toolbar. There will be more on this later, but you should understand that all of the instructions you place in a QlikView load script result in a single set of associated (in most cases) memory tables, which are the basis for the document's data model.

Creating a Load Script

Each QlikView document has one load script which can be edited from within the QlikView for Windows client software. To begin you must create a new QlikView document. This chapter has examples that assume you are not using the document creation wizard which automatically displays when you select *File>New* from the main pull down menu. You can cancel it and the result will be a blank QlikView document with no load script. Once you've created a new document you access the load script editor by selecting *File>Edit Script...* from the pull down menu. This will launch the script editor.

The script editor offers a variety of features that allow you to create and maintain the QlikView load script for your document. While it is possible to simply type in the statements necessary for loading and managing data in QlikView you will find that many of the features and wizards (dialogs) that are accessible from the script editor may help you to create script syntax and reduce the effort needed to create the load script. Keep in mind that in the end, the load script is nothing more than a series of statements which instruct QlikView on how to access, load and manipulate data. This is important because unlike other tools, you have a high degree of control over these instructions. The wizards and other features that help create script syntax are, for the most part, not necessary and therefore any limitations associated with them can easily be overcome. Figure 3-1 shows the key areas and features of the QlikView load script editor.

FIGURE 3-1 LOAD SCRIPT EDITOR

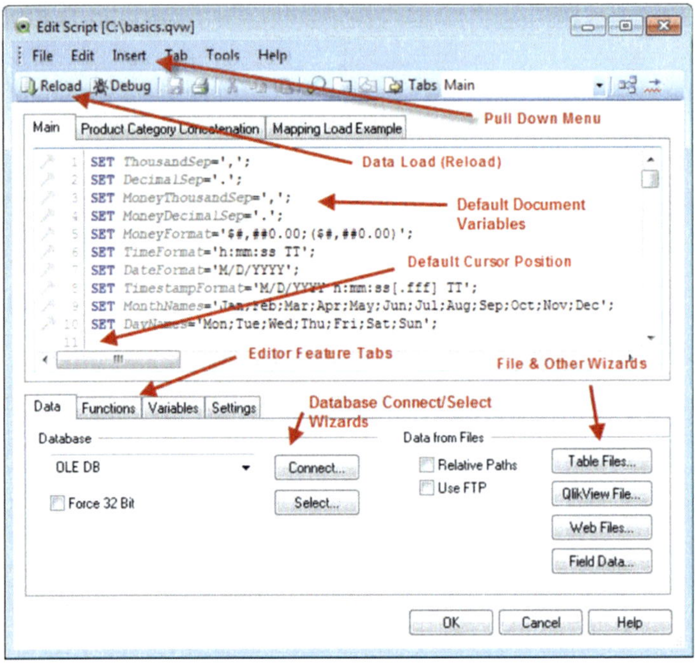

The load script editor provides an area in which load script statements can be typed. It also provides various features and functions found on toolbars, the feature tabs at the bottom and in the pull down menu at the top. The following are basic elements of the load script editor that you should understand before you get started:

- Reload Button: The reload button causes the load script to execute. This results in your QlikView document accessing the data sources, loading the data and the execution of anything else (any other commands) that are included in the load script.
- Default Document Variable Settings: The SET commands at the top of the load script are automatically generated

based on your local machine's settings (Windows settings). These settings result in global variables used by QlikView to determine how certain default values such as date formats should be set throughout the document. You can change and override them, but you don't need to.

- The Current Cursor Location: The blinking cursor indicates the current cursor location, which will be where the next statement or syntax you enter is placed as you type.
- *Connect...* Button: The *Connect...* button launches the connection wizard, which provides a graphical interface for creating a connection string to a database. Connection strings instruct QlikView on how to connect to databases using ODBC or OLEDB drivers on your computer. When used, this wizard will place the connection string syntax at the current cursor location. Be sure the blinking cursor is below the default document variables settings before launching this wizard.
- *Select...* Button*: The Select...* button will first launch a connection wizard if a connection string is not already in the load script above the current cursor location. After that it will launch a dialog that allows you to see a list of tables, views and fields from the database referenced in the connection string. This is covered in more detail in the chapter about *Creating a simple QlikView Document*.
- *Table Files...* Button: The *Table Files...* button launches a wizard that steps you through accessing data from a file based data source.

Database Sources

Perhaps the most common source of data you will use in building your QlikView documents is data from a database. Understanding some basics about relational databases is important if you are using them, and you likely are, as sources of data for QlikView. Many QlikView tutorials and examples begin by using file based data such as Excel files. QlikView is great at accessing and managing such data, but most developers have to access data from larger, structured data sources. If you do not have a background in relational database management, the following will help you understand some of the key concepts.

Relational Databasc Fundamentals

Introduced by E.F. Codd in 1970, relational database management systems (RDBS's) quickly became the standard for structured data storage across the industry. Today, relational databases are the most common form of structured data storage. Software vendors such as Oracle, IBM and Microsoft offer database systems that are part of this standard. Most of these vendors also incorporate the use of structured query language (SQL) as a means for accessing data. SQL has become the standard mechanism for accessing data from relational database systems. However, the use of SQL to retrieve data doesn't prepare you for what you will be doing in a QlikView load script. Understanding how SQL and relational data is structured and how it works is still important. Understanding it will help you can decide which parts of the data load process should use SQL and which parts should be done in the QlikView load script.

Relational databases provide a structure for storing data. This structure is accessible and maintainable using SQL statements. The structures of relational databases include tables and columns. Columns, elements of a table, store predefined types of data such as dates, numbers or characters. As rows are added to a relational table the data is structured according to the way in which the columns are predefined for that table. Each column must store a specific type of data. The column's data type requirement is sometimes referred to as a domain constraint. Not only will rows of data for given column have the same data type, but they will also have the same data length. If a column with character data has a data length of 10 characters no value within that column can exceed 10 characters. This is part of what makes a relational database "structured."

The concept of relational data is based on the relationships that can be established between tables. Each table in a relational database can (and should) include a *Primary Key*, which defines uniqueness for each row of data in the table. *Primary Key* values can never be repeated within the table. A *Primary Key* in one table can (and hopefully does) have corresponding value in a field found in another table. This makes primary keys a good candidate for associating data in your QlikView data model. The field in the second table may be defined as a *Foreign Key*, but not always. If it is, then then a formal relationship exists between the two tables. The purpose of such relationships is to ensure that data from one table properly relates to data in the other. Relational databases can enforce rules, known as constraints, to make this happen as data is entered and edited. Relationships and keys are not required to join tables together using SQL syntax, but understanding them helps to identify how relational data is structured.

Accessing Databases in QlikView

Before creating a load script using a database source, you should become familiar with a few script functions. These include: *CONNECT*, *LOAD* and *SQL SELECT*. These three functions control how, when and from where your relational data is loaded. Each data source within the load script uses one or more of these functions for accessing, retrieving and loading data into QlikView. Understanding each of these script functions and how to use them is important. You should note that in this chapter the examples and instruction, for the most part, are based on creating a load script manually. This is the best way to understand the power and importance of the QlikView load script and associated tools. However, there are wizards that make much of this easier and faster. In a few cases a wizard is referenced here, but where practical, wizards are not used in this chapter so you can focus on the script syntax. Some of these wizards are covered in more detail in the chapter on *Creating a Simple QlikView Document*.

When accessing relational data sources with QlikView, you may leverage several common database objects. As described above, the simplest of these are tables and columns. The QlikView *SQL SELECT* function presumes these are the objects in the database you wish to access. While it is possible to write a very complex *SQL SELECT* statement in the QlikView load script, it isn't usually at good idea because it requires anyone who maintains the document to have advanced SQL skills and makes the load script very complex. In many cases other database objects may exist which make accessing relational data easier. These include database *views* and *stored procedures*. These objects are created by your database administrator in advance and may have security rights associated with them. Database *views* are comprised of previously created SQL syntax that may involve joining dozens of tables together and may include complex sub-query syntax and calculations. Rather than recreating this SQL syntax every time it is needed, a view stores the syntax for reuse and gives it a name (the view name). You can use a *SQL SELECT* statement with a database view just as you would with tables. Stored procedures are database objects that, like database views, represent SQL syntax that was created in advance. However, unlike views, *stored procedures* can perform more complex manipulation of data and accept parameters that affect how data is returned. They can also update and delete data and even create or alter data structures. Executing stored procedures in QlikView is little trickier than using tables or views. The way in which stored procedures are executed is dependent on the type of database to which your document is connecting. There's more on leveraging stored procedures later in this chapter.

The CONNECT Function

The *CONNECT* function provides connectivity to relational data sources using either ODBC or OLEDB drivers. This assumes you have the appropriate drivers installed and configured on your computer and on the QlikView server to which you might deploy your document. Examples of these drivers would include the

MDAC installation for Windows, the SQL Server Native Client, the Oracle Client and various ODBC/OLEDB drivers. Creating a *CONNECT* function can be done in two ways. The preferred method is to use the built-in connection wizard which is launched using the *Connect...* button. The connection wizard uses the setting found on the *Data* tab of the script editor (bottom) under the *Database* section dropdown for OLEDB or ODBC. It launches a Windows Data Link Properties editor dialog, which facilitates the creation of a connection string. This process is not specific to QlikView. The same dialog is used in a number of tools for creating connection strings for database connectivity. When you close the dialog, the connection string is created based on the settings you selected. It is placed at the current cursor location in the load script. Using the *Connect...* button is a good way to get started with the *CONNECT* function because the syntax for connection strings can be complicated.

When created or entered manually, the *CONNECT* command is prefaced with either ODBC or OLEDB based on the selected type of connection. Typically, and according to Microsoft, OLEDB is preferred as it tends to perform better and has better threading. The *CONNECT* command is followed by a connection string. The connection string is used to configure the connection to use the correct server, database and user credentials as well as other settings that may be necessary. Contained within the connection string, among other things, is the user ID and password that is used to establish the connection. Alternatively, it may contain information indicating the use of Windows Authentication for connecting to the data source.

IMPORTANT: If you create a connection with Windows Authentication, it may not work on a QlikView server when you deploy your document. For this reason an actual database user ID and password is preferred. QlikView has an option to scramble the password so it doesn't appear in clear text within the load script. If you choose *Scramble Connect User Credentials* in *User Preferences>General,* the user ID and password in the connection string will be scrambled, otherwise they will appear in clear text.

Complete scrambling of user credentials is currently only supported for ODBC connections. Some parts of OLEDB connections cannot be scrambled, but passwords are scrambled.

The *CONNECT* function can be used to create three different types of connections. These include support for the combination of Windows 32-bit and 64-bit operating systems as follows:

- *CONNECT*: When using a simple *CONNECT* function the application uses the default database driver sub-system based on your operating system. If you are running on 32-bit Windows it uses the 32-bit database driver, if you are running on 64-bit Windows it uses the 64-bit database driver. Keep in mind that your workstation's default may be different than the QlikView server's settings if you plan to deploy your document to a server.
- *CONNECT32*: This version of the function forces the application to use the 32-bit database driver, even when you are running 64-bit Windows. This assumes 32-bit drivers are installed on your 64-bit workstation.
- *CONNECT64*: This statement forces the application to use the 64-bit driver. If you are running 64-bit Windows, this statement and the simple *CONNECT* statement will act the same.

CONNECT Function Examples:

The following examples help illustrate how statements using the CONNECT function appear in a QlikView load script. Please note that the connection strings in the OLEDB statements are abbreviated. The ODBC example references an ODBC DSN that must be set up in Windows prior to use by the load script. This is typically done using the Windows Administrative Tools application named *Data Sources (ODBC).* The following are examples of *CONNECT* statements using OLEDB and ODBC. You would not have all of these in this order in your load script: You would likely only use one of them followed by various *LOAD* statements. However, you can have more than one *CONNECT* statement in a load script, which allows for connections to more than one type of database.

```
OLEDB CONNECT TO [Provider=SQLOLEDB.1;...];

ODBC CONNECT32 TO CRMSampleODBC;

OLEDB CONNECT64 TO [Provider=SQLOLEDB.1;...];
```

Once you create a statement using the *CONNECT* function and a connection string exists in your script, all attempts to access data for that connection must follow (on the lines directly below it). If another *CONNECT* statement is added later in the script the data load instructions after it will ignore the first statement and use the second one.

The *SQL SELECT* Function

The *SQL SELECT* function in QlikView is similar to a standard SQL (Structured Query Language) SELECT statement. It is used to select fields and rows from a table or database view in a relational database. This means the preceding *CONNECT* statement is based on an ODBC or an OLEDB connection. A statement based on a *SQL SELECT* function includes a list of fields by name or uses the wild card asterisk (*) to include all fields from a database table or view. It also includes a "From" clause to define the table or tables from which the data is selected, just as it does in conventional SQL syntax. In fact, after the SQL part of the function name, the syntax that's entered is passed through to the underlying data source. We've been able to use fairly complex SQL syntax in these statements. However, ideally you won't lean on your SQL skills any more than you have to because QlikView's load script can do a great deal of data manipulation. The following is an example of a standard *SQL SELECT* statement:

```
SQL SELECT
     customer_id,
     customer_name,
     country
   FROM
     CRMSample.dbo.customers;
```

SQL SELECT statements can contain many optional standard SQL clauses as well. Here are few examples:

- *WHERE* – to define which rows to retrieve from the table.
- *GROUP BY* – grouping rows by common attributes so that an aggregate function can be applied (sum, count, average, etc.).
- *ORDER BY* – defines the order of retrieved records as ascending or descending by a column or columns.
- *HAVING* – selects specific records from a *GROUP BY* clause.

Using the SQL Function to Access a Stored Procedure

The *SQL SELECT* function is actually a combination of two functions. The SQL function tells QlikView that what follows is SQL syntax that is to be sent to a SQL database server (relational database system). The SELECT function is part of the SQL syntax that is sent. This means that you can use the SQL function to send other instructions to the database server. Among these are statements that call stored procedures. When calling a stored procedure you must use the SQL syntax supported by the database vendor. Calling an Oracle stored procedure will require different syntax than calling a MS-SQL Server stored procedure. The following is an example of how to call a SQL Server stored procedure in a QlikView load script:

```
SQL Exec dbo.GetCustomersByRegion 'CA'
```

In the example above, the name of the stored procedure follows the *Exec* command and a parameter value is passed into the stored procedure at the end of the line. In this case the procedure requires a region name to be passed as a string (that's why it is in single quotes). A preceding LOAD statement should be above this statement so you can control the field names and data as it loads, but the statement will work without it.

IMPORTANT: SQL Server stored procedure calls in QlikView also require you to configure two other settings:

1. You must add syntax to the end of your OLEDB CONNECT statement to allow it write back to the database. It should look like this:

```
OLEDB CONNECT TO [Prov…] (mode is write);
```

2. You must change the *Open Databases in Read and Write mode* setting on the *Settings* tab at the bottom of the script editor.

Both of these configurations are needed because of the way that the SQL OLEDB provider communicates with the QlikView load script.

Since you can use the SQL function to perform SQL commands other than a SELECT command, it stands to reason that other variations of conventional SQL syntax may follow the SQL function in your QlikView load script. We have included very complex T-SQL statements in load scripts for our projects in some cases. However, it is best to keep the SQL syntax simple if you can. As you will see in the chapter covering advanced data loading, there are many things the QlikView load script offers to help manage and manipulate data.

The LOAD Function

The *LOAD* function does exactly what its name implies; it manages the loading of data into your QlikView document. It is important to understand that the *LOAD* function doesn't access the data source; rather it manages the loading of the data after the data source connection is made. The data may come from a data file (table file), a *SQL SELECT* or similar relational database statement, from previously loaded tables that are already in memory or from other supported data sources. The *LOAD* function can also be used when creating static data in the load script. In this case you type in the data values necessary to establish a table structure. This is known as an *inline table.* Inline tables are tables that are created in the load script. They do not access data from an external file or data source. For this reason, inline tables are best used with data that is unlikely to change. The following is an example of an inline table used to store territory information:

```
LOAD * INLINE
[

territory_id, territory_name
1, East
2, Great Lakes
3, South East
4, Mid-West
5, West

];
```

In the load statement above, the square brackets define the syntax for both the structure of the inline table as well as the data. The two field names appear at the beginning, and the data for each row follows. Column values for each row are separated by a comma. The data for this table would appear similar to the following:

1	East
2	Great Lakes
3	South East
4	Mid-West
5	West

Using the *LOAD* function isn't always required. For example you can execute a *SQL SELECT* statement without using a *LOAD* function, in which case the results of the SQL statement are loaded and table and field names are derived from the results. However, this is not the best way to load SQL data into QlikView. It is better to use a *LOAD* statement before the *SQL SELECT* statement. The reason for this is that the *LOAD* statement allows you to manipulate the data from the SQL query as it is being loaded. You can change field names, concatenate fields together and perform calculations on the data. It is important to keep in mind that QlikView automatically associates tables based on field names. Using a *LOAD* statement before a SQL statement is important for this reason alone. When a *LOAD* statement is used before a *SQL SELECT* statement it is referred to as a *preceding load*.

When a *LOAD* function is used to create a *LOAD* statement it is followed by syntax that defines how the data will be organized and named in the QlikView data model. If you are using the *LOAD* function with a *SQL SELECT* statement it is followed by a comma separated list of fields and is terminated with a semicolon. Immediately following the semicolon is the *SQL SELECT* statement. A typical example looks similar to the following:

```
LOAD customer_id as [Customer No],
    date_placed as [Order Date],
    order_id as [Order Number]
    amount as Amount;
SQL SELECT "customer_id",
    date_placed,
    order_id,
    amount
FROM CRMSample.dbo.order_information;
```

In the example above take note of the following:

1. The fields are renamed using the reserved word "as."
2. Field names with spaces in them are enclosed in square brackets. Double quotes could have been used in place of the brackets as well.
3. If a field name is one word as with "amount" no brackets are needed when renaming.
4. Each field name from the SQL statement is referenced in the *LOAD* statement. If a field is not referenced in the load statement it will not become part of the data model and therefore will not be loaded into memory.

IMPORTANT: In order to control how QlikView names the table (the container for all of the fields) you can enter a one word name followed by a colon (:). This must be placed before the LOAD statement. Here is an example of the previous script syntax (first few lines only) with a table name added:

```
order_information:
LOAD customer_id as [Customer No],
    date_placed as [Order Date],
...
```

File Based Data Sources

A file data source, also referred to as a *table file* data source, is a data source based on a data file that is accessed from the operating system's file system. This differs from a relational data source because relational data sources involve accessing a database server and use SQL language to determine what data is made available to QlikView.

Types of File Data Sources

A wide variety of data file formats are supported by QlikView for the purpose of loading data. Each of the supported data file types are based on a structure that QlikView can interpret. The process of interpreting a data file format is sometimes referred to as parsing the data file. In some cases data files are provided in a text format, which means you can open and read them in a text editor. In other cases the files are in a proprietary format such MS-Excel, which require a specific software application if you want to see the data. QlikView also supports its own proprietary file formats, which are used to address various data loading scenarios. In these cases the file is referred to as a *binary* file and accessed with a *binary* load process. Supported file formats include the following:

- .TXT – TXT files store data as raw text. The way in which the data is structured for this file type uses fixed field widths. Many mainframe and mid-range computers produce data in this format. There is no delimiter separating one field (column) from the next. Delimitation is determined by character position and each row in the file is considered one record.
- .CSV – CSV files use a comma as a field delimiter. They are known as "comma separated value" files.

- .TAB – TAB files use a tab character as a field delimiter.
- .QVO – QVO files are created by QlikView when a user exports data from screen object. These files provide field names and field data in a text format based on fixed field widths.
- .MEM – MEM files are created by QlikView when you want to export the information about QlikView's memory use. This is done using *Settings>Document Properties>General Tab>Memory Statistics...* The file provides predefined fields of information about memory use in a text format based on fixed field widths.
- .SKV – SKV files use a semicolon as a field delimiter. They are known as "semicolon separated value" files.
- .PRN – PRN files are created by various software programs and usually provide data in a fixed field width format.
- .LOG – LOG files are created by various software programs to provide data about a process that occurred. They usually provide data in a fixed field width format.
- .XML – XML files store data in the popular eXtensible Markup Language format. More sophisticated than delimited or fixed width files, XML files store records of data in a hierarchical format.
- Excel (XLS, XLSX) – Excel files are commonly known and store data in a proprietary row and column format. QlikView can read them natively.
- HTML – HTML files are based on the markup language common to the Web (Hyper Text Markup Language). Usually when loading data from an HTML file (either locally or from the Web) the data is accessed from an HTML table in the file (on the Web page).
- .DIF – DIF files are an established standard for data sharing known as *data interchange format*. Often created and used by mainframe and mid-range systems, DIF files store data in text format. But unlike other text files, they store header and data information in limited chunks across

either two or three lines. Many systems support importing and exporting data in this format.

- .QVD – QVD (QlikView Data) files are data files created by QlikView and consumable by QlikView. These files store QlikView data in a highly optimized format which speeds up load times significantly. They are binary files and proprietary to QlikView. They often address data loading issues such as incremental loading and the need to share data across documents.

Loading Data from File Based Data Sources

QlikView consumes file based data in a manner similar to the way it consumes database data. The data contained in the file is loaded into QlikView and managed by a *LOAD* statement. One difference is that with file based data the *LOAD* statement is mandatory. The instructions that follow the *LOAD* function can differ depending on what type of file is being loaded. Data loaded from a file data source requires only the *LOAD* statement; the *SQL SELECT* statement used with relational database sources is not used when loading file based data. Although the *SQL SELECT* syntax is not used, the *LOAD* statement for file based data includes a *FROM* clause that describes the path and additional information related to the type of file being loaded. The *FROM* clause includes information such as:

- Whether the file contains embedded labels.
- The table name (tab name for Excel files).
- Codepage and delimiter for text files.
- Statements used to define any data transformations performed on the file data.

The following is a simple example of the finished load script for an Excel file:

```
LOAD
  hr_id,
  last_name,
  first_name,
```

```
  title,
  promotion_date,
  manager_id,
  yearly_payroll_load
FROM
[Datasources\hr_stats.xls]
(biff, embedded labels, table is Employee$);
```

Notice that the *FROM* clause references biff (Binary Interchange File Format), which is used by Excel. It also indicates that the file includes embedded labels and that the data is loading from the Employee worksheet in the Excel workbook.

While it may seem like a lot to remember, QlikView makes accessing file data sources relatively easy. It provides a *Table Files* wizard that walks you through the creation of the script syntax. When you click the *Table Files...* button on the *Data* tab in your script editor you are prompted to select a table file using Windows Explorer. Once you select a file, the wizard appears to step you through the process of preparing your file for automatic script generation. The wizard adjusts the steps based on the type of file you select (by file extension). The final output of the table file wizard is the appropriate script syntax for the file you selected.

The first screen of the table file wizard allows you to define the basic properties of your file based on the file type selected. This includes:

- The table name (tab if Excel).
- The header size, if any, in lines or bytes based on the file type.
- Whether or not your file contains embedded labels in the first row. If it does not, you can click on the column header and type in your own column names (Hint: pressing Enter after typing the name saves it so you can move on to the next column). This creates the *LOAD* statement syntax for renaming the column in the script.
- Delimiter and character set if text.
- Removing unwanted or unneeded columns.

The next screen allows you to enable a transformation step if you need it. The transformation step provides the following options:

- Remove garbage from the file by manually selecting rows or setting up filter conditions.
- Fill in missing data based on conditions within a cell.
- Add new columns to the file.
- Unwrap or rotate data based on selections or conditionally based on conditions within a cell. This is rarely needed, but can apply to HTML table data and similar situations where the data is not structured properly for loading.

The third screen of the file wizard provides a *WHERE* clause to extract only specific data from the file. It also allows you to define and manage a hierarchical (parent – child) relationship if one exists in the file or uncross a crossed table. This sometimes applies to XML and HTML based data.

The final screen allows you to review the script syntax that will be generated. Clicking the Finish button places the script into your script editor at the location of your cursor.

File Data Source Considerations

File data sources present several potential issues that are not present when using database sources. The most important of these include file location, file structure and data integrity. File data sources reside at a defined location on your workstation or network and may not be accessible to other QlikView developers or to QlikView servers. If they are not universally accessible then your QlikView document cannot be reloaded when it is distributed. Another primary concern is that the structure of your data file may change unexpectedly based on how and by whom the file is created. Files, by their nature, are often not managed formally and therefore data integrity may not be a concern of their providers. For example, data of various types can be contained within a single column and data types are often not defined properly or enforced. While this is not the intent, it can occur frequently. These issues make it important to create and enforce rules for how file data sources are created, distributed and updated. Failure to consider these potential problems can result in a QlikView document with no data, or worse, the wrong data. The following provides details and recommendations for how to address each of these issues.

File Data Source Locations

There are two ways QlikView can locate a data file: (1) By a fully qualified path or (2) via a relative path. The fully qualified path includes the drive letter or UNC with every subfolder in the path to the actual file. A relative path describes the location of the file data source relative to the location of the QlikView document (.QVW) file. When sharing your QlikView document this information is very important because when a data reload is performed it will fail if the file location is wrong. This is a major consideration when your document is deployed to a QlikView server. When your QlikView document is refreshed, regardless of how you share your document, the file data sources must reside at the location identified in the load script.

Another important consideration is file security. Actual file access is managed by the network permissions applied to the folder in which the file is stored. The user account under which the QlikView document processes is passed to the operating system when the file access is attempted. If that account does not have the appropriate permissions the file will not be accessible and the data load will fail. If you refresh the document from your workstation then your network credentials and user account will be used. If the document data is reloaded by a QlikView server then the user account used by the QlikView server services is used. Usually these issues can be avoided by creating and using a relative folder structure for data file sources. This may create challenges for keeping multiple developer environments in sync but it will greatly ease your transformation to a server-based shared environment.

File Structure

Depending on how your data files are created and updated their structure could become a problem. The order of the columns must not change. Also, new columns may be added or columns may be removed. This is especially true with files that have a human component to their creation (i.e. Excel files). Keep the following in mind:

- Be wary of files that do not contain embedded labels. In these cases you will be assigning column names based on their position in file. If the file's column-order changes your field names will misrepresent the data.
- If columns are inserted or removed you will get unexpected results. Unfortunately there is no way for QlikView to help you solve this problem. This is a business process issue and you must create and enforce rules for the governance of the file creation and update process.

Regardless of the rules you put in place, validation of all newly created files should occur in the development process prior to deployment or document sharing. At a minimum, it's a good idea to document the expected file structures so you can remind others of what your work requires when there's a breakdown.

File Data Integrity

The files you use as data sources may not always contain consistent and properly correlated data. The data within a single column may be incorrect or may not correlate properly to data in another column. This won't cause an error in QlikView, but it will produce inaccurate and unexpected results when the document is used. As previously mentioned, QlikView does not concern itself with data types. It stores all unique values from a column once and then creates pointers to all associated items in the data model. Even if that column contains numbers and text, it will still store each unique value and create the appropriate pointers. In some cases field values, especially those loaded from a data file, may not have proper associations. This may cause problems in list boxes tables, charts, and other screen objects throughout your QlikView document. This problem gets exponentially worse when the column in question is a field that QlikView uses to associate (link) tables or if it is used in an expression.

QlikView cannot resolve these problems for you. You must have rules in place to assure that data is provided in a consistent, complete and accurate manner. These problems are more likely to occur when using file based data because file based data is often manually maintained. Because such data isn't server based, as with database sources, rules may not exist to ensure integrity. Keep this in mind if data in your QlikView document doesn't look correct. It may not be a result of your work.

Associating Data across Disparate Data Sources

While it is possible to create your QlikView documents using data from well designed, integrated databases or a data warehouse, one of the benefits of QlikView is that such data preparation is not necessary. It is likely that you will use data from many disparate data sources. Before you can understand how QlikView handles the association of disparate data you should become a little more familiar with how QlikView stores data in general. This chapter provides some background on how the QlikView in-memory data model works and how it associates data. It is important to remember that when data is loaded into QlikView it is no longer subject to the rules and constraints often found in databases and data files. When loaded, data becomes "QlikView data," which means the rich set of features found in the QlikView load script and load process opens the door for a great deal of data management.

Understanding the QlikView Data Model

Each QlikView document contains its own associative database. This is referred to as the *QlikView Data Model*. The data model in QlikView results from how data is managed in the QlikView load script and organized when the load script completes a reload process. QlikView stores data at two levels. At the first level, unique values from each field of data are stored as a distinct list. This results in a series of in-memory lists that have no duplicate values. The second level of storage involves the creation of binary pointers from each item in these lists to their corresponding matches in other lists. These pointers are created based on field name matches that are defined in the load script. This is done without consideration for the type of data in each field. That means that QlikView doesn't care if the data in a field is number, character, or date. It will identify the data type if it can but it does that after the fact by evaluating the data stored in each list. If all of the elements in the list are integers it will identify that column as integer, etc. This allows for very efficient storage of data without affecting how data elements are associated with one another.

How QlikView Associates Tables

The way in which QlikView associates data is based on *Key Fields*. *Key Fields* are determined by field name only; two or more fields with the same name are interpreted as fields that link (associate) the data in two or more tables. Since each field is stored as a distinct list, a given category of data from one table is stored with the same category of data from another table in the same list. For example, a Product ID from the Order table is stored in the same list as the Product ID from the Product table. Since the data for this list comes from two different tables and potentially two different sources (fields in different tables or files) QlikView assumes the common field to be a *key field.* Key fields are the basis for how two or more tables are associated and are established by this process automatically. There are several ways to control or alter this behavior if the automated process does not yield the correct results. You can find more information about that in the chapter covering *Advanced Data Loading Techniques*. The critical thing to understand is how QlikView handles different fields of data, with the same name, from different sources. It associates them automatically. The only way to stop QlikView from associating them is to change the name of one of the fields. While this might seem laborious, the benefit is that getting data properly linked in QlikView is very simple and easy to change. In the load script syntax example below the two tables are associated by the *order_id* field:

```
Order:

LOAD customer_id,
    date_placed,
    order_id;
SQL SELECT "customer_id",
    date_placed,
    order_id
FROM CRMSample.dbo."order_information";

order_detail:
LOAD order_id,
    order_item_id,
    product_id,
    quantity;
SQL SELECT order_id,
    order_item_id,
    product_id,
    quantity
FROM CRMSample.dbo."order_item";
```

The resulting data model in the QlikView document would look like Figure 3-2:

FIGURE 3-2: QLIKVIEW DATA MODEL ASSOCIATION

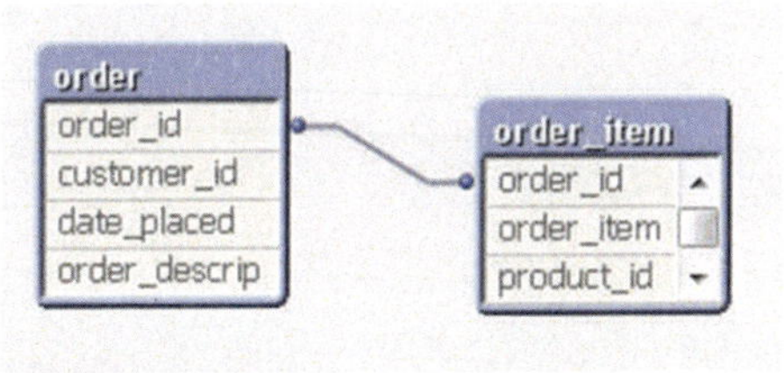

This is a simple example of how data can be loaded from an SQL database data source. Keep in mind that this data can be combined with data from other data sources including file based data. This often eliminates the need to use other tools and databases to prepare the data for analysis. Because QlikView has this advanced data management capability, it is possible to quickly address complex data integration needs. The chapter covering *Advanced Data Loading Techniques* goes into much more detail regarding the things you can do to manage data as it is loaded into your QlikView document.

Chapter 4: Creating a QlikView Document

QlikView documents provide users with the rich interactive experience for which QlikView is known. A QlikView document can include a wide range of user interface (UI) components ranging from list boxes, buttons and sliders to tables, charts and gauges. Creating a QlikView document is easy and can be done quickly. However, the ease with which a QlikView document is created should not lead you to believe that QlikView lacks depth and sophistication. QlikView is among the very few tools that blend ease of use with a robust, deep set of features and functions. Among these are such advanced capabilities as set analysis, statistical functions, pivot tables and data grouping.

It is important to understand that developing your first QlikView document is a process which, if followed properly, will result in a meaningful and rich analytical interface for your end users. Following a process based on the idea of beginning with a basic document and then enhancing it is the best way to get started. Often developers new to QlikView seek to create complex and comprehensive documents based on robust user requirements in their first effort. Such an approach may be frustrating for you. As with many technologies, the best way to learn is to begin with a specific goal and learn what's necessary to achieve it. Ideally, you will limit the scope of your initial effort so that you can quickly complete your first QlikView document and gain experience with the key aspects of QlikView before tackling more advanced features. Once you have a working document with data, you can enhance it and make it more functional. When determining the goal for your first document, choose something you believe will be useful to you or one of your users. Making up a trivial or fictitious scenario to drive your first development effort can help you learn, but sometimes results in confusion and doesn't always help you get a firm grasp on the technology. Also, make sure you limit your goal's scope to something relatively simple.

It is important to note that while this chapter includes the steps necessary to create a document, it is not a tutorial. A very complete tutorial comes with QlikView and is installed in the QlikView folder on your local machine. If you can't find the tutorial and materials provided by QlikTech, Inc., consider visiting the QlikCommunity web site and searching for them. Ideally, you will read this chapter before attempting to create your first QlikView document. It is designed to allow you to read through its entirety without having to do anything with QlikView. This offers a good foundation that will help as you begin your development effort. It also may serve as a helpful reference. However, even if you have experience with QlikView, you may find this chapter helpful. Several ideas about how to approach the creation of QlikView documents are shared and many specifics about QlikView are addressed along the way.

This chapter focuses on two scenarios for creating a QlikView document. The first leverages the Getting Started Wizard, which walks you through the creation of a simple QlikView document using an Excel file as the data source. The second uses a ground-up approach with a SQL Server database as the data source. Each of these projects includes a basic level of user interface design. They provide your user with charts, tables, pick lists and other screen objects to make it easy to understand and navigate the QlikView document.

Document Design Basics

When creating a QlikView document there are a few things you should consider from the beginning. First, it is often a good idea to include a tab sheet with basic instructions on how to use the document. This should include an overview of the QlikView associative data concept. Because most tools operate on the basis of queries and filtering, users are accustomed to an interface that removes data as they make selections. QlikView, due to its in-memory associative database, doesn't hide or remove data from the interface in most cases. Understanding that as selections are made, values across the document become either selected, associated (possible), or excluded is key to the user's success. By providing a brief overview of this functionality along with other specifics for how your document should be used can make the difference between a good user experience and a bad one.

Next, consider what data elements are necessary for you to create a meaningful user interface for your user. The best practices chapter of this book covers this and other recommendations for good design. While review of all best practices is not necessary to get started, limiting the data elements to what is necessary to achieve your initial goal is a good idea and an important habit to establish from the start. QlikView can load and associate a large amount of data, which tempts developers into being "sloppy." That is, many QlikView developers load more data than the document requires because they don't want to put forth the effort necessary to identify what's needed and produce a clean load script. While documents designed this way will work, it's a bad habit and will have consequences when you roll out documents to many users on a QlikView server or have to maintain the document later. Including too many data elements in your QlikView document can also create problems for users who run the document locally on their computers since the amount of memory and processor resources can vary.

Finally, since this is your first QlikView document, consider creating a mock up or least a list of what you want the document to do and how it should look to the user. While QlikView makes it very easy to change the layout and functionality of documents, it is important to have some idea of how the final document should look and work so you don't find yourself wasting time guessing. In figure 4-1 a sample mockup of a QlikView document is provided. Creating this took only took a few minutes. We used an inexpensive mockup tool we like called *Balsamiq* (http://balsamiq.com), but this can easily be done with pencil and paper. It is worth noting that once you have a handle on the data and user requirements for one document, it may not be necessary to mockup new documents in the future. QlikView makes prototyping very easy. Our recommendation for creating a mockup is centered on the idea that your initial effort may be reduced if you aren't learning QlikView at the same time you negotiate the basic user interface layout and ergonomics with your users. Having a mockup can make the process go more smoothly.

FIGURE 4-1: A SAMPLE MOCKUP OF A QLIKVIEW DOCUMENT

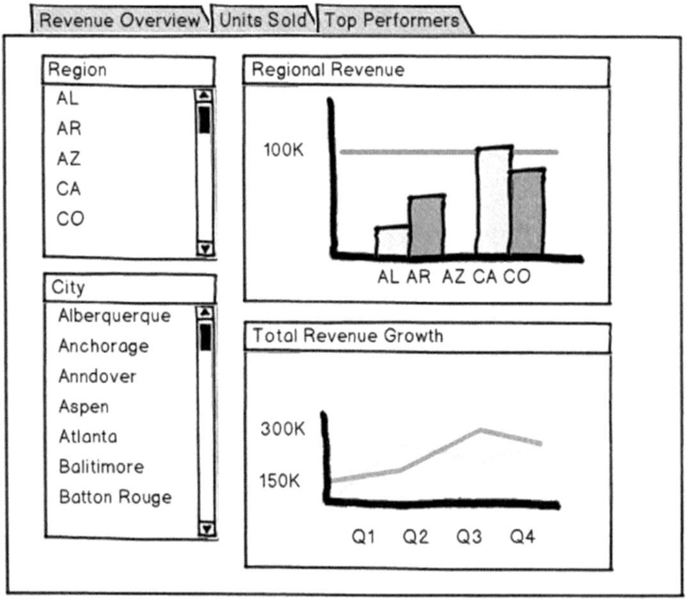

To get started with QlikView you need to have the QlikView for Windows software installed on your Windows based PC. You also need connectivity to the data on which your document will be based. If you've reviewed the chapter on accessing data, you already know this. If not, it is important to note that any and all data sources must be available to your PC before beginning document creation. This means Excel files and database connectivity should be reviewed and tested prior to beginning.

Using the *Getting Started Wizard* to Create a Document

After opening QlikView for Windows, you create a new document by selecting the *File>New* pull down menu item. The default behavior is to launch the *Getting Started Wizard*. You can toggle this option on and off in the *Settings>User Preferences* dialog. It appears on the *General* tab. The wizard is very basic and only serves to create a simple QlikView document based exclusively on Excel data. For this reason the steps below are very basic and only serve to describe the process. However, using the wizards can be helpful in getting you started with QlikView because it simplifies many of the steps and decisions necessary to create a document. In the next part of this chapter you will learn how to create a document without using the wizard, which is the method you will most likely use in most of your development.

When the wizard starts, it shows six steps and defaults to step one. Each step requires you to provide answers so the wizard can construct your document. An overview of each step is provided below:

- Step 1: This step requires you to locate and select an Excel file, after which you click *Next*. Notice that you can deactivate the wizard for future use of QlikView from this screen.
    - Click the *Browse* button to find your Excel file. Note that when searching for an Excel file the wizard looks for several Excel file extensions (xls, xlw, xlsx, xlsm) in order to accommodate several versions of Excel.
    - Click *Next* after selecting an Excel file with data.
- Step 2: Once selected, the Excel file is loaded into memory and the data appears in a grid. Note that only the first worksheet in the Excel workbook can be used. Other worksheets are not shown.
    - You are asked to indicate if the first row contains column headers. If you select Add column

headers, you can click on the header of each column and type in a name. The name is used by QlikView to set the corresponding field name.

- If you choose to add column headers, then you must type them in to replace the generic header (A, B...) on this form. To apply a typed header press *Enter*, and then click on the header for the next column. It is best to be sure your Excel worksheet has column headers in the first row.
- Click *Next* to proceed to step 3.

- Step 3: You are now required to name and save the QlikView document.
  - Click the *Save As* button to select a path and type a name for the document.
  - Click *Next* to proceed to step 4.
- Step 4: This step requires you to select a chart type. The resulting QlikView document has only one chart. In QlikView, straight tables and pivot tables are considered charts, so they appear in this section along with other popular chart types. You can experiment with these, but it's best to allow the first chart to be a bar chart so you can begin to understand how QlikView handles charting.
  - Click *Next* to proceed to step 5.
- Step 5: After selecting a chart type you must define one or two dimensions for the chart. A dimension represents the category of distribution for the chart. For example if you create a bar chart, the dimension defines what each bar represents. The list of fields in the drop down for the dimensions comes from the column headers defined when you loaded the Excel file.
  - Select the first dimension (what the bars will represent).
  - Click *Next* to proceed to step 6.
- Step 6: After you determine a chart type and define a dimension (or two), you must create an expression.

QlikView expressions, in most cases, are used to calculate a numeric value. This expression will SUM, AVERAGE or COUNT a value from one the fields brought in from Excel. SUM and AVERAGE functions are applied only to numeric fields, whereas the COUNT function can be applied to any field. This expression determines the value of the distribution in your chart. If you create a bar chart it determines the height of each bar.

- Determine the type of summary by clicking the radio button for *sum*, *average* or *number of*.
- Select a field to summarize.
- Click *Finish* to proceed and complete the creation of the document.

When you click *Finish*, the QlikView document is created and displayed. It is comprised of one tab sheet, a list box and a chart, assuming you completed all six steps before finishing. The list box is based on the field you used for the first dimension of the chart. You can see that this is a very simple document and only begins to represent what you can do with QlikView. However, using the wizard can be helpful in quickly getting Excel data into a QlikView document to produce a starting point for a more sophisticated design.

Creating a QlikView Document from the Ground Up

While the Getting Started Wizard can be helpful in your first efforts to create something with QlikView, it is very limited and is not likely to be adequate for you in the long term. The next step is for you is to begin developing a QlikView document from the ground up. By doing this you become familiar with many of the core features in QlikView. To create a new QlikView document without using the wizard you must either deactivate the wizard from the *Settings>User Preferences* menu option before creating the document, or cancel the wizard when it appears. Either action results in a new blank document with a single tab sheet named "Main."

Loading Data

The chapter on *Accessing Data with QlikView* covers data access and data loading in greater detail. However, this chapter covers some the basics for loading data so you can complete your first QlikView document. In order to create a QlikView document you must do some basic things to bring in data. This must be done before you do anything else because the user interface objects that you create, referred to as *sheet objects*, require a connection to data in order to render properly in most cases. Creating them without data, while possible, doesn't make sense and makes it difficult for you to layout the user interface.

All data access in your QlikView document is managed through the *load script*. The *load script* is comprised of a set of instructions that you create which control how the document connects to one or more data sources and how the data from these sources is loaded into memory. It is a very powerful feature and it is covered in more detail in other chapters of this book. The following steps walk you through using the load script editor to access and load data from a SQL Server data source.

1. To access the document's load script editor select the *File>Edit Script...* menu option. The editor will appear.
2. There are several script lines automatically generated at the top of the script. These script commands (SET commands) control some of the document defaults. The defaults are created based on your computer's settings and in some cases and can be changed for this document. However for your first effort, leave them as they appear. It is important that you position the blinking cursor below the SET commands before attempting to connect to a data source. By default, the cursor should already be below these lines. You may also notice line numbers on the left and if you have a version of QlikView earlier than version 11 other items may appear in a pane on the left. You can resize the window panes so the extra information on the left (to the left of the line numbers and icons) isn't visible if you like.

3. Select a Database Type: Below the script area there is a set of tabs with controls on them. The first tab is the *Data* tab. On that tab you can determine how to connect to one or more data sources. Each time you connect to a data source a line is added to the script. In the dropdown list on the *Data* tab select *OLE DB* to create an OLEDB connection to a SQL Server database. This presumes your computer has connectivity and drivers for connecting to SQL Server. If it does not then you may need to install the SQL Server Client or the Microsoft Data Access Components (MDAC) Utilities on your computer and obtain credentials from your database administrator.
4. Click the *Connect...* button and a standard Windows data link dialog appears. It allows you to connect to various types of databases. In this example we used the SQL Server Native Client provider and entered a server name and database name. To do this you must follow the steps for creating a connection string to your SQL Server database. These options may vary depending on which OLEDB drivers or version of MDAC is installed on your machine. One important note: If you use *Windows NT integrated security* and you plan to share your QlikView document, you may have problems, especially if you deploy to a QlikView server. This connection information can be changed later if necessary. Step through the Data Link Properties dialog and make the proper selections for SQL Server and enter the server and database names. Also, enter the appropriate options for logging in to the server and choose to save the password if you are not using Windows authentication.
5. After testing the connection click *OK*. This results in the creation of a connection string which is added to the load script. Statements that follow this connection sting (placed below it) automatically reference this connection. The connection string should look similar to the following, but may appear as one line in the script editor:

```
OLEDB CONNECT TO [Provider=SQLOLEDB.1;Integrated
Security=SSPI;Persist Security
Info=False;Initial Catalog=DATABASENAME;Data
Source=SQLSERVERNAME;Use Procedure for
Prepare=1;Auto Translate=True;Packet
Size=4096;Workstation ID=LOCALCOMPUTERNAME;Use
Encryption for Data=False;Tag with column
collation when possible=False];
```

6. Now that a connection to a database has been made and the connection information is in your load script, you can begin selecting tables and views of data from the database. This assumes your database credentials allow you see the tables and views of data you desire. If not, see your database administrator about your database rights. It is also worth noting that more advanced database objects such as stored procedures can be used, but this requires some special settings and syntax in some cases. See the chapter on *Advanced Data Loading Techniques* for more on this.

   Click the *Select...* button on the *Data* tab to select tables and views you wish to bring into the document. This launches a dialog from which you can select one or more tables and views from the database connection you previously created.

   Select a table first. The field list updates to show the fields for the selected table. Next, select one or more fields from the selected table. Use the *Ctrl* key while clicking to select more than one field. Ideally, you won't allow the *asterisk* to be selected. If you do select the asterisk, all fields for the selected table will be included. It is better to select only those fields you want (a best practice) to ensure that only the fields you need are retrieved from the data source. As you make selections, the script syntax is created for you in the tab labeled *Script* below. It is a good idea, and in many cases necessary, to check the *Preceding Load* check box (see Figure 4-2). Once you do this it will remain checked in the future. This is covered in greater detail in other chapters, but it's important to know that using preceding load syntax in your load script allows you to control critical aspects of how associations are made and how data is managed. You should always use it.

IMPORTANT: You must click the *Add* button after choosing the fields for a table or view before moving on to another table or view. This updates the script syntax. If you don't, when you move to another table your selections for the current table will not be included in the script. See figure 4-2.

When you click OK, the script syntax is added to the underlying load script and the dialog disappears. After the syntax is added to the load script you can edit it. In fact, you could have typed it in from the start. The select dialog is only there to make it easier to create the syntax in the load script. It is helpful in identifying which tables and fields you wish to include in the document without having to use a different tool to see the database schema.

FIGURE 4-2 SELECTING TABLES AND FIELDS FOR THE LOAD SCRIPT

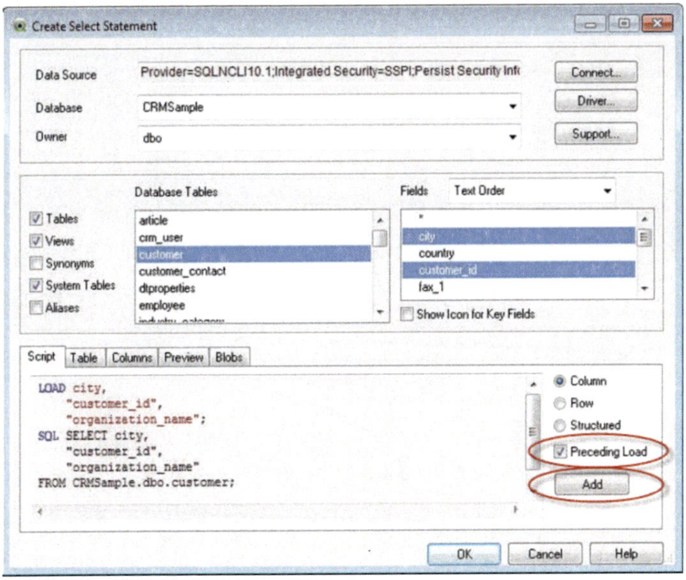

Once the load script syntax has been generated and edited, if necessary, you can load the data. This is done from within the load script editor by clicking the *Reload* button on the toolbar at the top, or from the main document screen by selecting the *File>Reload* menu item. It is advisable to save the document before attempting to load data. There is a user preference that will do this automatically each time a data reload occurs. This setting is accessed from the *Settings>User Preferences* menu item and is located on the *Save* tab; it is called *Save Before Reload.*

Using and Managing Tab Sheets

QlikView documents can be divided into separate areas by creating multiple tab sheets. A tab sheet is a canvas area onto which you place various sheet objects such as charts, list boxes, and tables. A tab sheet is accessed by clicking on the tab at the top of the tab sheet. There is no limit to the number of tab sheets a document can include, but ideally you will try to only create tab sheets where it makes sense from a user's perspective. Too many tab sheets make the document difficult to understand and navigate. On the other hand too few can result in a document with a cluttered interface. To create a tab sheet follow these steps:

1. Click on the *Layout>Add Sheet...* menu option. A new tab sheet appears to the right of the last existing sheet. It is automatically named with a sequential number and it becomes the active (selected) tab sheet.
2. To rename the sheet, or set its properties, right click on the sheet's canvas area (below the tab) and select the *Properties...* menu item from the popup menu. This launches the sheet properties dialog. The title can be edited on the *General* tab.
3. Click OK to save your changes and the sheet title changes and the properties dialog closes.

While the sheet properties dialog is open, you will notice that there are several sheet properties available. For example, you can change the background color of the sheet. You can also import a graphical image to use as the background and control the image's alignment and formatting. It is important that you understand the sheet is part of a *Tab Row*. The tabs that appear across the top for each sheet in your document comprise the tab row. There can be more than one tab row if there are enough sheets to require wrapping of the tabs. If you right click on any of the tabs and select *Properties...* from the popup menu, you can edit the sheet's tab row, rather than the tab sheet.

To construct a QlikView document you place various objects on to the sheets you create, or on to the main sheet that is created with the document. These objects are called *Sheet Objects*. They are created by right clicking on the sheet canvas and selecting *New Sheet Object...* from the popup menu. Sheet objects include a wide variety of user controls and objects for presenting and interacting with data.

Creating and Using List Boxes

QlikView is based on the idea of selecting data. Unlike other BI tools, QlikView does not query or filter data based on user selections. All of the data is in memory and available all of the time. For this reason *List Boxes* are a fundamental and popular component of QlikView documents. List boxes provide users with a list of values from which one or more selections can be made. As the user selects one or more values in a list box, those values drive changes in the other objects in the QlikView document. It would be unusual to create a QlikView document that does not contain list boxes. To add a list box to a QlikView document you do the following:

1. Right click on a tab sheet and select *New Sheet Object...* from the popup menu. A submenu appears and from there you select the *List Box...* item. The Properties dialog for the list box then appears.
2. Next, select a field for the list box to display.

3. You may also enter a *Title* for the list box, which appears as the caption in its header. By default the field name is used as the title, but this is not always desirable since field names are often poorly structured due to their technical nature.
4. Click *OK* to save your changes and create the new list box. The new list box is placed on the current sheet in the upper left corner.
5. You can move the list box by clicking and dragging the caption (header). You can also resize it by maneuvering the mouse pointer to hover over an edge of the list box and then clicking and dragging.

There are a number of more advanced properties and features of list boxes. However, they are not necessary to produce a basic selection list for your users. It is normal to have several list boxes that provide a variety of selections. It is a good idea to position list boxes in the same place on each tab sheet if they exist on more than one sheet. As with most sheet objects, list boxes can be copied and modified to save time. Standard Windows control keys (*Ctrl+C, Ctrl+V*) allow you to copy and paste list boxes and other objects once an object is selected.

Once you create a few list boxes you can review the data immediately. This is a good time to become familiar with the associative nature of QlikView. When you click on items in one list box to select them, items (field values) in the other list box should show a changed display state. These are the possible states for a field value in QlikView:

- **Selected**: This means the user has intentionally selected the item by clicking on it. Selected items appear with a green background or a checkbox or other indicator depending on how you set the properties of the list box. Multiple selections are made by holding down the *Ctrl* key and clicking several items, or by clicking and dragging over several items in a list box.

- **Excluded:** Items that are in the excluded state have no association to the items the user has selected. They appear with a gray background. However, this does not mean they are disabled. If the user clicks on an excluded item, the previous selections are replaced by the user's new selection.
- **Possible (Associated):** The term *Possible* is used to represent field values that are associated with the items the user has selected. These values appear with a white background and in most cases are moved to the top of their corresponding list box (this is a property you can change for a list box). If you want associated items to remain in their original sort order, set the *State* dropdown on the *Sort* tab of the list box properties to *Ascending*. This also occurs if the list box is fully expanded to display all of the values for the chosen field.

Collectively, these three states are sometimes referred to as the "green, white, gray" concept in QlikView. They are fundamental to the use of a QlikView document. It is a good idea to include a brief overview of this concept in the document by creating a tab sheet or other screen area with basic instructions. Figure 4-3 illustrates how these states appear by default.

FIGURE 4-3: SELECTION STATES IN QLIKVIEW LIST BOXES

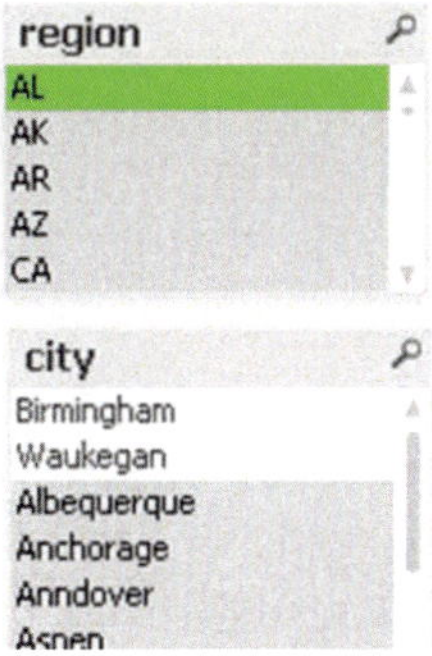

Adding Simple Charts and Gauges

Once you have loaded data and created a few list boxes to allow users to make selections, the next step is often to create data visualizations that summarize data. The most common visualizations are charts such as bar charts, pie charts and line charts. When considering which chart types to use think about what you want to show and how the end user will use the chart to make decisions. If you created a mockup, some of this has already been planned. It is helpful to know how the user will use the charts ahead of time. Different types of charts lend themselves to different types of analysis and conclusions. For example, if you wish to illustrate value distributions (how a total breaks out across categories) bar charts tend to be more effective than pie charts because if two items are close to the same value it is difficult see the difference in a pie chart. Trend analysis is usually best depicted with a line chart where the time dimension appears across the bottom from left to right.

While you may not want to spend too much time contemplating which charts best suites the users' needs for your first QlikView document, a little consideration for how the charts will be used will pay big dividends when you present your document to your users. Consider discussing the types of charts the users feel are most effective, but do so relative to specific values they want to see. There are two primary components to most charts. They are:

1. Chart Dimensions: These represent the categories of information that are compared or correlated in the chart. For example, consider what each bar should represent in a bar chart.
2. Chart Expressions (Values): Chart Expressions represent the numeric value that you are comparing, trending or correlating. This would, for example, determine the height of each bar in a bar chart.

To create a chart, you begin in the same manner as you did to create a list box. Right click on the tab sheet and select *New Sheet*

Object... from the popup menu. Next you select *Chart* from the sub menu. This launches the chart wizard, which walks you through the initial creation of the chart. Don't worry if you aren't sure about what to do in the wizard. When you finish the chart you can right click on the caption and launch the properties dialog, from which you can make changes to all of the chart properties. When the chart wizard appears it walks you through the following steps, each of which corresponds to a tab on the properties dialog of the chart after it is created.

1. **General** – This first step allows you to select the chart type. The default is set to a bar chart, but each type of chart is depicted. You can click on the chart image you desire, but we recommend beginning with a bar chart. Other types of charts may have more complex requirements. It is a good idea to type in a title for your chart rather than allowing the title to default to the syntax from the first expression.
2. **Dimensions** – A chart must have at least one dimension. Adding more than one dimension creates more divisions in the chart. For example, two dimensions create groupings of two bars in a bar chart. Be careful if you add more than one dimension. If the values for each dimension are vastly different, the chart may not be very useful because the scaling won't apply to both dimensions properly (this can be addressed in various ways that are more advanced). Also, try to select a field that does not have a lot of values. For example, if you have thousands of customers in your data, creating a dimension on the customer field would be a problem because you would have thousands of bars in your bar chart. We recommend beginning with just one dimension that has limited values. You do this by highlighting the field on the left and clicking the *Add>* button. Unless you have aliased field names in the load script, it is usually a good idea to type in a label for the dimension in the *Label* field below the *Used Dimensions* list. Otherwise the dimension label will default to the field name.

3. **Expressions** – You must create at least one expression to determine the value for each dimension item. This is what determines the scale and height of the bars in your bar chart. The wizard creates a default expression, so all you need to do is click the ellipsis (...) button next to the *Definition* text box on the right. This launches the expression editor. You can use the dropdown fields in the bottom of the expression editor to create your expression, or you can just type it in. A chart expression must summarize a field value. The most common summarizations are SUM, AVERAGE, and COUNT. However, more advanced summarizations are available in QlikView. The expression syntax should look similar to the following:

```
SUM(quantity)
```

4. You should note that you can also perform calculations in this expression. For example, you could multiply two fields such as quantity times unit price:

```
SUM(quantity * unit_price)
```

5. After entering the expression click *OK* to close the expression editor and return to the chart wizard.
6. **Sort** – This step allows you to control the order in which the dimension items appear in the chart. The default setting arranges them alphabetically in ascending order based on the dimension item name. However, you can change the order. For example, selecting the Y-value option and unchecking all other options displays the bars in your bar chart based on their height (value).
7. **Style** – This step provides options that affect the look of the chart. Graphical depictions illustrate various options. These options are specific to the type of chart you select. By clicking on an image of the *Look* you desire, various other properties are enabled. You can control certain aspects of 3D views as well as the chart's plot area.

Remember, all of these options are available for adjustment after the chart is created.

8. **Presentation** – The next step allows you to change various settings that control how the chart is presented. Many of these settings are specific to the chart type you select. Two notable settings are the ability to limit the number of dimension items shown in the chart by checking the *Max Visible Number* check box. If you are using version 11 of QlikView you will also see a tab with options for setting *Dimension Limits*. This option allows you to more easily show top or bottom values and addresses the issue of having too many dimension items to create a meaningful chart. If you are using an earlier version of QlikView you can sort the dimension by the Y-value in order to display the top or bottom of the distribution for the number you enter. The *Limit Legend (Characters)* check box is helpful when your chart dimension is based on a field with long text values. This allows you truncate the values to make the chart look better.
9. **Axes** – This step allows you to adjust how the X axis (dimension) and Y axis (expression) look and work. It, as with other options, is specific to the type of chart you select. For a bar chart you can adjust the expression axis to force inclusion of zero values, change the scale to use logarithmic values (helpful with numbers that span a very large range) and control various visual attributes. On the dimension axis you can control how the labels are oriented and formatted (very helpful in some cases) and adjust other visual attributes.
10. **Colors** – This step provides a variety of settings that allow you to control how the data appears relative to color, pattern and transparency. This affects how the bars (data), frame background and plot area border appear. Remember, you can adjust all of these later if you aren't happy with the way the chart looks.

11. **Number** – This step is important because it allows you to control how the data values are formatted. By selecting the expression on the left, you can choose a preformatted option such as Money or Integer. You can also control decimal precision and other formatting options. The Format Pattern text box is updated as you make different selections. You can also manually edit the pattern for custom formatting.
12. **Font** – This step provides options to set the default font characteristics for the chart. A sample of your selections appears in the text box in the middle of the dialog.
13. **Layout** – The layout step allows you to control the overall layout of the chart object. You can create a drop shadow around the object and set its border width. This also allows you to set various behavioral options. You typically won't want to change these settings. However, as you become more experienced with QlikView you may find some of these settings helpful. For example, you can conditionally show or hide the chart by using variables and the *Show-Conditional* setting.
14. **Caption** – This is the final step. It allows you to adjust the chart object's caption bar (header) and related items. These settings are common to most sheet objects. Notably, you can adjust which icons appear in the caption bar to allow users to perform actions such as print the chart, copy it as an image to the Windows clipboard or send its data to Excel.

Charting Tips

There are a few things you may want to consider when adding charts to your QlikView document. Charts have default properties that sometimes fail to provide an ideal presentation of the data. Here are few tips that may help your first charts look and work better for users.

- Dimension Axis Labeling: The default orientation for labels on the horizontal dimension axis of bar charts shows the label for each bar (dimension item) in horizontal text. QlikView will stagger these labels so they don't run into each other. This often makes the chart hard to read. Using the *Axes* tab of the chart properties (right click on the chart), change the *Primary Dimension Labels* option to use the middle or last radio button. This will force the labels to appear at an angle or vertically and may make the chart more readable.
- Null Values: If your chart includes dimension items for which there are no values, you may be showing irrelevant information. Consider checking the *Suppress When Value is Null* check box on the *Dimensions* tab of the chart properties.
- Non-Data Ink: A modern trend in data visualization is to eliminate unnecessary clutter from charts. Such clutter is often called "non-data ink," which means it is unusable information to the user. Examples of this include lines and backgrounds on charts and 3D rendering of chart elements. Consider reducing your use of non-data ink by selecting 2D styling on the *Style* tab and de-emphasizing things such as grid lines (*Axes* tab) in the chart properties.

Navigating Selection History

Because QlikView is fundamentally based on the idea that users make selections rather than filter data, keeping track of the selection status during a session is important. Users may start out selecting one set of data from various list boxes and then change the selection to explore different situations. This is what makes QlikView so powerful and such a great data discovery tool. However, it can become confusing. To address this QlikView keeps track of the user's selections in a manner similar to the way a Web browser keeps track of the sites a user visits. Additionally, QlikView allows the user to clear all selections across the entire document to create a new starting point for exploration. Basic selection navigation includes three things that users will commonly do:

- Clear Selections: By clicking the *Clear* button on the top toolbar, a user can deselect everything, which means all data is in the *Possible* state with a white background in list boxes. This will also result in charts showing values for all dimension items.
- Back Up to Previous Selection: Users may click the *Back* button on the top toolbar to revert to the last selection state. Even if the user clears the selection state, the *Back* button will allow navigation to the last selection state before clearing occurred.
- Go Forward: Users may click the *Forward* button to navigate to the next selection state after having navigated backwards.

It is very important that you make your users aware of these core navigation features. The *Clear*, *Back* and *Forward* buttons are available in all QlikView viewers including the Web client and Windows client. It's worth noting that you can also create buttons to provide navigation from within the tab sheet area.

Showing and Managing Current Selections

Since the user of a QlikView document may make a wide variety of selections across all dimensions in the document, it is easy to for the user to lose track of all of the selections made. For this reason a special sheet object exists called a *Current Selections Box*. This object shows all of the dimensions on which the user has made selections and displays either the actual values selected or a summary of them. The *Current Selections Box* also allows users to erase (remove) the selections from within the box, rather than going back to the list boxes originally used to make the selections or using the *Clear* button (which clears all selections). If you are using version 11 then the Current Selections box also allows selections to be changed from within the box by clicking on the little down arrow icon in the row for a given dimension.

To add a Current Selections Box to your document you right click and select *Add Sheet Object...* from the popup menu, just as you've done with other objects. Select *Current Selections Box* from the list and the properties dialog appears. There is a wide variety of options for how the box appears and works, but no changes are necessary to use it. When you close the properties dialog it is placed on the tab sheet and can be moved by dragging the caption with your mouse pointer.

Helpful Hint: Current Selections Boxes can be resized and the columns within them can be adjusted to different widths. This can help in achieving a high quality interface. Also note that you cannot apply labels to fields in the Current Selections box; another good reason to ensure that fields are aliased in the load script.

Creating and using Bookmarks

While the ability to navigate the user's selection states and see the current selection status is helpful, sometimes users wish to save a predetermined set of selections. Allowing for this is critical because users often wish to perform the same analysis on a regular basis. If the user must select certain values on a number of dimensions each time analysis is performed, the user will become fatigued and the QlikView document may not be used for long. To address this, QlikView includes bookmarks. Bookmarks are collections of selections that can be named and recalled at any time. This is done by making one or more selections and then using the *Bookmark>Add Bookmark...* dropdown menu, which displays the *Add Bookmark* dialog.

The *Add Bookmark* dialog allows you to enter a name, but creates a name based on the date and a sequence number. It is recommended to modify the name to reflect the nature of the selections to be stored in the bookmark. It also includes options for several features:

- *Make this bookmark a document bookmark*: This option forces the bookmark to be saved with the document and makes it available to all users. If the document is deployed to a QlikView server, users (depending on the version of the server) can create their own personal bookmarks. However, you, as the developer, may want certain bookmarks to always be available. These are "document bookmarks."

- *Include Selections in Bookmark*: This is checked by default and should remain that way. However, there are some circumstances with newer versions of QlikView when a bookmark is used only to affect input values. As a sub-option you check *Make bookmark apply on top of current selections.* This will force the bookmark to be layered on top of the current user's selections (added to them). The default behavior is to replace the user's selections with those saved in the bookmark. If you choose this option, it is a good idea to have the bookmark name show that it is being added to current selections.
- *Include Input Field Values*: This option allows the bookmark to keep track of data the user entered into input fields that are used to create "what if" scenarios.
- *Info Text*: The Info Text field in the dialog allows you to create a description of the bookmark and provide the users with additional information on how to use it. A good example of this might be when the bookmark is being applied to current selections. The info text is stored, but it won't show up unless you also check the *Pop-up Message* check box, which displays the message in a popup menu after the user selects the bookmark. Note that the message does not appear when hovering over the bookmark. This is an important consideration if you plan to deploy your QlikView document to mobile devices that employ touch-screen technology.

Deleting a Bookmark is something that must be done from time to time. You can delete a bookmark from your document by selecting *Bookmark>Remove Bookmark* from the dropdown menu. The available bookmarks will be listed and you can select the one you want to remove. You can also edit bookmarks by selecting the *Bookmark>more...* dropdown menu item. This shows a dialog with a list of the bookmarks and options for changing them. However, editing a bookmark is limited to a small set of options. In some cases you may have to remove and recreate the bookmark.

Chapter 5: Advanced Data Loading Techniques

In earlier chapters you were introduced to the standard methods for loading data into QlikView. For some QlikView documents, these basic approaches to loading data are adequate. However, during development of other QlikView documents it will become necessary to have a deeper understanding of data loading techniques. Understanding the more advanced methods for loading data will also help you optimize your load scripts and produce leaner, more efficient QlikView documents. Such efforts not only solve a variety of problems concerning data structuring, but also address issues with memory use, performance of your QlikView document and simplification of user interface design. Additionally, by understanding and using these advanced techniques you will be able to enhance how the user interacts with the data model by providing meta-data. This can be important for users who wish to leverage QlikView to create tab sheets, charts and other user interface objects for themselves.

This chapter also addresses some of the traps associated with loading data into QlikView and provides solutions for these situations. Methods for optimizing your data loads and increasing functionality within your QlikView documents are also covered.

Synthetic Keys

The chapter covering *QlikView Document Design Best Practices* introduced the concept of synthetic keys and synthetic tables. Remember that synthetic keys are really compound keys comprised of more than one field. This occurs automatically in QlikView whenever there is more than one field in common between two or more tables. Whenever a synthetic key is created, at least one synthetic table will also be created that acts as a bridge between the two original tables. Documents with synthetic keys can work and can produce accurate results, but documents that include synthetic keys are typically considered a problem as these keys and tables add overhead and complexity and may cause improper associations in some cases.

Many of the examples in this chapter demonstrate how synthetic keys and their corresponding synthetic tables can be eliminated by using more advanced load script functions. It is a good idea to eliminate synthetic keys even though they sometimes work and produce correct results. Understanding this is fundamental to being able to optimize your load script and plays an important role in situations where data and user volume is high.

Managing and Optimizing In-Memory Tables

Unlike conventional BI tools, QlikView loads all data into memory. This offers the advantage of allowing you to associate and manipulate the data in memory after it has been retrieved from various underlying data sources. The simplest example of this is when you control how two tables are associated by changing the name of one or more fields in the *preceding load* statement. However, there are many other things you can do with tables of data once they are loaded into memory. In fact, you can even manipulate the data as it is being loaded, making it possible for QlikView to address a wide variety of data management needs.

Joining Tables

A common, but often overlooked feature of the QlikView load script is the ability to join two or more tables together. Joining tables in QlikView should not be confused with associating tables. An association, which occurs when there is a common field name between two tables, cross references the two tables to each other. A join in QlikView creates a single table from two tables, which effectively eliminates one of the tables. This can address issues with performance as well as data model complexity.

Joining tables occurs horizontally; that is, fields (columns) from both tables are combined with the rows from both tables. When two tables are joined, a key field that is common between them is used to determine how the rows in one table correlate to the rows in the other. This means that in most cases values from one of the tables are repeated for each occurrence of a corresponding value in the other. This duplication of data is one reason why you may want limit how often you join tables. But, keep in mind that the extra overhead used by the repeating data is often a worthwhile trade off to accomplish other things in the load script. Also keep in mind that QlikView does a good job of handling duplicate data internally, so the extra memory requirements for the duplicated data are not as significant as it may seem.

Why join tables? First and foremost, it is important to understand that every association you create in your document data model carries with it a cost. When the data is loaded and the user interacts with the document, some operations require data from more than one table. When this happens extra time and processing is needed to find and use associated data. This overhead is finite and because all data is in memory it is unnoticeable in most cases. Documents with hundreds of thousands or even millions of rows of data rarely show an impact from data model associations. However, when very large amounts of data are loaded (hundreds of millions or billions of rows), reducing the number of associations can have a profound effect on performance. If you are accessing all data from a relational database that supports SQL syntax, it may be desirable to perform table joins in the SQL statement. However, if you need to join tables from disparate data sources (i.e. one table from SQL Server, another from Oracle, another from a CSV or XML file), this is not an option because of the different data formats and source systems. Joins between QlikView tables can accomplish this because as the data is loaded into QlikView it is joinable. Also, if by associating two tables in QlikView with a common key field the same result is achieved, why should tables ever be joined? The fact is that in a complex QlikView data model, having everything in its own table can cause problems. In some cases it can become difficult or impossible to maintain unique key field names for every table, which often results in synthetic keys or circular references. In other cases having a large number of tables and associations combined with a high volume of data can result in very poor performance. Such performance problems manifest themselves when complex expressions that use fields from multiple tables must be calculated in QlikView expressions after the data is loaded. In some cases our team has seen simple user interactions such as navigating from one tab sheet to another take an unacceptably long time due to issues with table associations. These and other problems can often be addressed by joining tables together in the load script.

An example of joining two tables together is represented by the need to combine order detail information and order header information into a single table that includes both order totals and order line item details. The reasoning in this case is that the number of order and line item details is very high and having them in two tables results in poor performance. By combining them the QlikView document may consume more memory, but will perform better. Consider the following conventional table association shown in Figure 5-1.

FIGURE 5-1: CONVENTIONAL TWO TABLE ASSOCIATION

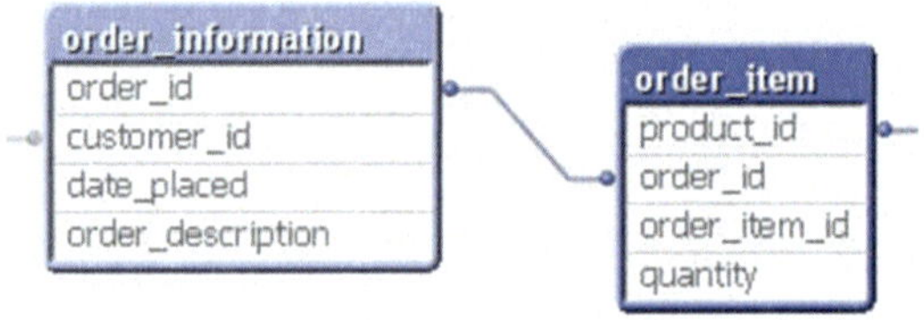

In this example order details are linked to order header information using the common key field named *order_id*. This works well until data volumes become very large. When that happens, expressions in the user interface that summarize order detail values such as *quantity* don't perform well. It should be noted that the data volumes would have to be very high (hundreds of millions or billions of rows) before this would be a concern. However other associations in the data model may compound this, so assume there are many more associated tables in the data model and a very high volume of data. The load script syntax for these tables is simple:

```
order:
LOAD customer_id,
    date_placed,
    order_id;
SQL SELECT "customer_id",
    date_placed,
    order_id
FROM CRMSample.dbo."order_information";

order_detail:
LOAD order_id,
    order_item_id,
    product_id,
    quantity;
SQL SELECT order_id,
    order_item_id,
    product_id,
    quantity
FROM CRMSample.dbo."order_item";
```

The association between these tables is obvious because they both contain a field named *order_id*. To combine these tables a join function is used. It is placed between the two tables.

```
order:
LOAD customer_id,
    date_placed,
    order_id;
SQL SELECT "customer_id",
    date_placed,
    order_id
FROM CRMSample.dbo."order_information";

JOIN

order_detail:
LOAD order_id,
    order_item_id,
    product_id,
    quantity;
SQL SELECT order_id,
```

```
    order_item_id,
    product_id,
    quantity
FROM CRMSample.dbo."order_item";
```

The addition of the JOIN function doesn't change the data, but effectively eliminates the second table. The resulting single table is the first table and retains its name. Figure 5-2 shows the revised data model.

FIGURE 5-2: JOINED TABLE RESULT

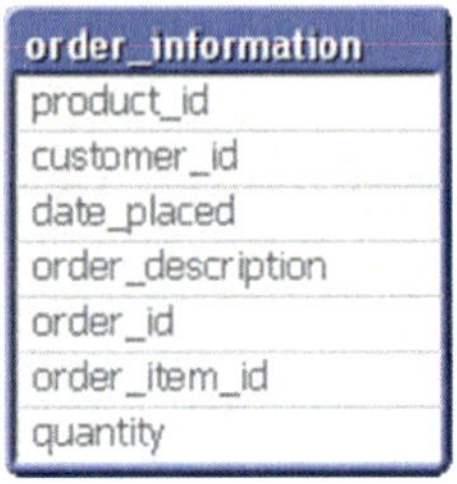

Notice in the result of the join syntax that the *quantity*, *order_item_id* and *product_id* fields have now been added to the order table eliminating the need for both tables.

There are different types of table joins in QlikView similar to joins in SQL and other data management languages. The default join type is known as a *Natural* join, which matches rows in both tables on one or more common fields (keys). It only returns rows from both tables where there is a match on both for at least one of the common fields. Other join types include:

- *INNER JOIN* – An inner join includes only rows from both tables where all common fields are matched. This is different from a natural join where rows are included with a match on any of the common fields.
- *OUTER JOIN* – An outer join combines both tables with all combinations of rows from each table. No matching is required.

- *LEFT JOIN* – A left join includes all rows from the first (left) table and only rows with a match on common fields from the right table.
- *RIGHT JOIN* – This is the opposite of a LEFT join.

Concatenating Tables

The idea of concatenating tables is a little different than that of joining tables. In the case of concatenation one table is combined with another vertically. That is, the data set from the second table is added to the data set from the first. The two data sets are essentially stacked on top of each other. A join will append fields (horizontally) from the first table to the second table resulting in duplication of the first table's data where matches to more than one record in the second table exist. A concatenation of data won't duplicate data from the first table because the rows, not the fields (columns), from the second table are being added to the bottom (vertically) of the first table. This presumes that both tables have the same fields, but as you will see even if the fields are different in the two tables, a concatenation can be performed.

Why concatenate tables? The reason for concatenating two tables is the same as joining two tables. Ideally you want to eliminate unnecessary associations between tables. Concatenating tables may, in some cases, be more efficient than joining them. This is especially true if the fields are the same or very similar in both tables. The value in concatenation is that the data model and document become more efficient. Outside of very specific and rare user interface behavior, there's no benefit to having two tables with identical fields.

If two tables are loaded in the QlikView load script and they have identical field names, they will automatically be concatenated into a single table with all rows from both. This can be confusing if you don't realize that it happens automatically, but QlikView does this because it does not alter the result of the load script instructions and it makes the document more efficient. The resulting table will have the first table's name. It doesn't matter if they are loaded sequentially, or if other tables are loaded between them. The fact that all fields in both tables are named the same results in automatic concatenation. Knowing this is important, because when you look at the data model it may seem as though one of your tables isn't loading. The way you can know it is concatenated is to look at the data.

In some cases, you will find that although two tables do not have identical fields, you still want to concatenate them. One reason you may want to do this is that one of the tables has extra fields that further describe each row, but otherwise the fields are the same in both tables. You may not want to omit the extra fields even though they don't apply to the first table. Figure 5-3 shows the results of a data load where two tables, one from an SQL database (*product_category*) and one from an Excel file (*Sheet1$),* both represent product category data. The Excel data contains a field not found in the SQL data. Other than the *note* field in the Excel data, the fields in both tables are identical. Because of this one difference, QlikView will not attempt to automatically perform a concatenation. The result is a synthetic table and key because more than one field in each table matches.

FIGURE 5-3 CONCATENATION NEEDED

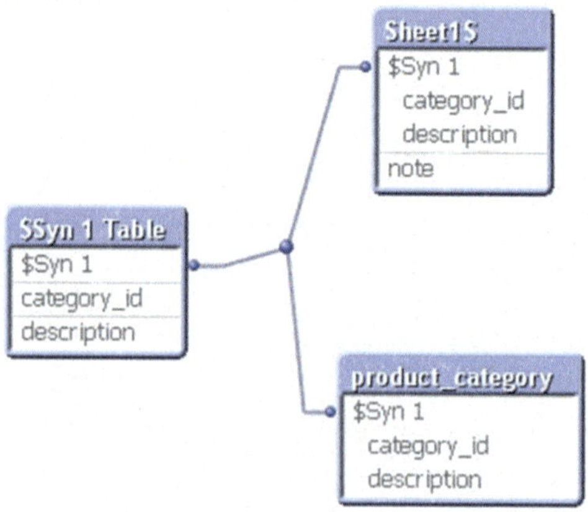

This data model will function properly and return the correct data. However, it is not efficient and should not be allowed to exist in this form. By forcing a concatenation between these two tables, the synthetic key and table is removed and a single *product_category* table results, containing all the data and fields from both tables. To force a concatenation you add the *CONCATENATE* command between the two table loads in the load script syntax. Here is an example:

```
LOAD "category_id",
    description;
SQL SELECT "category_id",
    description
FROM CRMSample.dbo."product_category";

CONCATENATE

LOAD category_id,
     description,
     note
FROM
[product_cats_new.xls]
(biff, embedded labels, table is Sheet1$);
```

The resulting data includes all fields and rows from both tables. Rows from the SQL table have no note, but rows from the Excel table do. Here is an example of the data:

category_id	description	note
1	Supplies	
2	Office Equipment	
3	Computers & Networking	
4	Parts	
5	Misc	
200	Cell Phones	limited carriers
201	Tablet Computers	Apple only
202	MP3 Players	Apple only

The effect on the data model is that there is now only one table named *product_category*. The synthetic table and key as well as the Excel table are automatically eliminated.

Performing Lookups with a Mapping Load

Depending on the structure of your source data, there may be many situations where the data necessary for a coherent view of a subject is spread across a variety of tables. This is common when developing QlikView documents from normalized database systems. Such situations can result in loading a lot of unnecessary data as well as a complex set of unnecessary associations in the data model. One load script feature that can help with this problem is the *MAPPING* function. The mapping function allows you to use a value from one table to look up a value from another table. This effectively eliminates the need to retain the first table because it retrieves the needed data values and incorporates them into the second table. As with joins and concatenations, the result is a single table, reducing the number of tables and joins. This makes for a more efficient document data model that is easier to maintain. When using the mapping function the first table, the table from which data is retrieved, is called the "mapping table." The second table is the table into which the retrieved values are placed. The mapping table (first table) is automatically removed from the data model and from memory upon completion of the load script.

Consider a situation where you wish to load customer contacts with their respective regions, but the region information is in the main customer table, not in the contact table. Figure 5-4 shows how these tables would be associated if you wanted to load both tables to accomplish this.

FIGURE 5-4 MAPPING LOAD SCENARIO

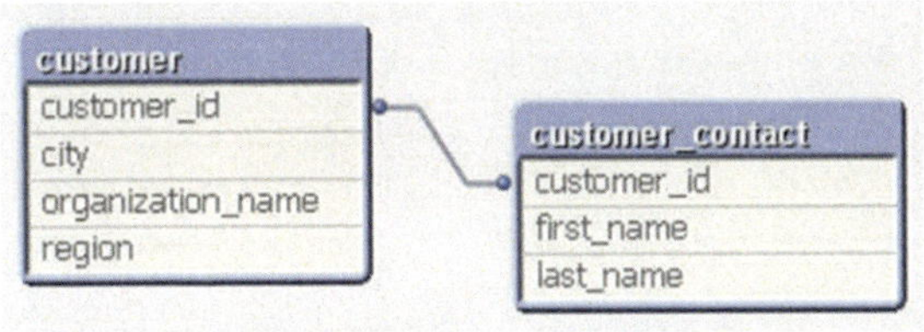

To bring the *region* field into the *customer_contact* table so that there is only one table and no associations, you must first designate a mapping load. This is done by adding the *MAPPING* script command in front of the *LOAD* command. The rest of the load statement is the same as it would be for any data load. So, for example, if you are loading a table from an SQL database the load statement uses a *SQL SELECT* after the *LOAD* command. The use of the *MAPPING* command allows the results of the load to be used as a look up. When creating a mapping load, the result from the load statement must return only two fields. The first field must be the key that is used to look up a match. The second is the value that is returned by the lookup. The following is an example of a mapping load that returns the *region* value when a *customer_id* is used to perform the lookup.

```
customer_region_map_table:
MAPPING LOAD "customer_id",
    region;
SQL SELECT "customer_id",
    region
FROM CRMSample.dbo.customer;
```

Once a mapping table has been created in the load script using the *MAPPING LOAD* syntax, an *APPLYMAP* function may be used to perform a lookup. The *APPLYMAP* function is used in a preceding load to create a new field. The syntax requires that you first pass in the name of the mapping table (the table created with the mapping load). This value must be a string constant. In other words the name of the table should be enclosed in single quotes. The second value is the name of the field from the current load that represents the value used to perform the lookup. This could also be a constant value or an expression, but by using a field name from the current load each row in the final table will have a corresponding value based on the field value passed to the mapping table. Here is an example of an *APPLYMAP* function.

```
customer_contact:
LOAD
    APPLYMAP('customer_region_map_table',
             customer_id) as region,
    "customer_id",
    "first_name",
    "last_name";
SQL SELECT "customer_id",
    "first_name",
    "last_name"
FROM CRMSample.dbo."customer_contact";
```

Notice that the first field returned by the *LOAD* statement uses *APPLYMAP* to lookup a region. The first value is the name of the mapping table, the second is the *customer_id* field from the *customer_contact* table, which is used to find the corresponding region in the *customer* (mapping) table. The result is a single table name, customer_contact, which includes the region field. The mapping table is automatically removed from memory and does not appear in the data model. The reference to the mapping table does not appear to be case sensitive, but the reference to the field in the current load is. If you get an error, consider case correctness in your *APPLYMAP* statement. A third value can also be passed to the *APPLYMAP* command. Following the table name and field (or expression) values, you can also pass a default value that is used when a value cannot be found during the lookup.

Addressing Complex Associations, Circular References

The QlikView in-memory associative data model is different from a traditional relational database. Relational databases are comprised of tables that "relate" to one another by one or more fields. In conventional data models the concept of relating two tables is based on the idea that when both tables are used in a query, a single data set is created containing fields from both tables. The way in which conventional table relationships are established often involves the use of several fields (columns) from each. The QlikView associative database, however, requires that two tables "associate" by only a single field. Rather than combining a predetermined set of fields from both tables, as you might in a conventional SQL query, QlikView automatically associates all of the fields in both tables based on a match from a single field in each. The result is essentially two lists of data that, once associated with a single field, can be combined in whatever way is needed.

QlikView's associative data model also differs from conventional relational data models in another significant way. When two tables are joined using SQL syntax in a relational model, the output can show all of the data that is related between both of the tables, as well as data that is not related. An example of this would be an outer join in SQL. However, such results from a SQL query do not correlate exceptions. For example, there is no way for a user to see which values are NOT related to a given row in the results. Exceptions must be engineered using specific criteria in SQL and other database languages; this cannot happen on an ad-hoc basis after data is returned.

The associative model in QlikView allows all of the data returned by the document data load to be associated and accessible. In turn, the user may see all of the values associated with a selected value, as well as all of the values that are NOT associated with that value. Understanding how an associative data model works requires a paradigm shift for developers who have experience with conventional database technologies. The results produced by QlikView's in-memory associative data model are much more intuitive for the end users. This is because they allow users to interact with the data in the same way that the human brain naturally associates information and memories.

At first glance the association of tables by a single field may seem like an impediment to creating a coherent data model. This challenges the idea of "natural keys" in relational data design. However, once you understand how QlikView associates data, you will find this approach is easy, quick and powerful. It is important to remember that the field used to associate two tables in QlikView does not require unique values in either table. You should think of an association as a way of matching table values, rather than a way of joining the tables together. The first, and most important, step is to limit the fields in each table so that no field, except the field used to create an association, exists in both tables. For example, if a field named *unit_price* exists in both the *product* table and the *order_detail* table, you need to make a determination as to which table should act as the source for unit price values. In this case, you might choose the *unit_price* field from the *order_detail* table since that table would contain the unit price of each item on the order at the time that it was ordered. By contrast, the unit price value attached to the product record might change over time. By loading the field from only one of these tables, you have effectively eliminated another association between the two tables and you have reduced the amount of data needed to facilitate the needs of the document.

Multi-field Keys in QlikView

Although it is usually preferable to associate tables in QlikView with only one common field, you will likely experience situations in which you need to associate two tables on more than one field. Consider a scenario where a discount can be applied to individual line items on an order based on product promotions. The discount detail information may be stored in a separate table from the order information, so the two tables need to be associated by the order_id and product_id fields. To address this, these two fields may be concatenated to create a single field with both values. The following example of load script syntax shows this.

```
LOAD
       "order_id" & "product_id" as key_field,
       "order_item_id",
        quantity;
SQL SELECT "order_id",
    "order_item_id",
    "product_id",
```

```
    quantity
FROM CRMSample.dbo."order_item";
```

In the above example the first field uses the *order_id* and *product_id* fields to create a new field called *key_field*. They are concatenated. The resulting number is a combination (not a math operation) of the two numbers. This is occurs because the concatenation operator (&) is used. QlikView can perform this operation and return a number because it is loose about how it treats data types once data is in memory. It is obvious such concatenation would work for text values, but we find it interesting that the same operation can occur on numeric values. If the fields needed in such a compound key are text values, QlikView can use the text values to generate a unique numeric value to reduce data and make the key more efficient. This is done using the *AUTONUMBER* function which returns a unique integer value for unique text passed into it as an argument.

Slowly Changing Dimensions: A Common Data Challenge

You may also encounter even more challenging situations where there is a more complex type of association needed between several tables. A common example of this is the need to address slowly changing dimensions, or SCDs. At a high level, slowly changing dimensions are descriptive values (dimensions) that need to be tracked as they change over time. For example salespeople change territories, employees change positions and departments within an organization and people change addresses over time. In each of these cases, you need to decide if tracking and reporting those changes is meaningful and if so, how you should handle the changes when the document reloads data.

In general, there are three different types of SCDs, though some schools of thought suggest there are even more. Type 1 SCDs are dimensions where there is no need to track changes. Once a change takes place, the historical record is overwritten and now appears as if the new value existed for all of time. A person moving to a different address might be an example of this. If there is no need to track the history of someone's residences, it is acceptable to overwrite old address information with the new. In this case, history is not preserved.

Type 2 SCDs are what many people envision when they think of situations that represent slowly changing dimensions. In these situations, it is necessary to track the new values and the old values for every change in the dimension. In other words, history is preserved for all of time. Consider a scenario where orders are placed with customers over a long period of time. The sales person, who is an employee, for a customer's account may change during that period. This means some orders are associated with one employee while other orders are associated with different employees. At any given point in time only one employee is associated with the account. To get a summary of a sales person's performance it is necessary to know for which intervals of time the employee was associated with the customer's account. In this scenario the *customer*, *employee* and *order_information* tables are stored in a SQL database, but the sales history information, which correlates when an employee was assigned to a customer account, is stored in Excel. The Excel file tracks the customer ID, employee ID, a start date and an end date. There is no data in either the *customer* or *order_information* table to indicate association with an employee. The goal is to add an *employee_id* field to the *order_information* table so that we can summarize orders by employee. To make this happen the following steps must occur:

1. Load the customer and order_information tables from the SQL database.
2. Load the sales_history table from the Excel file
3. Load the employee table from the SQL database
4. A LEFT JOIN with and INTERVALMATCH is performed between the *employee* table and the *sales_history* table.
5. The *sales_history* table is joined to the *order_information* table.
6. The *sales_history* table is dropped from memory.

Steps 1, 2 and 3: The following load script syntax shows the loading of the *customer, order_Information, sales_history* and *employee* tables. There's nothing special about how this occurs. The loading is based on standard load script syntax.

```
customer:
LOAD "customer_id",
    "organization_name",
    region;
SQL SELECT "customer_id",
    "organization_name",
    region
FROM CRMSample.dbo.customer;

order_information:
LOAD "customer_id",
    DATE("date_accepted", 'MM/DD/YYYY') as
date_accepted,
    description,
    "order_id";
SQL SELECT "customer_id",
    "date_accepted",
    description,
    "order_id"
FROM CRMSample.dbo."order_information";

sales_history:
LOAD employee_id,
     customer_id,
     date_start,
     date_end
FROM
[sales_history.xlsx]
(ooxml, embedded labels, table is training_history);

employee:
LOAD "employee_id",
    "first_name",
    "job_title",
    "last_name";
SQL SELECT "employee_id",
    "first_name",
    "job_title",
    "last_name"
FROM CRMSample.dbo.employee;
```

Step 4: The next segment of load script syntax shows that after the tables are loaded a *LEFT JOIN* is performed in conjunction with an *INTERVALMATCH* command. This is done between the *employee* table and the already loaded *sales_history* table. The *RESIDENT* command allows for reference to the *sales_history* data that has already been loaded into memory. This must be done because the *INTERVALMATCH* function does not load data.

The *INTERVALMATCH* command uses the *date_accepted* and *customer_id* fields to find a match in the in the *sales_history* table. The match occurs by determining if the value from the *date_accepted* field falls between the *date_start* and *date_end* values. If it does, then the *customer_id* value is compared to the *customer_id* from the *sales_history* table. If the *customer_id* also matches then the results from the INTERVALMATCH are added the fields in the *order_information* table. The following syntax represents the next set of load script commands, which perform step 4.

```
LEFT JOIN (order_information)
INTERVALMATCH(date_accepted, customer_id)
LOAD
        date_start,
        date_end,
        customer_id
RESIDENT sales_history;
```

Steps 5 and 6: The *sales_history* table (already in memory) is joined to the *order_information* table to ensure that the *order_information* table includes the *employee_id*. This allows the *employee* table data to be associated with order data so fields such as *last_name* may be used in the document sheet objects. Finally, in step 5, the *sales_history* table is dropped because it is no longer needed. Its fields and values are joined to the other tables where necessary. The reason *RESIDENT* loading is used with the *sales_history* table is because it is used several times to add fields and data to other tables and then dropped. If it were used in a conventional join, it would have to be reloaded to be used subsequently. The following syntax represents the next set of load script commands, which perform steps 5 and 6.

```
LEFT JOIN (order_information) LOAD * RESIDENT
sales_history;

DROP TABLE sales_history;
```

The final result of this load script is a set of three tables where the *date_start*, *date_end* and *employee_id* fields are added to the *order_information* table. Figure 5-5 shows the document's data model after load script execution.

FIGURE 5-5 DATA MODEL ADDRESSING SCD TYPE 2

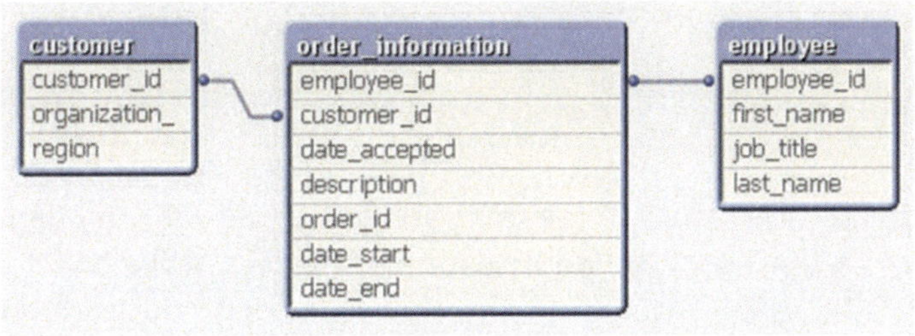

Upon completion of executing the *INTERVALMATCH*, and associated load script syntax, the document may now show summaries and details that illustrate how employees are associated with customer accounts, as well as specific order summaries for employees, within specified periods of the time. Figure 5-6 shows such results.

FIGURE 5-6 INTERVALMATCH SYNTAX RESULTS

Data

customer_id	order_id	date_accepted	date_start	date_end	last_name
45	428	09/19/2001	1/1/2001	12/31/2001	Devinsherm
45	1573	12/01/2001	1/1/2001	12/31/2001	Devinsherm
2607	936	08/13/2002	1/1/2002	12/31/2002	Madison
2607	1448	09/19/2002	1/1/2002	12/31/2002	Madison
2607	1835	10/28/2002	1/1/2002	12/31/2002	Madison
2935	354	09/05/2001	1/1/2001	12/31/2002	Mederia
2935	1072	12/25/2001	1/1/2001	12/31/2002	Mederia

Note that the results in the table are associated with an *alternate state* so that all of the detail data may be seen while the Orders chart shows the result of the user's selections. In this case notice that only one employee has activity between the start and end dates for the year 2001.

By using the extended *INTERVALMATCH* syntax, you can successfully solve the Type 2 SCD challenge in your data while at the same time maintaining a synthetic table-free data model.

Circular References

Circular references pose a different challenge to building an efficient and functional data model in your QlikView document. Circular references occur when there are associations within the data model that cause a loop between tables. In other words, the association between some of your tables will bend back around to include the original table. This is problematic for an associative data model because it can cause unpredictable results. If a selection is made on a field from one table, QlikView will find all of the data in the second table that is associated to the selected value. If that table then associates to a third table, all of the corresponding values from that table will also be associated. This is the default behavior in QlikView and part of what makes it so powerful. However, if that third table then associates back to the original table by way of a different field, the values from the initial selection may not relate properly to the values QlikView attempts to associate. Simply put, the loop back to the original table will result in undesirable results most of the time.

QlikView handles this automatically with a process called "loosely coupling." When a table is loosely coupled, the first thing you notice is that the association to that table seen in the Table Viewer appears as a dashed line instead of a solid line. In addition, if you navigate in QlikView to *Settings>Document Properties>Tables* you will see the "Loosely Coupled" checkbox selected next to the table. QlikView has determined that this table should be loosely coupled. QlikView will always loosely couple the largest table in terms of row count when determining how to mitigate a circular reference. Figure 5-7 illustrates a document data model with a circular reference. Notice that both the *customer* and *order_detail* tables have a common field. This, combined with the fact that the *order* table provides a path between these tables, results in a loop.

FIGURE 5-7 CIRCULAR REFERENCE IN DATA MODEL

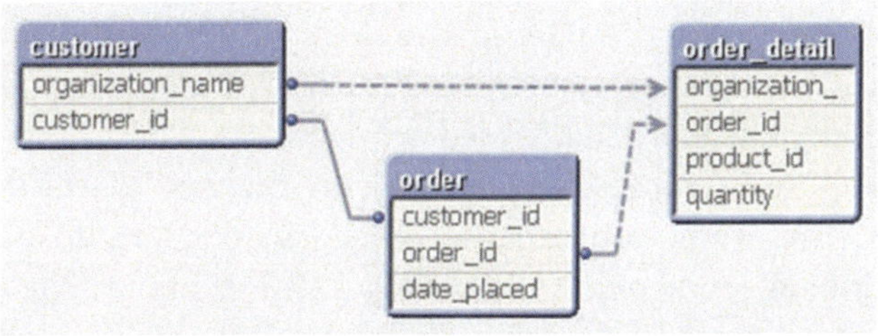

Loosely coupling a table breaks the association from continuing down a given pathway, forcing associations to only work in a single direction from what was previously a circular reference. In Figure 5-7, the path would be taken through the *order* table if selections involving fields from *customer* and *order_detail* occurred. Seasoned QlikView developers will immediately see why this is also an undesirable result. The solution is to not create circular references in the first place. Often this can be accomplished by renaming the field that is creating the association or removing it entirely from one of the tables. For example in this case there's no reason to have the *organization_name* field in the *order_detail* table. In this case, you need to identify which table is the correct table from which the value should be loaded.

Creating Custom Date and Calendar Options

Dates and times are difficult elements of data to manage when building analytical solutions. Old paradigms and misunderstandings about how date/time data affects onscreen results challenge even the most experienced QlikView developers. This chapter provides you with a variety of options for how you can make date/time values a functional part of your QlikView document. It also helps you address common pitfalls associated with incomplete date/time data.

Basic Manipulation of Date and Time Values

When QlikView loads a date/time field into memory, it is stored as a number. However, the date/time field also has a format associated with it, and both the number and the format can be manipulated in the in the document's load script. For example, if a date value of 9/19/2001 6:27:57 AM is loaded into memory; the actual value stored is 37,153.26941. This is because 6:27:57 AM is stored as a decimal on the end of the integer 37153. Therefore, you can use standard functions to perform some manipulation of date/time values. For example: The *FLOOR* function truncates the value to an integer, which effectively removes the time and leaves only the date. This can be handy in making sure comparisons are accurate since dates with time values can return different (or no) matches than those without. The chapter covering *Best Practices* shows you how manipulating date/time fields in the QlikView load script can reduce uniqueness in your data model, which is desirable for reducing the memory needed by the document. One easy way to achieve that goal is to remove the timestamp on any date/time fields if they are unnecessary within the QlikView document. Removing the timestamp from a date/time field requires only one line of syntax in the load script. For example, if the *date_placed* field in the *order* table contains a timestamp, the following syntax eliminates the timestamp and produces a result that truncates the date value to the day (no hours, minutes or seconds), while renaming the field to *Order Date* and formatting the date for use in the user interface (via the *DATE* command):

```
DATE(FLOOR(date_placed), 'MM/DD/YYYY') as [Order Date]
```

You can also abstract other components of a date/time field in the QlikView load script by using simple functions such as *YEAR*, *MONTH* and *DAY*:

```
YEAR(date_place) as [Order Year],
MONTH(date_placed) as [Order Month],
DAY(date_placed) as [Order Day];
```

This syntax creates *Order Year*, *Order Month* and *Order Day* fields in the *order* table for every row that exists in that table. These fields can be used in list boxes to allow users to select specific years, months and days. By using such syntax in the document load script, you can significantly reduce data duplication and optimize the in-memory data model.

Creating a Custom Calendar in the Load Script

Using basic dates and date parts such year, month and day is an easy thing to do in a QlikView document and provides users with selection options based on one or more date fields. However, because the date values are based on data in the document data model it is possible to have gaps in the date range. For example if you provide list boxes for certain months to show order information and no orders exist for a given month, the month will not appear in the list box. This can be confusing to users. It can also create problems when comparing fiscal dates to calendar dates. To address this and other issues, it may be desirable to create a table to hold all dates and date parts within a given range based on the earliest and latest dates in the data model. This type of table is typically referred to as a *master calendar*.

The creation of a separate table to store date information is not a concept exclusive to QlikView. However, in most data modeling endeavors, an arbitrary time period is selected for which to create prior and future dates: You don't want to create dates too far into the future because it stores useless dates, but you need to make sure you cover any dates that may need to be joined to the calendar table in order to accept those values. QlikView offers a unique ability in this space to dynamically create a table that only contains dates in a range for which there is corresponding data, while still filling in the holes.

Storing all date-related data in a single table offers several benefits. First, it reduces data redundancy which can improve the performance of the QlikView document. Redundancy is created when you add date parts such as year and month to the same table that contains the date field. Second, it gives QlikView developers a single location from which to create all date-related objects such as list boxes and calendar/slider objects. Finally, creating custom calendars can extend the functionality of your QlikView documents by adding more meaningful and easier to use date selections in the user interface.

A master calendar stores a single row for every unique date within the database along with corresponding date-parts such as year, month and quarter as fields. It can also include fiscal date information. Fields such as *year*, *quarter*, *month*, *day*, *fiscal year*, and *fiscal quarter* are typically found in a master calendar table. Mapping tables, as shown earlier in this chapter to provide lookup capabilities; can be used in conjunction with master calendar tables to provide fiscal calendar information. Mapping tables are often created as in-line tables because there is no need to have such data stored in a database since it rarely changes. Inline tables are tables are that are created within the load script. In the following example, the load script syntax creates an inline mapping table called *fiscal_quarter_map* to add fiscal quarter information to a master calendar table. The fiscal year, and therefore the first fiscal quarter, begins in July. The master calendar table is created after the mapping table has been loaded into memory.

```
Fiscal_quarters_map:
LOAD * INLINE
[

Month, Fiscal Quarter
1, 3
2, 3
3, 3
4, 4
5, 4
6, 4
7, 1
8, 1
9, 1
10, 2
11, 2
12, 2

];
```

Creating the master calendar requires several steps. You begin by determining which date field in the document's data model will be used for the calendar. Then you must determine the date range for the calendar and create a temporary table in which the dates for each day in the range are generated. This is important because you don't want to load date values that are before or after the date range of your data, but you want every day that occurs within the range even if there's no data in the other tables for a given day. Remember, this range will be updated each time the document data is reloaded, so if the range needs to expand or contract, it will.

In this example, the *date_placed* field from the *order_information* table has been identified as the source field. It determines the minimum and maximum date values that bookend the number of dates that need to be created. The syntax below uses a script function called *PEEK* to make this happen.

```
LET v_start_date = NUM(PEEK('date_placed', 0,
  'order_information'));
LET v_end_date = NUM(PEEK('date_placed', -1,
  'order_information'));
```

The *PEEK* function retrieves the data value for a specific record in a field. If the table containing the *date_placed* field has been sorted in ascending order by *date_placed*, the first record will contain the minimum date value and the last record will contain the maximum date value. The numbers 0 and -1 in the code example correspond to the first and last records respectively. These date values are then stored in variables that will be used later in the load script.

Note: It is possible to avoid the need to load the date field data in ascending order. This is done by creating a temporary table and using the MIN and MAX functions to retrieve the earliest and latest dates in the data. You could then use the PEEK function with a second argument of zero on each of the fields returned in the temporary table (one field for the minimum value, one for the max) to move the values into the variables. However, if you sort the date field as it is loaded (earlier in the script), the extra temporary table can be omitted.

The next step is to create a temporary table that stores a record for each date between the *v_start_date* and *v_end_date* variable values. In this example, the *AUTOGENERATE* function is used in association with the *ITERNO* function, which increments the *v_start_date* variable for each iteration of the loop in order to create a record for each value. *AUTOGENERATE* creates the values while *ITERNO* refers to iteration count. This happens within a WHILE statement evaluation, which causes the process to loop until the last date record created is equal to the *v_end_date* value.

```
temp_cal_table:
LOAD
  DATE($(v_start_date) + ITERNO() - 1) as temp_date
  AUTOGENERATE 1 WHILE $(v_start_date) + ITERNO() -
    1 <= $(v_end_date);
```

Finally the *temp_date* field created in the last step is referenced in order to build the master calendar table.

```
LOAD
  DATE(FLOOR(temp_date),'MM/DD/YYYY') as
    date_placed,
  DAY(temp_date) as calendar_day,
  WEEK(temp_date) as calendar_week,
  MONTH(temp_date) as calendar_month,
  CEIL(MONTH(temp_date) / 3) as calendar_quarter,
  YEAR(temp_date) as calendar_year,

  APPLYMAP('fiscal_quarters_map',
    NUM(MONTH(temp_date)), NULL()) as
    fiscal_quarter,

  IF(MONTH(temp_date) < 7, YEAR(temp_date),
    YEAR(temp_date)+1) as fiscal_year

RESIDENT
  temp_cal_table
ORDER BY
  temp_date ASC;

DROP TABLE temp_cal_table;
```

This LOAD statement creates a master calendar table based on data from the *temp_cal_table* created previously. The RESIDENT command is effectively the same as a FROM clause and acts as a directive that tells the LOAD statement from where to get its data. The ORDER BY clause simply sorts the table results in chronological order.

The first line in this LOAD statement associates the table to the *order_information* table by aliasing the *temp_date* field as *date_placed*. This creates the link to the other data in the data model. The next five lines use the *temp_date* field to create date parts. This is a fairly straight-forward use of the *DAY*, *WEEK* and similar script functions. However, you may notice the use of the *CEIL* functions and some math to create *calendar_quarter*. This syntax takes the highest month number and divides it by 3 (3 months in a quarter) and uses the *CEIL* function to round up any fractional amounts that result from doing division. The result is the quarter for each day that is placed in the calendar table.

The *APPLYMAP* function (see the section in this chapter on Performing Lookups with a Mapping Load) performs a look up to the *fiscal_quarters_map* table that was previous loaded as an in-line table. It results in a fiscal quarter number field. If no match is found then a NULL value is returned. The IF statement, immediately following the *APPLYMAP* statement tests to see if the month is less than 7 in which case the fiscal year is the same as the current calendar year. If it is greater than 7 then the fiscal year is one year higher than the current calendar year.

Note that unlike a mapping table, the *temp_cal_table* which is a temporary table needs to be manually dropped at the end because it is no longer needed and will create problems if left in the script.

When this script is executed during a data reload the new master calendar table is added to the data model and associated with the *order_information* table based on the *date_placed* field. The data model is shown in Figure 5-8.

FIGURE 5-8 MASTER CALENDAR IN DATA MODEL

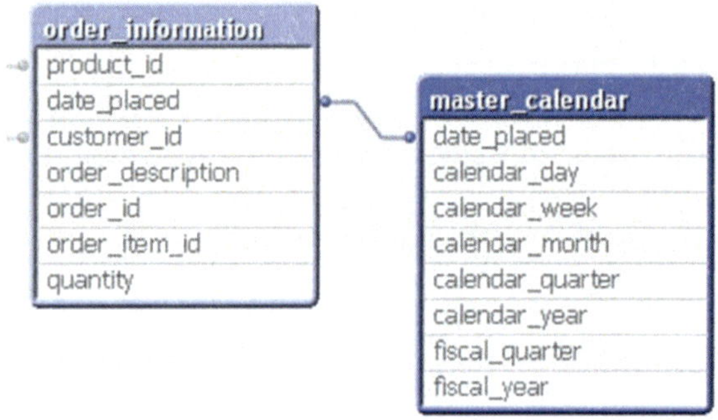

Once a master calendar has been created, you can use standard sheet objects, such as list boxes, to enable users to make date selections. Figure 5-9 shows a series of list boxes using the master calendar table created in this example.

FIGURE 5-8 MASTER CALENDAR USER INTERFACE EXAMPLE

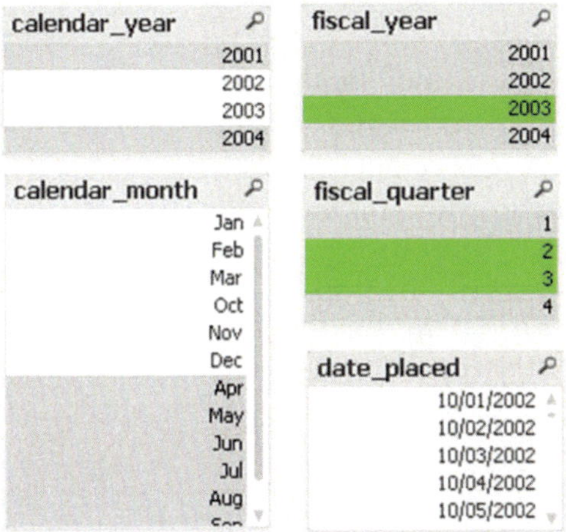

Notice in the list boxes above that fiscal year 2003 and fiscal quarters 2 and 3 are selected. Because fiscal years span calendar years, the calendars years 2002 and 2003 are associated (showing with a white background). Also, all of the months associated with fiscal quarters 2 and 3 are displayed as associated. Master calendars not only provide a means of providing all of the date and date parts in a given range, they also can be helpful in showing the relationship between different types of calendars. In this example, the relationship between the normal calendar and the fiscal calendar are clear to the user.

Translating Source Data Values into Meaningful Semantics

Data is rarely organized, named or described in a manner suitable for non-technical users to consume. For this reason most BI tools require those responsible for developing content to understand the complex relationships and idiosyncrasies associated with source data systems. To make data usable by business analysts, executives and information workers data is often organized and described in business friendly ways. The term used for this business friendly presentation of data is "semantics." Semantic presentation of data doesn't alter what the data represents, but it does change how the data is described and organized. It may also provide calculations and summarizations of the data that are likely to be commonly needed by user. The simplest example of this is field aliasing. As you have seen in several chapters of this book, it is common to rename fields in the QlikView load script. The most important reason for doing this is to control how tables in the data model associate with each other. However, it is perfectly reasonable to rename fields for the purpose of making them easier to understand. By placing aliased names in square brackets, you can use multi-word names that are very business friendly. While this makes it easier for developers of QlikView documents and users engaging in Web based collaboration to understand the data model, it is not always adequate. For this reason QlikView 10 introduced a feature that allows you to provide descriptions and to tag fields with other data while it is being loaded. This chapter describes more advanced methods of translating the data loaded from source systems into values and descriptions that more accurately reflect the needs of the users.

Adding Metadata to Enhance Usability

The processes involved in translating data from source systems into something meaningful in a business context involve the use of metadata. Metadata is often defined as "data about data," which does not go very far in explaining the purposes of metadata. While metadata can take a variety of forms, the concept is typically associated with describing the lineage, logic, structure and use of data. Generally speaking there are two types of metadata. The first is descriptive metadata. This type provides information that explains the data as exemplified by field and table descriptions. The second is structural metadata. This type describes how data is structured and organized. The focus of QlikView's metadata features is to address the need of descriptive metadata. However, structural metadata does exist within a QlikView document. In fact, the data model and its graphical depiction is an example of structural metadata.

Field Commenting

The most common use of metadata in most BI tools is directed at providing descriptions for fields from the source data. Since much of this data can be derived or calculated while it is loaded, the rules and intended use of each field need to be known by developers. Once comments have been added to fields in the load script, they appear as popup text when a developer hovers over the field in the properties dialog of a chart or other sheet object. This makes it possible for the developer to better understand which fields to use in expressions and for dimensions. Comments can be added to tables, fields and variables in order to aid with development and analysis of the data.

Comments can be added on a field-by-field basis as data is loaded. However it may be desirable to add them from a predefined table such as an in-line table, Excel file or database table that stores metadata and fieldnames. The *COMMENT* command can be used with both tables and fields to associate comments. It is typically used in conjunction with a mapping table. The first field in the mapping table lists field names while the second field contains the comments (descriptions). The following example uses an in-line table and creates and associates comments for three fields in the data model.

```
Field_comment_map:
MAPPING LOAD * INLINE
[
fieldname, description
organization_name, The legal name of the organization.
unit_cost, The standard (not actual) cost associated
with item.
unit_price, The MSRP (retail price) of an item
];

COMMENT FIELDS USING field_comment_map;
```

The script above occurs after the fields have been loaded earlier in the load script. The *COMMENT* command assumes that a mapping table exists. In this case the *field_comment_map* is the mapping table. Remember, because it is a mapping table it will automatically be removed and won't appear in the data model. If you wanted to add comments to a field without using a mapping table, the syntax would be similar to the following. This example allows you to add comments one field at a time.

```
COMMENT FIELD unit_cost WITH 'The standard (not
actual) cost associated with item.';
```

Figure 5-9 shows how the comments appear when you select fields for a sheet object.

FIGURE 5-9 USING COMMENTS FOR SHEET OBJECT SELECTION

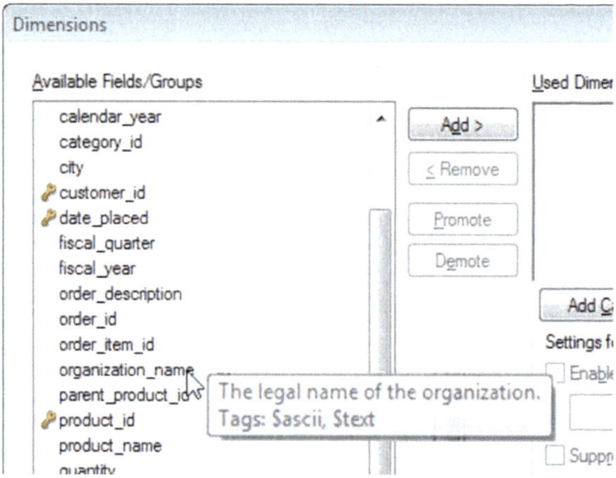

Data Abstraction Using QlikView Data Files

The basic concept of how data is loaded and used in a QlikView document should be clear to you by now. All data is loaded and associated in the load script process. It therefore is available to all expressions and objects. QlikView doesn't need to go back to the data sources when users request various combinations of dimensions and calculations. While this in-memory, associative functionality is powerful and makes it easy to quickly create robust content, it comes at a price. Each time a QlikView document needs to be updated, the entire load script must be run and all of the data must be reloaded. Generally, this is not a problem. In most cases reloads occur at night or at times when there are few users online. Additionally, the QlikView server does a very good job of managing the scheduled reload process and presenting updated data, even if users access the document during a reload. However, in some cases the sheer volume of data combined with the number of QlikView documents that must be reloaded presents a problem. When there is a large number of high volume data loads needed, the time it takes to complete all of these processes may become too long. To address this, QlikView includes a feature known as QlikView data files or "QVDs."

A QVD is a highly optimized data table stored on disk as a file. It is the result of a load script and allows for all of the same features and functions used to load a QlikView document. In fact a QlikView document (QVW) is used to create a QlikView data file (QVD). Once created, a QVD file offers several benefits:

- Loading multiple documents: Rather than having documents directly access data from the underlying data sources, it is possible to load a QVD file once and use it to feed data to any number of QlikView documents. This eliminates multiple connections and data extractions that would be necessary if each document directly accessed the data sources. It can dramatically reduce the load on the source system, and because QVD's are optimized, the time to load each document is much less; one tenth the normal load time in most cases.
- Simplified Document Development: Without a doubt the hardest part of QlikView document development is getting the load script right. It requires knowledge of the underlying data sources and significant technical ability with QlikView scripting. A QVD file or set of QVD files can eliminate the need for some of the developers to have this knowledge and skill set. Once a QVD file exists, a developer can access it and get the fields and data without understanding the underlying data structures or complexities of the load script that created it. This is a great solution for business analysts, managers and other

users who don't possess SQL or advanced scripting capabilities.

- Incremental Loading: In many situations data is updated or created incrementally: For example each month of accounting data for the preceding month is made available. The previous month's data in such situations rarely changes. QVD's allow you to create a series of incremental data files that eliminate the need to return to the source data to load older data.

When using QVDs you load them into your document in the same way you load other data sources. However, because they are already designed for use in QlikView, you don't have to worry about how associations occur or how to manipulate field values unless you want to. Each QVD represents a single table. But that one table could be created by a series of complex load script processes such as mapping loads, interval joins and concatenations. Additionally, QVDs, if designed properly, can include the metadata descriptions for each field.

Creating a QVD

QVD's are created in a regular QlikView document's load script using the same syntax normally used to load data. The only difference is the use of one of the special commands as part of or following a *LOAD* statement that results in QVD creation. We won't cover all options here, but the most common is to use the *STORE* command. This command is executed after the work has been done to create a table. It pushes the table structure and data into a QVD file based on a file name you provide. The following syntax shows an example that creates an *order_info.qvd* file based on several *LOAD* statements with some joining.

```
order_info:
LOAD "customer_id",
    DATE(FLOOR("date_placed"), 'MM/DD/YYYY') AS
"date_placed",
    description as order_description,
    "order_id";
SQL SELECT "customer_id",
```

```
    "date_placed",
    description,
    "order_id"
FROM CRMSample.dbo."order_information"
ORDER BY date_placed;

JOIN

LOAD "order_id",
    "order_item_id",
    "product_id",
    quantity;
SQL SELECT "order_id",
    "order_item_id",
    "product_id",
    quantity
FROM CRMSample.dbo."order_item";

STORE * FROM order_information into order_info.qvd;
```

In this example the final line using the STORE command is what creates the QVD file. Since no path information is provided as part of the file name the QVD file will be created in the same directory as the document's QVW file.

Using a QVD file is easy. You load it as you would load any other table file data source such as Excel or CSV. In the load script editor click on the *Table Files...* button and navigate to where the QVD file resides. Select it and the File Wizard will walk you through the process of selecting which fields you want. If you want all data in the default format click the *Finish* button. The result will be load script syntax that looks similar to the following, which you could type into the script as well:

```
order_information:
LOAD order_id,
     customer_id,
     date_placed,
     order_description,
     order_item_id,
     product_id,
     quantity
FROM
[order_info.qvd]
(qvd);
```

Once the load is completed, and it will happen very fast with a QVD file as the data source, the fields and data are available for use with tab sheet objects. You can also combine the QVD file load with other QVD file loads or other conventional loads. The following example shows the QVD file load being combined with a SQL load to bring in the customer table.

```
order_information:
LOAD order_id,
     customer_id,
     date_placed,
     order_description,
     order_item_id,
     product_id,
     quantity
FROM
[order_info.qvd]
(qvd);

OLEDB CONNECT TO [Provider=SQLOLEDB.1;Integrated...

customer:
LOAD city,
    "customer_id",
    "organization_name",
    region;
SQL SELECT city,
    "customer_id",
    "organization_name",
    region
FROM CRMSample.dbo.customer;
```

Notice in the syntax example above that after the QVD file is loaded, an OLEDB connection is created so the SQL load can work. The order of the two loads doesn't matter since the data model results in two tables: One from the QVD file and on from the SQL statement. They are associated by the *customer_id* field which is common to both tables. One important note: If the QVD file was created at a different time than when the document was loaded it might not include all of the necessary data. For example, if the QVD file was created on Monday and a customer was deleted on Tuesday and then the document load occurs on Wednesday, there may be orders for the deleted customer still in the QVD.

When the processing is managed by a QlikView server these problems can be avoided.

Chapter 6: Expressions and Set Analysis

All Business Intelligence tools have some ability to perform calculations and derive values from the data. The ability to do this is often referred to as "formula writing" or "expression writing." QlikView provides this capability through the use of expressions. This chapter presents not only the fundamentals associated with creating and using QlikView expressions, but it also includes a number of more advanced techniques and examples. Your ability to create and use QlikView expressions is important. Without skills in this area you are limited in what you are able to do with QlikView. Even the most basic QlikView documents use expressions to summarize data for visualization. Creating a simple expression for a QlikView chart is easy. However, there is much more to expression writing in QlikView than most QlikView developers realize. Mastering the development and use of expressions opens the door to creating powerful and meaningful content with QlikView.

What are QlikView Expressions?

In QlikView, the term *expression* refers to a calculation or manipulation of data that you create and embed in your QlikView document. It is important not to confuse this with the load script, although at times you will see similarities between the two ideas. In fact, the QlikView online help documents the functions and expression details in a section called "scripting" and it is possible to create expressions in the QlikView load script. These are referred to as *script expressions*. Script expressions differ from other QlikView expressions in that they reside in the load script syntax and execute only once: During the data load. Normal QlikView expressions, which are commonly referred to as "chart expressions," recalculate values dynamically based on user interaction with the document. Expressions are associated with sheet objects or similar aspects of the user interface. This includes such objects as list boxes, charts, text boxes and others. Expressions are best described as calculations that you, as the developer, create and use to produce results on the screen.

The most common use of an expression in QlikView is to provide a value for a chart. You cannot create a chart in QlikView without also writing an expression. Charts use your expression syntax to determine how to render a summarized value visually. For example, you may want a bar chart to show the number of orders for each region. The expression for the bar chart counts the orders so the chart can determine the height of each bar in the chart. In this very simple example of an expression, the bars on the bar chart are determined by the chart's dimension (region in this case) and the height of the bars is determined by the expression result. The expression is calculated for each dimension member; in this case, for each region.

QlikView expressions can be very complex and can include very powerful language that does fascinating things with the data in your document. Since QlikView materializes all of the data in memory, expressions can operate on unusually large volumes of data and at very high speeds. The ability to do this is one of the advantages QlikView offers over other tools. QlikView expressions can, and often do, perform calculations and summarizations over billions of rows data.

Expression Fundamentals

QlikView expressions are comprised of syntax (language) that you create. The syntax for expressions is similar to the syntax used in the QlikView load script. The key components include QlikView functions, operators, field values, variables and constants. Some of these are things you create; others such as field values exist after the document performs a data reload. The functions used in expressions are, in many cases, different from the functions used in the QlikView load script. However, in some cases the load script and expressions use the same functions.

Expressions presume that all of the data has been loaded and is available for use. Expressions have no ability to access and load external data. They only operate on what is already in memory. An expression is normally associated with a chart or other object. The way you create expressions is by accessing the properties dialog of the desired object. For example, you may wish to create a text value that appears on the main tab sheet that shows a calculated value rather than static text. To do this you right click on the sheet, select *New sheet object* and select a *Text Object....* The text object properties dialog appears. You can type text into the *Text* box in the dialog and your text appears in the object on the sheet when you close the dialog or apply changes. However, you may also type an expression that calculates or derives a value. The result of the expression appears as text in the text object. When accessing the properties dialog of a sheet object you will usually see an ellipsis button (...) associated with the text box into which you type expression syntax. If you click that button the *Expression Editor* appears as a separate window. Figure 6-1 shows the expression editor.

FIGURE 6-1 EXPRESSION EDITOR

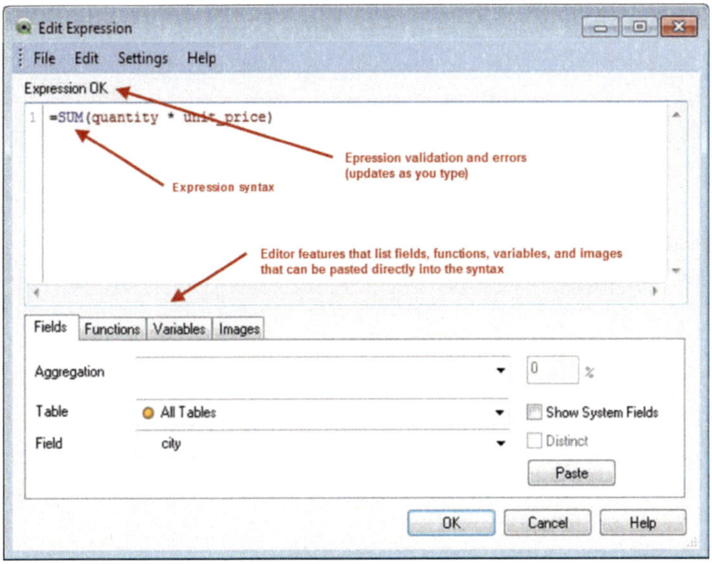

The expression editor has several features that make expression writing easier. At the top of the editor is the editor text window into which you type your expression syntax. The expression syntax is automatically color coded to help clarify how the expression editor interprets what you type. You may also notice the words "Expression OK" at the top left. This label indicates whether there is a problem in your expression syntax as you create or edit it. At the bottom of the expression dialog is a set of tabs. The first tab (*Fields*) allows you to select various aggregation functions (functions that summarize data). You are not limited to using these functions, but these aggregate functions are the most common, so they are provided in the list. It also provides a list of fields from the data model. By using these features you can create a simple summary expression without typing the syntax. Clicking the *Paste* button creates the syntax for you based on your selections. The second tab (*Functions*) lists all of the QlikView functions, making it easier to find a function by name. When you select a function, a syntax example is provided to help you understand how it is used. There is more on functions later in this chapter. The other two tabs provide access to variables and images. We cover these expression capabilities later in this chapter as well.

You don't have to use the expression editor. You can create an expression by typing an equal sign then the expression syntax (similar to Excel formulas) directly into the sheet object's expression text box. However, the expression editor may make expression writing, especially for complex expressions, easier. The equal sign is only needed in situations where the value typed can be interpreted as text. For example, the *Label* for expressions on the *Expressions* tab of the *Properties* dialog can either be entered as text or as an expression. If you wish for the value entered to be interpreted as an expression, then you need to use the equal (=) sign. Alternatively, if you type a value into the box for the expression itself, it will be interpreted as an expression regardless of whether you use the equal sign.

All of the expressions you create in your QlikView document can be reviewed and edited from the *Expression Overview* dialog. This dialog is available from the *Settings* pull down menu (*Settings>Expression Overview*).

FIGURE 2: EXPRESSION OVERVIEW DIALOG

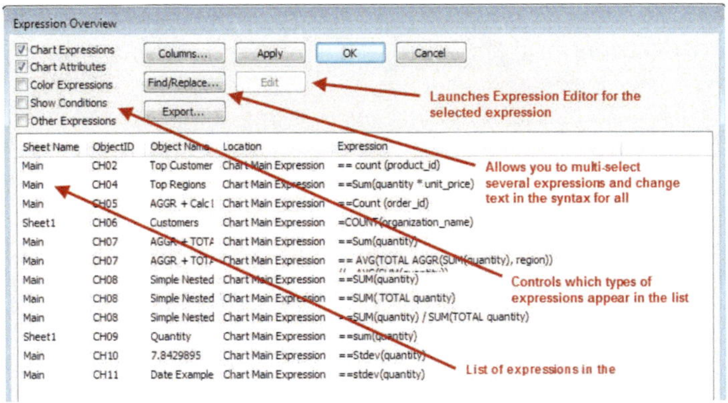

The *Expression Overview* dialog lists all of the expressions in your document and allows you to edit them by launching the Expression Editor for the selected expression. You can also use this dialog to export expression syntax. Among the other features of the *Expression Overview* dialog is a very helpful feature that allows you to find and replace text in one or more expressions without having to edit each expression individually. This is done by multi-selecting expressions in the list (*Ctrl+Click*) and using the *Find/Replace...* button. The Apply button applies the changes to the document object properties, which is nice because if you make changes and decide you want to cancel them, you can cancel the dialog and your changes will be ignored.

Expression Elements

Expressions in QlikView are comprised of one or more basic elements (parts). These elements, when combined, allow you to create both simple and sophisticated rules for producing a value. It is important to understand that an expression always results in a data value of some sort. Parts of an expression include values that come from the QlikView data model (fields) or from what you type. All values have a predefined type of data. For example, if you type something surrounded by single quotes it is considered a string (or character) data type. If you type in a number, without quotes, it is considered a numeric data type. You will find that the elements of a QlikView expression are similar to those of an Excel formula. The following list contains a short description of the components that, in some combination, make up an expression:

- Constant Values: These are data values you type directly into the expression and do not represent built-in functions or other predetermined features. They do not change and therefore are referred to as "constant." They might include such things as: 1023, 'This is text', 'Ohio', 43.21. You can perform calculations using constant values such as: 123+12 because the plus sign (+) is a predetermined feature called an operator.
- Operators: Operators are combinations of characters that the expression engine in QlikView understands. They allow you to perform mathematical, text and other operations using values from the data model or other values. They include such symbols as the following:

+	Adds two numbers together
-	Subtracts one number from another
/	Divides one number into another
*	multiplies one number by another
&	concatenates (joins) two string values

- QlikView Functions: Functions are predefined commands that you can use to manipulate data in an expression. They are similar, and are sometimes the same, as the functions used in the load script. However, the load script includes functions that are not valid for use in an expression. Functions receive values and return values. For example, the *round* function receives a numeric value, rounds it to the nearest whole number (unless otherwise instructed) and returns the rounded whole number value. The value placed inside of the parenthesis after the function name determines what the function returns. These values are referred to as *arguments*. For example: `round(123.6233)` returns `124`.Functions may receive more than one argument, but always return a single value. The fact that QlikView functions return a single value makes them "scalar functions." All QlikView functions are scalar.

- Field Names: Any valid field name from the QlikView data model may be used in an expression. The actual field value is the value of the field used based on the selections made in the document by the user. In other words, if you use a field in an expression and the user selects something, the way the fields are used may change. For example, if your expression counts the *last_name* field and the user selects a region, the count reflects the number of last names in the selected region rather than last names for all regions. This behavior can be controlled with advanced syntax.
- Variables: You can define document wide variables that hold values. Variables are temporary storage areas for values that can be used across expressions in the document. Variables can be used to set properties on a sheet object, pass values from one expression to another, as well as for other purposes.
- Reserved Characters and Words: Many combinations of characters are known to the QlikView expression engine. For example two forward slashes (//) tell QlikView the remainder of the line is a comment and should be ignored. There are a variety of such reserved character combinations. One of the most common is the equal sign (=), which begins each expression (similar to Excel formulas). All QlikView functions, operators and similar syntax are reserved words. This means you cannot use them for any purpose other than what QlikView expects.

For example, you cannot use a function name as the name of a variable.

Commenting

When writing expressions it may be helpful to provide some commentary that explains how the expression is designed and what it is intended to do. In QlikView you can include comments by first typing two forward slashes (//). This tells the QlikView expression engine to ignore everything after the second slash until the end of the current line. When you create a comment the text of the comment is a different color (green by default) and font, which makes it clear that it is a comment and will not affect how the expression executes. It can sometimes be helpful to comment actual expression syntax to test portions of a complex expression. If you highlight text (including multiple lines of text) and right click, you will see popup menu items for commenting and uncommenting the highlighted text. This can make commenting large segments of your syntax easier and allows you to uncomment multiple lines in a few mouse clicks. It's worth noting this same capability exists in the load script editor.

Understanding Functions

The QlikView functions used in expression syntax provide a wide variety of data operations and standardized calculations. Functions allow your expression to produce calculated values, derived text, and summarized data. Remember that a function always returns a value. Each function in QlikView follows a standard format for use. Functions are reserved words that cannot be used for other purposes. You pass values into a function by including them within a comma separated list surrounded by parentheses immediately following the function name. The values you pass to a function are called *arguments* and they can be created from combinations of constant values, field values, variables and other function statements. The following example illustrates the basic format for using a function:

```
=function_name (arugment_value1, argument_value2)
```

Expressions may include more than one function and in some cases it may be necessary to nest functions. Nesting is the concept of using one function's result as an argument to pass to another function. The first function is "inside" the second function. The following is an example of a nested function statement:

```
=ROUND(SUM(quantity), 1000)
```

In the example above, the first function is the *SUM* function. We consider it the first function because it is inside of another function. The order of operation for functions is from the inside to the outside. There is only one argument being passed to the first function. The argument used in the first function is a field value (the *quantity* field). The second function is the *ROUND* function. It has two arguments being passed to it. The first is the result (the return value) of the first function. The second is the constant value of one thousand (1000), which tells the function to round the value to the nearest 1000. This example demonstrates the use of nesting with expression functions.

Performing Calculations

Perhaps the simplest operation an expression performs is a calculation. QlikView expressions can calculate values based on any of the valid elements of expression syntax. For example, constant values may be combined with field values. A very simple calculation might result in multiplying a field value. For example, you may want to calculate and display a tax amount based on a predetermined (constant) percentage of a sales amount field, as illustrated below:

```
=unit_price * .15
```

In the example above, the field unit_price uses the multiplication operator and a constant value of .15 to return the dollar amount that represents a 15% sales tax. Calculations may also be nested. That means, as with Excel and other tools, an order of operation determines how values are used progressively within the expression. The following is an example of a nested calculation:

```
=quantity * (unit_price * .15)
```

In the example above, the calculation inside the parentheses occurs first and results in the sales tax amount. That result is then used in the next calculation. Excel and other tools allow you to nest several levels of calculations inside of the parentheses. The inner most calculations occur first. Their results are then used in the next outer calculation.

String Manipulation

QlikView expressions may also be used to operate on text, or string, values. These values cannot be used in mathematical calculations because the data type is not numeric. However, expression syntax may be used to affect string values. Common string manipulation includes such procedures as:

- Concatenating: Bringing two or more strings together
- Parsing: Locating and extracting a portion of a string
- Converting Strings to Numbers: Converting strings that have numbers into numeric values so math may be performed
- Other operations

Among the most common string manipulations you might encounter while writing expressions is the need to combine two or more strings together. For example, you may wish to show first, middle and last names as a single value in a list or as a calculated dimension in a chart. The following example demonstrates a simple concatenation of three string values:

```
=first_name & ' ' & middle & ' ' & last_name
```

In the example above, there are three fields used from the data model (first_name, middle, last_name). The ampersand (&) character is the operator that concatenates them together. But, a constant value of a space character is added inside of the single quotes so the names don't run into each other. The result of this expression would be something like "James Albert Smith."

Another common need when working with strings is to parse string values to extract pieces of a string. For example, you might have email addresses in your data and wish to pull out the domain (last) part of the email address. The following example shows how to use the *MID* and *INDEX* functions to do this.

```
=MID(email_address, INDEX(email_address, '@') +1)
```

In the example above the *MID* function parses the email_address field. Its first argument is the field name (the string from which its result is derived). The second argument is the starting point (the first character in the string) to start the parse. The *INDEX* function is used to find the position of the at-symbol (@) character. Its first argument is the field to search, which is the same field. Its second argument is the character to find, which is enclosed in single quotes because it must be a string (character) value. The plus one (+1) syntax increases the starting point to the character following the at-symbol so that the at-symbol is not included in the result. A third argument could have been provided to indicate the position to stop the parse, but since the remainder of the email_address field includes all desired characters it isn't needed in this case. There are many other string functions in QlikView. You should explore them using the online help and other materials available. A few noteworthy examples include the following:

- *TRIM, LTRIM, RTRIM*: These functions remove leading and trailing spaces from a string.
- *UPPER, LOWER*: These functions convert case to upper or lower case.
- *CAPITALIZE*: This function makes the first character of each word in a string upper case. This is often used for names.

- *LEFT, RIGHT*: These functions perform parsing and return the desired number of characters from the left or right side of a string.
- *SUBFIELD*: This function returns a part of a string based on delimiter characters such as quotes that exist in the original string.

It is likely that you will have a need to convert and format numeric values in a QlikView document. This can be done in the object properties dialog for most chart types. However, you may need to format numeric values for text objects or other objects that don't provide formatting options in the properties dialog. You may also find that the number values in your data model are provided as string values, not true numeric values. Ideally, you would convert such string values into number values in the load script, but the same conversion can take place in an expression. There are two basic numeric functions that serve similar purposes in QlikView. They are *NUM* and *NUM#.* The difference between them is important to understand.

- *NUM* – The *NUM* function <u>formats</u> a numeric value based on a format string that defines the date format you want returned.
- *NUM#* - The *NUM#* function <u>converts</u> a string value to a number based on a format mask that defines how the string value is formatted.

Because both of these functions return a numeric value it is easy to confuse them. The following is an example of a field that stores numbers as strings that you want to convert to numeric values for use in the document.

```
=NUM#( string_value, '#.0000')
```

In the example above, the string_value field stores numbers as strings in a format that includes four decimal places and no other formatting. The *NUM#* function reads the string value from the field in the data model and returns the value as a numeric value, making it possible to perform mathematical operations on the result. The next example shows how this expression can be used within a NUM function to change the format of the numeric result.

```
=NUM(NUM#( string_value, '#.0000' ), '###,###.00')
```

In the example above, the result from the first expression (*NUM#*) is passed as an argument to the *NUM* function. A format mask string in single quotes is also passed as the second argument. It instructs the *NUM* function to use a comma as a thousand separator and show only two decimal places. The resulting number would appear similar to this: 234,256.04, if the entire expression is used in a text box.

In some cases numbers are stored in conjunction with text in data fields. Ideally, you would deal with this in the load script, separating the numbers into their own numeric field. However, in some cases this may not happen or make sense. You can convert text to numbers and numbers to text with QlikView functions. Converting text to numeric values assumes that the text that represents numbers that can be separated from other nonnumeric characters in the string. The following example demonstrates how string parsing and conversion functions combine to return a numeric value. The result of the expression can be used in numeric aggregations such as *SUM* or *AVG* functions and may also be used to perform math operations.

```
=NUM#(MID(customer_id, INDEX(customer_id, '-') +1))
```

In the example above, the customer_id field stores both characters and numbers separated by a dash (-). The *MID* function, in conjunction with the *INDEX* function, parses the string and returns only those characters that are to the right of the dash. Those characters are numbers in this case. The *NUM#* function, on the outside, converts the result of the *MID* function into a numeric value. The *NUM#* function may also be used to format the numeric result with a thousand separator and decimal precision.

Working with Date Values

It is very likely that you will have to perform some sort of date manipulation in QlikView expressions. While QlikView provides a good formatting feature for dates and other values, at some point you will need to do more than format date values. The load script often includes date manipulation to create new fields and in many cases managing date values is best done in the load script. However, the same date manipulation functions may be used in expressions. Common date operations include:

- Converting and formatting date values
- Determining future and past dates
- Retrieving the current date and time
- Determining date increments such as weekdays and weekend days
- Determining the start and end dates of a given year, quarter or month
- Determining if a date value falls within a predefined year, quarter, or month
- Many others

Converting and formatting date values in a QlikView document is a common need. This can be done in the object properties dialog for most chart types. However, you may need to format date values for text objects or other objects that don't provide formatting options in the properties dialog. You may also find that the dates in your data model are provided as string values, not true date-time values. Ideally, you would convert such string values into date values in the load script, but the same conversion can take place in an expression. There are two basic date functions that serve similar purposes in QlikView. They are *DATE* and *DATE#.* The difference between them may seem subtle, but it is important to understand them as they do not both serve the same purpose even though their syntax and arguments are the same.

- *DATE* – The *DATE* function formats a date value based on a format string that defines the date format you want returned.
- *DATE#* - The *DATE#* function converts a string value to date based on a format mask that defines how the string value is formatted.

Because both of these functions return a date value it is easy to confuse them. In some cases the DATE# function is used inside of the DATE function. This is because the dates in the data model are stored as formatted strings and you not only wish to convert them to date values, but you also wish to format the date values. The following is an example of a field that stores dates as a string that you want to convert and format.

```
=DATE(DATE#( string_date, 'YYYY.MM.DD' ), 'YYYY-MMM-
DD')
```

In the example above, the string_date field represents a field in the data model that stores a string value, but the value represents dates. The format of the string is a 4 digit year, a 2 digit month and a 2 digit day separated by periods. The DATE# function is passed the field value and a string mask telling it how the string data is formatted. It converts the string value into a date value. The result from the DATE# function is used as the first argument to the DATE function, which formats the result with 4 digit year, abbreviated month name and 2 digit day separated by dashes. If this expression was used in a text box the result would look similar to: 2010-Mar-20.

Another common need is to show results based on years, quarters or months. Unless these date-oriented groupings are available when the data is loaded, you will need to create expressions to convert date values into a higher level grouping. The following example demonstrates how a date value can be used in an expression to return quarter descriptions:

```
=QUARTERNAME(date_placed)
```

In the example above, the *QUARTERNAME* function is used to provide quarter descriptions for a date value provided by the date_placed field in the data model. When used in a calculated dimension in a chart, this expression produces a series of quarters with the month range and year shown for each quarter. The resulting data appears for each dimension member in the chart legend similar to this: Jan-Mar 2010. This same operation could be performed using the *YEAR*, *MONTH*, *WEEKDAY* and other date functions.

Another common need is to determine the start date of a given year, quarter or month. For example, you may wish to show an aggregate value for the first day of every month to analyze a trend. The following example shows an expression that does this.

```
=MONTHSTART(date_placed)
```

In the example above, the *MONTHSTART* function returns a single date (the first day of the month) for the month of the date passed in as an argument. When used in a calculated dimension, a trend can be shown based on an aggregated value for the first day of each month. This type of result can be obtained using the *YEARSTART* and *QUARTERSTART* functions. You should note that *YEAREND*, *QUARTEREND* and *MONTHEND* functions also exist.

In some cases it may be necessary to use two date values to determine the difference in days between them. This is commonly referred to as "date math." The result is usually a number representing days, weeks, months or some other segment of time. Before you can perform date math you must ensure you are working with date values and not string values. Previously in this chapter you were introduced to the *DATE#* function, which converts string values to date values. A common example of date math is to find the difference in days between two dates. The following example demonstrates how by using the minus (-) operator you can do this without a QlikView function in your expression.

```
=date_shipped - date_placed
```

In the example above, the date_shipped field represents when an order actually shipped. The date_placed field represents when an order was placed by a customer. By subtracting the date_placed date from the date_shipped date, a number is calculated and returned. It represents the number of days between when the order went out and when it was placed.

Summarizing (Aggregating) Data

The process of summarizing data is also referred to as "aggregating" because it involves combining values in some way. You will see this term in the QlikView interface and documentation. To perform summarization on data in QlikView an expression is created that uses one or more aggregate functions. Typical aggregations of data in QlikView include such functions as *SUM, AVERAGE* and *COUNT.* These functions are quick and easy to use, and you have doubtless used one or more of them if you have created a chart in QlikView.

Basic Data Aggregation

Although there are many other reasons to create expressions in QlikView, perhaps the most common use of expressions is to summarize data for charts. Since charts must present data visually, the data must be organized into categories called dimensions and then summarized for each dimension value. The summarization of data across one or more dimensions in a QlikView chart is a built-in feature of the tool. However, you must create an expression to tell the chart how to aggregate (summarize) the data. The following is an example of each of the basic aggregation functions as they are used to summarize a field value in an expression:

```
=SUM (quantity)
=COUNT (product_name)
=AVG (quantity)
```

Each of these examples performs a common aggregation of data. Only one of them would be used in a given expression unless it was necessary to perform additional math on them. Some of the built-in QlikView aggregation functions include the following:

- *SUM, COUNT, AVG* (the common ones): These functions should not require extensive description, though it is worth noting a few things. *COUNT* is a function that can operate on any type of field. Text fields can be counted. However, it is a bad idea to use it, or any aggregate function, on a key field (a field used to associate tables) since such fields are duplicated across tables. *SUM* and *AVG* perform conventional mathematical summary and averaging operations.
- *MAX, MIN, NULLCOUNT*: These functions are helpful in finding top and bottom values in a field (*MAX, MIN*). The *NULLCOUNT* function is helpful in identifying where data is missing from a field. In some cases databases treat a NULL value as legitimate; in other cases NULL values may reflect problems in the data. For these reasons the ability to count NULL's is important.
- *STDDEV* (standard deviation): The *STDDEV* function performs a standard deviation calculation on a field. Standard deviation is used in statistical analysis to determine variability or diversity of data set elements from the average (mean). When used in a chart, the *STDDEV*, returns the standard deviation for all of the chart data in a single value for the chart title (if the expression is used in the chart title). It also shows the standard deviation value for each dimension member.

These are just a few basic examples of aggregation functions. There are many more built into QlikView, including advanced statistical functions such as *KURTOSIS* and *SKEWNESS*. In our experience some customers have been able to replace statistical analysis software such as MiniTab and SAS with QlikView. QlikView also includes a wide range of financial functions such as *FV* (future value), *PV* (present value) and *PM* (Payment) to name a few.

You can use aggregation functions in conjunction with calculations that you wish to perform within an expression. For example, the data may have detail level values that need to be calculated before an aggregation occurs. In the following example, the quantity field is used as a multiplier for the unit_price field. This operation is performed within the parentheses for the *SUM* function:

```
=SUM (quantity * unit_price)
```

In the example above, the word *SUM* is the function name. The calculation results in a single value that is used as the argument value for the function. If the field names are not typed correctly (don't match the field names in the load script) the expression results in an error. The *SUM* function isn't performed until the multiplication is complete (order of operation is driven by the parentheses). Other common aggregation expressions include summarizing non-numeric values (by counting) and locating the highest (*MAX*) or lowest (*MIN*) value in a given field.

Controlling Aggregation Scope (TOTAL, ALL)

It is possible to control how the aggregation occurs in a QlikView expression. The previous examples assume that the aggregation should be driven by the set of possible values (values associated with the user's selections) in the data. That means if those expressions are used in a text object to show a value on the screen, the total for all data appears (assuming the user makes no selections). If the user selects a given region, the total recalculates to show the value for the selected region. When an aggregate expression is used in a chart, the summarized value is calculated for each dimension value in the chart (i.e., each bar in a bar chart). Dimensions in charts are determined by the field you select on the *Dimensions* tab of the Chart Properties. If you create a bar chart based on the region field, each bar shows the relative value (based on the aggregate expression in the chart) for each region. Even though there's nothing in the chart expression to indicate it should aggregate for each chart dimension (region), it does. This is automatic for chart expressions in QlikView.

There are several ways through which you can force QlikView to use a different scope -a scope other than the set of possible values- when aggregating data. The most advanced of these is through the use of set analysis, which is covered later in this chapter and arguably a more powerful and versatile option. However, there are some basic qualifiers that when added to a simple aggregate function, forces an aggregate function to use a specified scope without requiring the more complex syntax associated with set analysis. These are the *TOTAL* and *ALL* qualifiers. A qualifier affects how a function performs; that is, it can be thought of as a predefined argument value. These qualifiers are added to the syntax of an aggregate statement, such as *SUM*, *AVG* or *COUNT*. The word *TOTAL* or the word *ALL* is placed inside of the parentheses ahead of the first argument value. In the example below, the *TOTAL* qualifier is used within a *SUM* function:

```
=SUM(TOTAL quantity)
```

When the *TOTAL* qualifier is used, the aggregate function operates on all dimension values in a chart. Normally, the function operates on one dimension value at a time. In a bar chart, each bar represents a dimension value and the aggregate function summarizes the desired value for each of them. However, when the *TOTAL* qualifier is used the summary occurs for all dimension values at one time. When using the *TOTAL* qualifier the aggregated value will be same for all dimensions, but it still operates on the set of possible values (the values associated with the user's selections). This may be helpful when performing calculations. For example, you may wish to have each bar in a bar chart show the percentage of the total for the chart. To do this you would use the *TOTAL* qualifier to return an amount that can be divided by for each bar (dimension) value, as shown in the next example:

```
=SUM(quantity) / SUM(TOTAL quantity)
```

The expression above, when formatted as a percentage on the *Number* tab of the Chart Properties, shows the percentage each value (each bar in a bar chart) represents of the chart total. The *TOTAL* modifier also allows you to force the aggregation to occur on a different dimension, one that is not used in the chart. For example, suppose you want to show the percentage of units sold in each city as a percentage of each city's respective region (rather than as a percentage of all cities). The chart uses the city field as the dimension, but you need to perform a calculation to include aggregations on both city and region. The following example demonstrates how the *TOTAL* qualifier, with some additional syntax, can do this.

```
=SUM(quantity) / SUM(TOTAL <region> quantity)
```

In the example above, there are two aggregate functions used in a division calculation to derive the percentage of a given city's quantity relative to its region. Notice after the *TOTAL* modifier in the second function the *region* field is added and enclosed in angle brackets or chevrons. This tells the expression engine to force the aggregation on the region field even though the chart for this expression uses the city field as the dimension. The result is a percentage of each city's quantity for its region. The entire expression is still subject to the set of possible values (values associated with the user's selections).

The *ALL* qualifier works in a way similar to the *TOTAL* qualifier. The only difference is that it ignores user selections (possible values) and calculates over the entire data set (all records). The *ALL* qualifier forces the aggregate function to always summarize all values for the field in the data model no matter what the user selects.

Nesting Aggregated Values (AGGR)

The idea of nesting may be applied to aggregated (summarized) values. However, QlikView doesn't allow simple nesting of summaries without the use of some advanced functions. For example, you cannot nest a *SUM* function inside of a *COUNT* function. This is because there are inherent problems with nesting aggregate values. The way in which the expression engine performs aggregations won't allow this to be done. For this reason, if you try to nest aggregated functions without special syntax, QlikView ignores your expression syntax and no value is returned. This can be misleading. When used in a chart, the expression won't show bars or a line. No error is raised; it is just ignored as though no data met the criteria for the expression. Our team has experienced similar challenges with a wide variety of analytical tools. We especially notice problems when trying to nest summaries inside of averages. Because of these problems, QlikView includes an advanced function that helps when you need to nest aggregation functions.

In order to mitigate the issues discussed above, QlikView provides a function known as the advanced aggregation function (*AGGR*). This function performs an aggregation based on a dimension (field) that you pass to it. It returns an aggregated value for all possible (user selected) values associated with the dimension field you choose. In this respect it is similar to using the *TOTAL* qualifier, with additional syntax, in a normal aggregate function. However, the value returned by the *AGGR* function is usable within another aggregation function such as *SUM*, *AVG* or *COUNT*. It is designed to work in combination with a calculated dimension, but can be used in other ways too. All QlikView charts require you to select one or more fields to use as dimensions. A chart dimension determines how the data will be categorized and displayed. For a bar chart, each bar is a summarized value representing the members (values) in the dimension you chose. Another option for establishing a chart dimension is to create your own *calculated dimension*. A *calculated dimension* is a dimension based on an expression that you write. The expression returns a list of values, which are used to establish the chart's dimension values. Creating a calculated dimension is easy. From the *Dimensions* tab in the Chart Properties you click the *Add Calculated Dimension* button. The expression editor appears and you type in the syntax that defines the dimension. A simple example of this is to create an expression that references a field.

The result is the same as selecting the field as the value for a regular dimension.

The *AGGR* function can operate in conjunction with a calculated dimension. It essentially performs an aggregation relative to a field value. The field value, when used within a chart, can represent one or more values for one of the chart's dimensions (i.e. bars in a bar chart). The way the *AGGR* function works is to act as an aggregator of aggregators. It allows you to nest another aggregation inside of it. The first argument for the *AGGR* function is a nested aggregation function such as *SUM, COUNT* or *AVG*. It is specifically designed to tell the QlikView expression engine how to handle the nested aggregation. The second argument for the *AGGR* function is the name of a field. This is what makes it a fit for use as a calculated dimension because it allows summarization of a value before the normal chart summarization occurs.

All of this may seem somewhat academic, or even confusing, until you encounter a situation where nested aggregation is needed. For example, you might want to show a line on a bar chart that represents the average value for all of the bars. While this can easily be done in QlikView without creating an expression, it serves as a good example for understanding nested aggregation. Also, if you use the built in *trendlines* expression property to do this (which eliminates the need to create an expression to show a trend or average), you cannot format the line. So using an expression may still be necessary. In this example you have a bar chart that shows order item quantities by region. Each bar is the sum of a given region's order item quantity. There are two expressions. The first is the normal aggregation that drives the bars in the bar chart. The second is an advanced aggregation that allows an average to be nested within a sum. Here is the example:

```
=AVG(TOTAL AGGR(SUM(quantity), region))
```

In the example above, an average for all of the data in the chart is calculated. Because the average must be across all dimension values, the *TOTAL* modifier is used in the outside function. In order to summarize the quantity field for each region within the *AVG* function the *AGGR* function is needed. It allows the nesting of the *SUM* function and forces it to aggregate data at the region level. The result is an average amount for the entire chart. The value from this expression is the same for each bar in the bar chart. Therefore it is a good idea to show this expression as a line, which is done in the *Display Options* on the *Expressions* tab of the Chart Properties. Other uses of the *AGGR* function are shared later in this chapter. See the section on *Grouping Values into Buckets.*

Grouping Values into Buckets

In some cases it is necessary to show summarizations based on ranges of values. This type of presentation is often compared to creating buckets or brackets. For example, it may be desirable to show order counts based on customer purchasing at several levels (i.e. 1,000, 2,000 etc.). Further, you may want to show how many orders are placed with customer purchasing at each increment of $1,000. To do this you can use the *AGGR* function in combination with a chart's calculated dimension capability. As you discovered earlier in this chapter, the *AGGR* function allows you to control how an aggregate function such as *SUM* or *AVG* performs. The *AGGR* function allows for the summarization of an aggregate function (nested aggregation). When used in an expression to define a calculated dimension, the *AGGR* function makes it possible to create a dimension based on value ranges from data in the QlikView data model. A calculated dimension performs the same duties as a regular dimension in a chart. It defines how the chart elements are categorized. In a bar chart it defines what constitutes each bar. The chart's expression determines the height of each bar. Normally, the bars in a bar chart are automatically created by values in the data field used for the chart's dimension. When you create a calculated dimension the bars in a bar chart are determined by the result of an expression that you create.

The *AGGR* function allows you to summarize a value for each value in a field. This results in a set of values that can become the dimension members in a chart. For example, you might want to show sales amounts in groups (buckets) of $5,000. Each $5,000 increment becomes a dimension value (bar in a bar chart). The following example shows how an expression used for a calculated dimension can do this:

```
=AGGR(ROUND(SUM(quantity * unit_price),
5000),organization_name)
```

In the example above, the *AGGR* function is used to summarize an aggregated value for use as a calculated dimension in a chart. The internal *SUM* function calculates and summarizes a sales amount. The *ROUND* function uses this amount as an argument and returns values in increments rounded to the nearest $5,000. This is done for all customers by using the organization_name field as the dimension for the *AGGR* function. When used in a calculated dimension, this expression creates a dimension value for each $5,000 increment of customer sales. If the chart is a bar chart there will be bars for increments of $5,000, $10,000 etc. The chart must also include an expression to determine the height of each bar.

Set Analysis

Because QlikView expressions always assume that aggregate functions should operate on the set of possible values (values associated with the user's selections), it can be difficult to show certain types of comparisons. If you want to show the grand total for all regions and the user selects one or two regions from a list box or chart, your expression will recalculate based on the user's selections. For this reason, (beginning with QlikView version 8.5) support for advanced expression functionality known as *set analysis* was added to the QlikView expression engine. Set analysis in QlikView is represented by enhanced, and sometimes confusing, syntax used in expressions. It applies primarily to aggregation expressions in which you are summarizing data. Set analysis syntax allows you to control how aggregation functions such as *SUM*, *AVG*, and *COUNT* operate with respect to user selections and other criteria. It can become very complex. For the purpose of introducing you to a more advanced example of expression writing, this part of the chapter uses moderate examples of set analysis. However, you will find that even though these examples are not very complex, they are powerful and very helpful.

Set Identifiers

The first thing you need to understand when using set analysis syntax is that it is designed to work with aggregation functions. That means you always begin with an expression that summarizes data. By adding set analysis syntax to the expression you change way the aggregation behaves; you change the scope of the aggregation. In the first example below, syntax is added to force the aggregation to occur for all data, irrespective of user selections. That means all values are used, not just possible values.

```
=SUM( {1} quantity * unit_price )
```

In the example above, the only thing that's been added to the aggregation expression is the curly brackets and their contents (the number 1). All set analysis syntax is placed inside of curly brackets at the beginning of the contents for the aggregate function. The number 1 is what forces the aggregation to occur across all values irrespective of the user's selections. If the number 1 is replaced with a dollar sign {$} the expression uses the possible values (the same as if no set analysis syntax is used). The area inside and inclusive of the curly brackets is called a "set expression." The number 1 or the $ are called the *set identifier* because they identify, at a high level, how the data set for this expression is established.

You may combine separate set analysis expressions to perform calculations. For example, if you want to show the percentage for the user's selection of the grand total you could use the following syntax:

```
=SUM(quantity * unit_price) / SUM( {1} quantity *
unit_price)
```

In this example there are two aggregate statements separated by a division operator (the forward slash). Each statement completes and the results are used in the division operation, resulting in a fractional number that is determined by what selections the user makes. If all values are selected the result is 1 or 100%. If you use this statement in a text box, you may wish to format the result so it appears as a readable percentage. Since the result may be a fraction (0.45 for 45%) all that is needed is to multiply it by 100:

```
=SUM( {1} quantity * unit_price ) * 100
```

In the example above, the entire previous expression is multiplied by 100, resulting in a friendlier representation of the percentage. However there is still a problem. The decimal precision, depending on the document settings, may go out five or ten places. This is not friendly or easy to read. So, to resolve this, the *NUM* function can be used to force the result to two decimal places.

```
=NUM(SUM( {1} quantity * unit_price ) * 100, '##0.00')
```

In this example the *NUM* function is passed the result from the aggregate expression as the first argument and the second argument for the *NUM* function is a format mask (string that directs the *NUM* function to mask the result so that zeros appear as place holders for small values and there are only two decimal places used).

There are other options for controlling aggregation with set analysis syntax. The set identifier may also include a reference to a bookmark or to an alternate state (alternate states are only available in version 11 and later). This allows other mechanisms to control the contents of a set. For example, if you have a bookmark in your document that is made up of the regions in the area of the Great Lakes, you could reference the bookmark in an expression. The following example demonstrates how a bookmark identifier is used as a set identifier:

```
=SUM({BM01} quantity)
```

In the example above, the bookmark identifier (BM01) is used as the set identifier. This forces the *SUM* function to only summarize the quantity field for regions selected by that bookmark. It works independently of the user selecting the bookmark. The user may make any desired selections but the value for this expression will always be based on the regions selected when the bookmark was created or last updated (replaced).

Set Operators

When working with set analysis you can use *set operators* to further control how the expression's data set is created. This is one of the features that distinguish set analysis from the *TOTAL* and *ALL* modifiers. For example, by using the minus sign (-) as an operator immediately following the set identifier you can invert the result. For example, if you use the dollar sign identifier ($) in an expression, the default behavior is to include all possible values (values associated with the user's selections). However by adding the one (1) operator which includes all values, followed by a minus sign before the dollar sign (1-$), you will create a set of all excluded values (values not associated with the current user selections). This can be a powerful addition to your document because it performs exception reporting. Showing exceptions is something most BI tools don't do well, if at all.

Set Modifiers

Another common need that set analysis syntax addresses is the need to force a summary on a predetermined dimension (field) value: In other words, summarize for a specific field value or set of values. For example, imagine you wish to show the total sales for a specific region in a text box. You may wish to show the total for the region no matter what selections the user makes, so you want to ignore possible values. To do this use can use set analysis *modifiers*. Modifiers are elements of syntax placed inside of the set expression (inside the curly brackets) that specify a field name (the dimension) and a field value (the dimension value). This syntax gets a little tricky because it includes curly brackets inside of other curly brackets. But it works well and it is very powerful. The following is an example that sums the sales amount for the CA region irrespective of user selections in the *region* field. The syntax to format the result has been left out for the sake of clarity. But, they could have been added and would work the same.

```
=SUM({1<region={CA}>} quantity * unit_price)
```

In this example, additional syntax is added between the greater-than and less-than <> characters. This segment is where the set analysis *modifier* syntax resides. The first part of the modifier is the name of the dimension field (region). The next part of the expression includes an operator telling the expression that the region must equal a specific value. Now comes the tricky part, the values that are used in the modifier must be enclosed in curly brackets. In this case there is only one value (CA), but a list of region values could be included with each value separated by commas (`region={CA,CO,OH}`). The result is a summary of the quantity multiplied by the unit price for the CA region irrespective of *region* selections made by the user.

The above examples demonstrate how to ignore a user's selections within a field by hard-coding specific values within a set modifier. However, there may be times that you want to ignore selections in a field other than the one for which you are providing a value. For example, if you want to hard-code the region value of 'CA', but ignore any selections made in the order_year field, you need to include additional syntax within the set modifier to account for the order_year field as well. Each field you need to reference within the set modifier is separated by a comma (,). If you wish to ignore the selections in a field without hard-coding a value then you simply add the equal sign(=) after the field without providing a value. For example:

```
=SUM({1<region={CA}, order_year=>} quantity *
unit_price)
```

Dollar Sign Expansion and Previous Period Comparison

In many applications there is a need to compare current values to those of a previous period. When evaluating BI solutions this is often fundamental to making a purchase decision. Previous period comparisons can include comparing the current year, quarter, month or fiscal period to the corresponding period at some point in the past. For example, you may want to compare the current month to the same month last year, or you may want to compare the current month to last month. In order to do this in QlikView you must use a set analysis modifier to force your expression to summarize data for the previous period. This can be done using a constant value for the period. However, it may be desirable to dynamically determine the current and previous period values based on what the user selects. For example, if your QlikView document has an *order_year* field (created in the load script based on the order date: `YEAR(order_date)`), then the user might use a list box to select a year. The selected year is considered the current year. Your expression uses the current year value to determine the previous year. If the user selects 2008 from the list box, your expression uses the 2008 value to determine that it should summarize a value based on 2007. To do this you must use a feature of set analysis called *dollar sign expansion*. By using dollar sign expansion you can nest expressions inside of the modifier syntax for a set expression. This allows you to dynamically calculate values used to control the set. Before exploring dollar sign expansion consider the following set expression that summarizes a value based on constant values:

```
=SUM({$<order_year={2007}>}quantity)
```

In the set analysis expression above, the *SUM* function summarizes the quantity field. The set analysis expression inside of the outer curly brackets uses a set modifier to force the summarization to occur only for the year 2007. This presumes that data model includes an *order_year* field. This expression works well, but it is not versatile. Conceivably, for each year you would have to update the expression syntax to reflect the correct year value.

To address the issue created by using a constant value for the year, you must be able to perform a calculation inside of the set modifier syntax. This is not allowed unless you use special syntax. The term for this is *dollar sign expansion*. Using the dollar sign ($) and parentheses that follow it, you can create an expression inside of the modifier syntax so that the modifier value is calculated. Consider the following enhancement to the previous expression:

```
=SUM({$<order_year={$(=YEAR( TODAY() )-1 )}>}quantity)
```

In the example above, the *order_year* modifier is being sent the result of an internal expression. The dollar sign expansion (the $ followed by parentheses) is what allows the internal expression to work within the set analysis expression. The internal expression uses the *TODAY* function, which must be followed by parentheses to indicate it is a function even though no arguments are needed. The result of the *TODAY* function is the current system date, which is passed as an argument to the *YEAR* function. This results in the current year value as an integer. The value of one (1) is then subtracted to return the previous year.

IMPORTANT: There are idiosyncrasies with all syntax. The QlikView expression engine is no exception to this. In this expression the equal sign (=) must be placed inside the dollar sign expansion and it must immediately follow the open parenthesis. If a space is placed between the open parenthesis and the equal sign the expression will not return a value. Keep this in mind any time you use dollar sign expansion.

In the last revision of the expression, a dynamic calculation of the previous year is created using dollar sign expansion within the modifier syntax of the set analysis expression. In some cases this result is adequate. However, it may be desirable to allow the user to determine which year is considered current. This is done in QlikView by providing a list box on the year field and the year field is usually created in the load script. To use the user's selection to drive the current and previous year expression results you again use dollar sign expansion. However, in this case you don't use the *TODAY* function to determine current and previous year values. Instead, you use the year field value provided by the user's selection in the list box. The following expression syntax shows this:

```
=SUM({$<order_year={$(=order_year-1 )}>}quantity)
```

In this example, the internal expression that is enabled by dollar sign expansion uses the user selected value for *order_year* and subtracts a value of one to return the year before the one selected by the user. This replaces the *YEAR* and *TODAY* functions from the previous version of the expression. When a user selects an *order_year* value in a list box or other tab sheet object, the expression automatically summarizes the quantity amount for the previous year.

Yet there is still a potential issue with the set analysis expression as it is written thus far. In the example above, QlikView expects a single value to be returned to the set analysis expression for *order_year*. If a user selects more than one *order_year*, no result is returned. This can be misleading and disconcerting to the user. In order to ensure that a single value is returned for *order_year*, you can use either the *MAX* summary function or a function called *ONLY*. Consider the two expression options below:

```
=SUM({$<order_year={$(=MAX(order_year)-1 )}>}quantity)

=SUM({$<order_year={$(=ONLY(order_year)-1
)}>}quantity)
```

If you use the *MAX* summary function, the expression will always be sent an *order_year*, even if more than one is selected. If you use the *ONLY* function and multiple *order_year* values are selected, the expression will return an error. If you opt to use the *ONLY* function, you should also write a calculation condition expression in the Object Properties of the chart to ensure that it only renders the chart if a single value is selected for *order_year*.

You should also customize the error message returned so that the user understands what must be done in order to render the chart.

Set analysis syntax can do much more than what is reviewed in this section. But knowing just these basic elements can address a multitude of needs. Most tutorials and introductions to QlikView do not include a review of set analysis, but our feeling is that until you can write expressions at this level you're very limited in what you can make QlikView do.

Conditional Calculations

In some cases an expression must return a value based on a predetermined condition. For example, you may want a label for a chart or value in a text box to show different information based on specific circumstances. A common example of this is the need to change the column header in a straight table to show how the values (rows) for the column are being calculated. Consider one of the earlier examples where by using set analysis, a summarization is performed based on the year a user selects. If the user selects 2003, you would want the column header to show 2003. If the user selects a different year, you want that year to show. This is easily accomplished by using the year field in an expression for the column label. No special conditions apply to this situation, because the user's action determines which year is shown. The expression is simple and looks similar to the following:

```
=order_year
```

However, this presents a problem if no selections have been made. If the user clears all selections and no year is selected, the column's data reflects a calculation for all years. But the column header will be blank because there is no *order_year* value selected. To address this you must create expression syntax that controls what the expression does based on a condition. The condition is based on whether or not a selected year value exists. To accomplish this you can use a control structure based on an *IF* function statement in your expression. QlikView *IF* statement syntax is very straight forward. It follows a conventional IF-THEN-ELSE structure. The only syntax for an *IF* statement is the *IF* keyword, parentheses and commas. The following example shows how the scenario introduced above can be addressed with a simple *IF* statement:

```
=IF( order_year > 0 , order_year, 'All Years')
```

In the example above, the *IF* function is passed a condition as the first argument. The condition returns true or false. In this case the condition determines if an *order_year* value is selected by evaluating the *order_year* field for a value greater than zero. The second argument is the return value of the expression if the condition is true. In this case it shows the selected year. The last argument is the value returned if the condition is false (the ELSE value). In this case the constant string of “All Years” is shown.

More complex conditions and structure can be used and such scenarios may include nesting of control structures. Consider, however, that if your document contains a lot of data and a complex data model, conditional calculations in expressions may have a negative impact on performance. If this seems to be the case, consider reviewing your load script to see if some conditions can be addressed as flag fields in the data model.

Working with QlikView Variables

If you’re unfamiliar with the concept of variables, you should take this opportunity to learn it because it will increase the versatility and value of your QlikView documents. Variables are a fundamental aspect of almost every programming and scripting language. They play an important role in facilitating the development of applications, reports and other content. As a QlikView developer, you will likely encounter the need for variables at some point in your career. The basic concept of a variable is that it stores information on a temporary basis. Variables are not databases; they are in-memory storage areas for small amounts of data. In most cases variables are volatile.

That is to say when you close your QlikView document, any values you've placed inside of variables are lost. However, QlikView will retain the value for a variable when the document is saved, but this capability does not exist in all versions of QlikView. In our experience, QlikView version 10 SR2 and later allows for this, but earlier versions do not, due to a bug that was later corrected. QlikView bookmarks may also be set to retain variable values, which make it easy for users to create their own scenarios and reuse them.

What do Variables do in QlikView?

The purpose of variables is to allow different parts of your QlikView document to share and update data values. QlikView variables can serve several purposes including the following:

- Controlling the visibility of sheet objects based on user input
- Storing and using data values that users create while interacting with a QlikView document, which allow for the creation of user-driven scenarios with the data
- Storing global values that are used by multiple objects throughout the QlikView document
- Standardizing expression syntax to make it easier to maintain and make it more dynamic

Variables can be created and updated in a variety of ways. The QlikView load script can define and set variable values. Examples of this are created by default when a new document is created. The SET statements that perform this function appear at the beginning of the QlikView load script. These standard variables are used in the document to determine how common formatting and settings should be used. Variables can also be defined in the document properties (*Settings>Document Properties>Variables tab*). Variables can be updated by user input objects such as sliders, buttons and input boxes that allow users to scroll, click or type to create values. Variables can be used in QlikView expressions as values or as extensions to expression syntax. The scope of QlikView variables is document wide. That means once a variable is created and contains a value, it is accessible from virtually anywhere in the document. Variables must have a predefined name, which cannot be the same as any reserved word. For example, you cannot name a variable with the same name as a function (i.e. *SUM*). Variables can only store a single value; they are scalar. Variables cannot store a set of records or a list a values unless such values are contained in a single string of characters.

Variable Overview: Managing Document Variables

Variables can be created in the document load script or from within the document settings. There is also a dialog called *Variable Overview* that is dedicated to creating and managing variables. You can access it from the *Settings* pull down menu (*Settings>Variable Overview*) in QlikView for Windows. The dialog lists all document variables. It allows you to select a variable by clicking on it, whereby you can set or change the variable's value. You can also create new variables in the *Variable Overview* dialog. The dialog also allows you create comments for variables to help you keep track of what the variable is used for.

FIGURE 6-3 VARIABLE OVERVIEW DIALOG

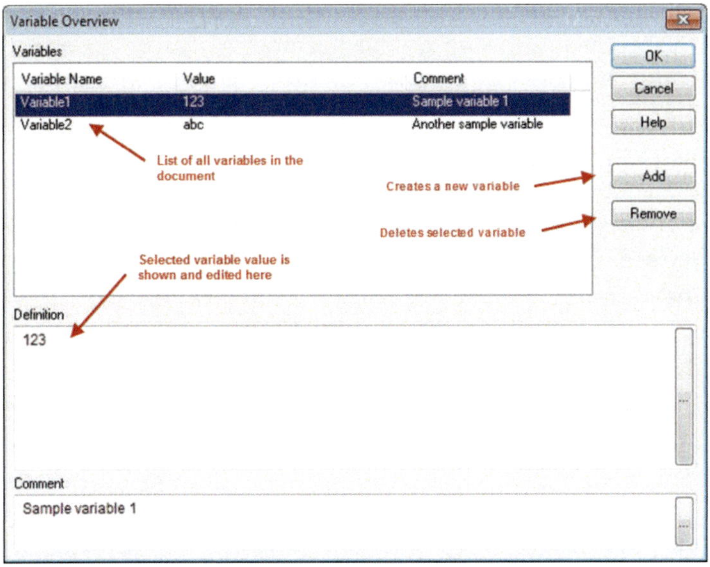

SET v. LET Statements

To place a value in a variable from within the load script, you use either a *SET* command or a *LET* command. If you set a value in the *Variable Overview* it will be the same as using the *SET* command in your document's load script. A value can also be placed in a variable from within an expression or in an input object. Variables can contain two types of values. A variable may contain any standard alphanumeric or numeric data type such as a string, number or date value. A variable may also contain expression syntax (as a string) or the value created by an expression. When a variable contains expression syntax, it can be used a part of another expression (more on this later). The *SET* command places a scalar (single) value into a variable. The following example shows a constant value being stored in a variable.

```
SET v_region_id = 12;
```

This example would be used in the document's load script to populate a variable named *v_region_id* with a default value of 12. The value might change as the document is used because the variable may be connected to a user input control. The *SET* command is used to store standard values in variables. However, in some cases it may be necessary to calculate a value and store the result in the variable. If you wanted perform a math operation or some other calculation, and you used the *SET* command, then the result of the calculation would not be stored in the variable. Instead the calculation syntax would be stored. For example if the variable was in the load script as follows:

```
SET v_region_id = 12+6;
```

The variable would contain the string "12+6" and not the value of 18. This happens because QlikView variables can be used to store expression syntax as well as basic values. For this reason the *LET* command exits. If you create the variable with the *LET* command, as shown below, the result of the calculation is stored.

```
LET v_region_id = 12+6;
```

In the example above, the variable named *v_region_id* stores a value of 18 because the *LET* command causes the calculation to occur before the value is placed in the variable.

Using Variables

Variables are available for use within QlikView expressions and with certain sheet objects. Common examples of variable use in QlikView include such things as using a button object to set a variable and then using the variable's value to control the visibility of objects on a tab sheet (or even tab sheets themselves). Most objects have a visibility property found on the *Layout* tab. It is called *Show*, and when set to use the *Conditional* option an expression may be used to toggle visibility of the object. If the expression returns zero (0) the object disappears, otherwise it is shown. If the expression references a variable, the value of the variable will determine when the object is shown on the tab sheet. The variable can be updated by a button object or any other object that allows you to set *actions* making it possible for users to show and hide objects by clicking on buttons.

Since QlikView variables may contain standard values or expression syntax, different methods for referencing a variable in expressions may be used. If you reference the variable by name, the value stored in the variable will be treated as a standard scalar value, even if it was populated with expression syntax. In order to use the contents of a variable as expression syntax you must reference it with dollar sign and parenthesis. This is similar to the dollar sign expansion syntax used in set analysis expression. The following shows a variable being referenced in a way that adds the variables value as syntax to an expression.

```
=$(Variable1)
```

In the example above the contents of Variable1 is used as syntax in the expression. If the content reads "1+1", the expression would return a value of 2. However if the expression references the variable by the variable name without the dollar sign and parentheses as shown below, the result would be the text "1+1".

```
=Variable1
```

This difference in how variables are used and referenced may seem esoteric, but consider the fact that you can place complex expression syntax into a variable and use it as part of the syntax for several expressions throughout your document. The variable could be set in the load script and the syntax could even be created conditionally. If the logic for the expression syntax needed to change, you would only have to change it one place.

Variables are often used in conjunction with sliders, input boxes and expressions to create "What If" scenarios that greatly increase the interactivity of a QlikView document. Understanding and using variables is an important part of developing feature-rich documents that offer your users an enhanced experience. These types of capabilities can reduce the number of QlikView documents you need to create and reduce the amount of maintenance needed for existing documents because they make a single document applicable to a wider variety of user needs. This, in turn, can simplify your deployment and may have a positive impact on your licensing cost.

Expressions with Images

When using certain types of screen objects it may be appropriate to show images to help illustrate the differences in data values. A common example of this is a scorecard that uses images to show the status or trend of an item. QlikView has a number of built-in image files that may be referenced within an expression. It is important to keep in mind that if you are referencing an image file (built-in or otherwise) in an expression, the expression must be used with an object property that expects a reference to an image file. Chart expressions allow you to set the *Display Options* (*Chart Properties>Expressions>Display Options*). If the chart is a *Straight Table* or *Pivot Table* you will be able to set the *Display Option Representation* to "Image." This option assumes that the result of the expression is a string that represents a path to an image file. There are built in images that you can use as icons. The *Images* tab in the *Expression Editor* allows you to select image paths and paste them into the expression syntax.

For example, you may want to create a *Straight Table* that lists all of the regions and includes a column with an icon that indicates each region's status or performance. To do this you would create the table, add a dimension for region, and add an expression that determines which image to show under certain conditions. In the example below, a green icon is shown if the region's quantity is over 500 and a red icon is shown otherwise. An *IF* statement is used to set the condition:

```
IF (SUM(quantity) > 500,
'qmem://<bundled>/BuiltIn/check_g.png',
'qmem://<bundled>/BuiltIn/exclamation_r.png')
```

In the example above, an *IF* statement is used to create a condition on the *SUM* of quantity. If the sum is more than 500 (the condition), the built-in "check_g.png" image is used. If the condition is not met the built-in exclamation_r.png image is used. The result looks similar to the following:

FIGURE 6-4 EXPRESSION WITH IMAGE IN STRAIGHT TABLE

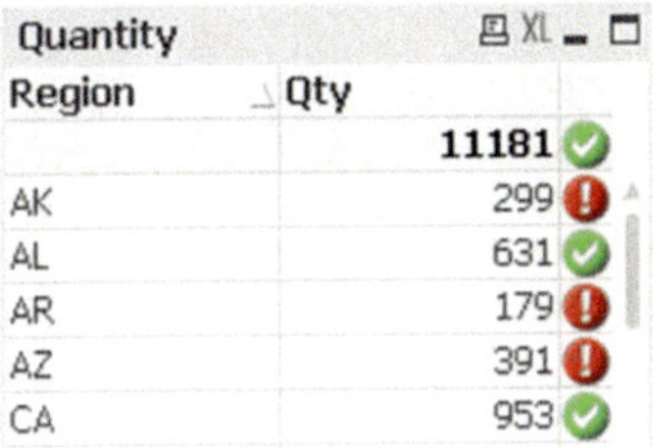

It is important to consider a few things when creating a table with image expressions:

1. The image will, depending on properties you set, adjust its size to the width of the column. If it doesn't show properly, you may have to resize the column by dragging the column border in the table.
2. The vertical size of the image may be too large to fit in the cell. To correct this consider increasing the font size on the *Font* tab (*Font>Size*). This will increase the height of each row.
3. If you don't use a built-in image, keep in mind that the path to the image file must be available to the QlikView server or user's local client if you distribute the document. If you deploy to a server, the Windows account for the server's services must also have rights to the folder in which you placed the image.
4. Try to use .PNG files with transparency. We're not sure what other files may be supported, but if you use a file that doesn't support transparency, you may find the image looks bad in your document

5. It is always considered a best practice to manually adjust the size of the image used prior to using it in QlikView. In other words, if you display a 10 MB image in QlikView and scale it within QlikView, it will still occupy 10 MB of space in memory. Rather, if you resize the image outside of QlikView to 5 MB and then use it in QlikView, the image will only need 5 MB of memory.

Using image references in expressions allows you to create rich, customized content with QlikView. This capability is often overlooked. Some QlikView developers completely miss the fact that through this feature you can quickly and easily create a scorecard interface.

Chapter 7: Advanced Document Design

Getting started with QlikView is easy. Many feel it is easier to begin developing content with QlikView than with other software tools. This is in part because QlikView combines the process of loading data with the necessary tools to display and interact with data. The fact that these distinct operations occur within a single development environment contributes greatly to the success of QlikView. While getting started and creating meaningful documents with QlikView is easy, there is much more you can do than a basic tutorial offers.

This chapter will provide you with a deeper understanding of QlikView's user interface features and functionality. You will learn about managing user selections, advanced techniques for data visualization, managing screen real estate, how to work with large tables of data, how to search for values in the data, and much more. After mastering some these features, you will be able to produce very sophisticated content. It is important to move beyond the basics of chart and user interface design because the real value in dashboards and analytical documents lies in the users' ability to compare and correlate multiple values in ways defined in part by the user. Predefined dashboards and static representations of summarized values do not address the ever increasing demand from users to better understand what the data represents. This chapter will help you design and build more flexible and comprehensive interfaces that enable the user to do more.

List Boxes and User Selections

At its core, QlikView's value is based on offering users the ability to select data. Unlike other tools, QlikView does not, in most cases, filter data and it does not perform queries designed to retrieve a subset of the data based on user input. Rather,

QlikView is better thought of as an associative selection engine. This means that in almost every case a QlikView document incorporates a means for allowing the user to choose which data are relevant. The most common way this is done is through the use of list boxes. List boxes are sheet objects that are based on a field from the document's data model. By now you have no doubt created many list boxes and you should understand that when selections are made in a list box, the selected data appears with a green background. You should also understand that associated values (possible values) in other list boxes will appear with white backgrounds and disassociated values (excluded values) appear with gray backgrounds.

Changing Selection Appearance

This green-white-gray functionality and interrelationship of list boxes with other list boxes and charts is automatic in QlikView. No special consideration or effort on your part is needed to make a list box function. However, in many cases the default characteristics of a list box are not adequate or desirable. The default appearance of a list box presents the field data in a vertical list. When items are selected in a list box, their status and appearance is based on several defaults, including the following:

- Background and Foreground Colors: Selected items appear with a green background and white foreground.
- Selected Items on Top: When items are selected they automatically move to the top of the list.
- Associated (Possible) Values in other List Boxes on Top: As selections are made in one list box, associated (possible) values in other list boxes move to the top and appear with white backgrounds. NOTE: If the list box that contains associated (possible) values is sized in order to show all values for the field, then possible values will not rise to the top of the list, but rather will retain their position relative to other sorting options.

- All Items Appear in a Vertical List: In all list boxes the default layout displays the field values vertically with a scroll bar.

This default behavior is built into QlikView for very specific reasons. For example, if the user selects three items in a list of one thousand items, it may be problematic to leave the selected items in their original positions in the list box. Some of the selected items may be well below the bottom of the list box, requiring the user to scroll down to see what is selected. For this reason the selected items automatically move to the top. While this makes sense when explained, it can be confusing to a new user because as selections are made the sort order of the list box appears to change. The same situation exists with associated (possible) values in other list boxes. Therefore it may be preferable to force items in list boxes to remain in their original positions. This is done by unchecking the *State* checkbox in the *Sort By* grouping in the properties dialog for the list box (*Properties>Sort>State*).

The way in which selections are rendered can also be problematic. Imagine a user who is color blind making selections or reviewing a document with predefined selections or bookmarks. Such a user may have difficulty differentiating between a green and gray background making it difficult to distinguish between selected and associated values. For this reason and others, you may wish to show selections differently. List box selections in QlikView can be shown in several ways:

- Standard green background
- Corner tags that show a colored triangle in the upper left corner of the item when selected
- Check boxes that are commonly used in other applications (checkbox lists)
- LED indicators (illuminated circles)
- LED with check boxes

This is done by changing the *Selection Style Override* on the Presentation tab (*Properties>Presentation>Image Options> Selection Style Override*).

Another default behavior that may not be desirable is the presentation of the data in a vertical list. If the field for the list box includes a limited number of values, it may be preferable to display it horizontally. This is done by unchecking the *Single Column* property on the presentation tab (*Properties> Presentation>Single Column*). List boxes with multiple columns tend to work best when there are a finite, knowable number of values in advance. Common scenarios where this makes sense include list boxes to provide a list of years, months or even days. Changing the orientation of a list box can free up space on the tab and make the user interface easier to understand.

Some aspects of selection appearance and behavior in your QlikView document should be consistent across the document. If you decide to use checkboxes to show selections, it is a good idea to do that in all list boxes. Having some list boxes with check boxes, others with LED's and others with the default green background will make the user interface very confusing to both new and seasoned users. However, other list box properties may only apply to certain situations. For example, it wouldn't necessarily make sense to have multiple columns for a list of hundreds of items, but it would for a list of years or months.

Adding Columns to List Boxes

QlikView list boxes appear as a single column of values based on the fields used in the list box properties. As previously indicated you can force the values of the field to appear in multiple columns. Prior to version 10, list boxes could not show other data such as other field values or expression results. One exception to this is that earlier versions of list boxes could include a frequency number by checking the Show Frequency check box (Properties>General>Show Frequency). This property adds a column that displays the number of selectable combinations associated with the item in the list box. For example, if a region has 9 customers, and customer is the lowest level of detail in the data model, the frequency for that region would be 9. This value can also be shown as a percentage of the total number of entries.

While forcing the list box field values into multiple columns or showing the selectable combination frequency may be helpful, it is likely other values that you define would be more helpful. Beginning with version 10 QlikView includes support for adding one or more expressions to a list box. This feature opens the door for you to add virtually any value as a column to a list box. This is done by using the Expressions tab in the list box properties. Adding expressions to list boxes is similar to adding expressions to charts. Each expression appears as a new column in the list box. The most common example of an expression in a list box might be to add another field. For example, if you had a list of cities, it may be desirable to add an expression the shows each city's region since the same city name can exist in multiple regions. The following simple expression is an example of the expression syntax for this scenario:

```
=region
```

More complex expressions may also be used. This makes the basic list box a more versatile sheet object because it allows you to show summarized data, while providing a selection mechanism for the user. For example, it may be helpful to show the number of orders associated with each city. The expression syntax for this would be as follows:

```
=COUNT(order_id)
```

It is important to note that such expressions will calculate relative to the item (row). However, when the user makes selections and some items are excluded the calculation will not return a value for the excluded items in the list box. This can be confusing to the user. This can be addressed by using a Set Analysis Identifier that forces the aggregation to occur without regard for the possible values (see the chapter on expressions and set analysis). Here's an example:

```
=COUNT({1} order_id)
```

There is no obvious limit to the number of expression columns that you may create in a list box, but keep in mind that if you wish to show many columns, a *Table Box* or *Straight Table* may be more appropriate.

Spark Lines and other Mini Charts

Adding expressions to list boxes makes it possible to show more meaningful information about items, which makes it easier for users to decide which items to select. Additional list box features take this a step further. It is possible to show the results of a list box expression (column) as a mini chart or gauge. This effect is common to scorecards that show the status of an item. Another common use for this is to show what are commonly known as spark lines. These are small line charts that appear on each row of a list box showing a trend for the list box item. List box expressions may be visualized inside of the list box in several ways. A summary expression (*SUM, AVG, COUNT,* etc...) can be shown as a gauge, which shows the calculated value relative to a minimum and a maximum value. The expression result can also be shown as a mini-chart, which uses the value in conjunction with a selected dimension (selected separately from the field used in the list box). To do this you must change the *Representation* property for the expression (*Properties> Expressions>Display Options>Representation*). The default setting displays the expression result as text. Other settings include image, various types of gauges and mini-chart. If you select a gauge, for example a *Linear Gauge*, the button below the *Representation* drop-down allows you to adjust the gauge settings. This button displays a dialog from which you can set minimum and maximum values for the gauge, thereby controlling the range for the gauge. The value from the expression determines where the indicator falls within the gauge. Setting a maximum value for a gauge may not be as simple as it seems. Consider the list box expression below, where the expression counts the number of orders for a list box showing regions (orders per region).

```
=COUNT(order_name)
```

This expression is simple enough, and will return an order count as an integer for each region in the list box. However, if you want to show this as a line gauge, it will be necessary to calculate a maximum value for the gauge. An expression can be created for the Max value field in the Gauge Settings dialog, but a simple expression using *MAX* will not work properly. The expression must return the maximum count of orders for all regions. This means you must create a nested aggregation (see the expressions chapter for more on this). To do this you must use an advanced aggregation function as follows:

```
=MAX(AGGR(COUNT(order_name), region))
```

In the expression above, the *COUNT* function is nested inside of the *MAX* function. This cannot be done without using the *AGGR* function, which requires the count to occur relative to a dimension; in this case the region dimension. The result of this expression is the number representing the highest count of orders across all regions. In figure 7-1, you can see how the gauge looks in the list box after the proper maximum value calculation is performed and other properties of the gauge are set in the *Gauge Settings* dialog.

FIGURE 7-1 LIST BOX GAUGE COLUMN

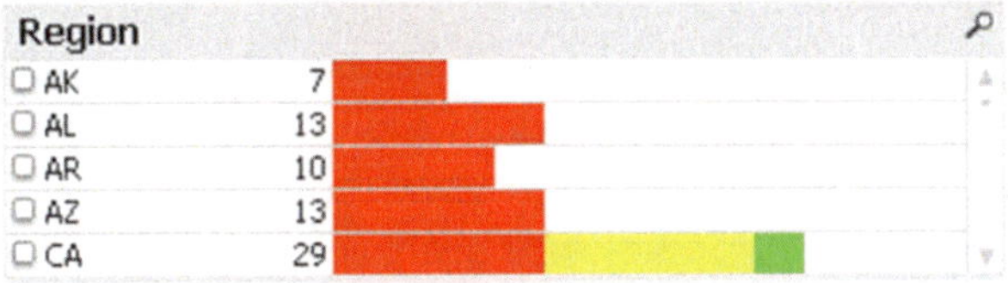

In Figure 7-1 the linear gauge's size is based on each region's value as it measured against the maximum order count for all regions. Various other settings have been configured to manipulate the way in which the gauge works and looks. These include creating segments to show when a given value is good or bad (red, yellow, green) as well as adjustments to the gauge's outline and boundary properties. Additionally, the list box *Cell Borders* property (*Properties>Presentation>Cell Borders*) has be activated to provide some separation between the rows. The list box *Selection Style Override* property has also been set to use LED checkboxes. The numbers do not automatically appear to the left of the gauge. A separate expression represented as text must be added if you want to show the numbers with the gauge. Although this list box provides graphical information, it remains a fully functional list box. Users may select multiple values, see excluded values and perform other list box operations.

Mini charts are similar to list box expression gauges. You create a mini chart by selecting the mini chart option from an expression's *Representation* property (*Properties>Expressions> Display Options>Representation*). This causes the button below the *Representation* property list box to show that it represents *Mini Chart Settings*. Clicking it launches a dialog from which you configure the mini chart. Mini charts are different from gauges in that they represent the list box expression's value relative to a dimension (field). The dimension usually is not based on the same field shown in the list box. A common dimension type for mini charts is a date value: Usually, a year, quarter or month value, but it could be a date field resulting in a day value. However, if you have too many increments in the dimension, for example a lot of day values for the expression, the mini chart will look very flat. For this reason consider summarizing the dimension in the load script. If you are using a date value, consider breaking it into year-month or year-quarter increments and use the resulting field as the dimension. In the *Appearance* grouping on the Mini Chart Setting dialog, a *Mode* property exists. The Mode property allows you to choose what type of mini chart you would like. There are several options. The most popular tend to be the following:

- Sparkline: Displays a line chart with color coded dots to show maximum and minimum values

- Bars: Displays a bar chart where bars are color coded for maximum and minimum values
- Whiskers: Displays bars that are above or below a middle line based on the how the values fall compared to an average (with color coding)

Once you have selected a dimension and mode for the mini chart it should work. Other settings in the dialog allow you to control colors and a few other things, but usually the default values are adequate. In Figure 7-2, a Sparkline mini chart is shown using a year-month combination field that was added to the document's load script.

FIGURE 7-2 SPARKLINE MINI CHART

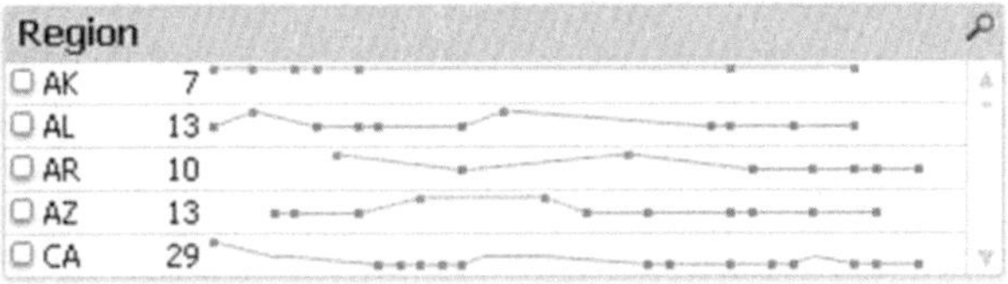

In Figure 7-2 the mini chart column is the third column in the list box. It is the second expression. The first expression shows the regions' order count value as text.

Showing and Managing User Selections

Since QlikView is fundamentally based on the idea that users select data values in which they are interested, it is important to represent user selections. If a user selects several regions and other items from list boxes or charts, it is easy for the user to forget what is selected. As a result the user may misinterpret the data. The default characteristics of list boxes address this by showing user selections with a green background and by moving them to the top of each corresponding list. This, however, does not address the user's need to see selections when viewing different tab sheets unless the same list boxes exist on every tab sheet. Additionally, some selectable objects such as charts don't clearly show that a selection has been made. If a user clicks and drags across a chart, the resulting rectangle will determine which elements of the chart's dimension will be used for selection. After a user makes a selection in a chart (when the user releases the mouse button) the chart will show only the selected items, making it unclear which items were selected unless a list box is shown for the chart's dimension.

To address the inevitable need to communicate what the user has selected, QlikView includes a sheet object that shows the user's selection: The *Current Selections Box*. It can be added to any tab sheet by right clicking on the tab sheet and selecting *New Sheet Object* (*New Sheet Object >Current Selections Box*). The *Current Selections Box* object automatically shows each field for which selections have been made and the corresponding values that were selected. If the user has selected a large quantity of items from a list box or chart, the *Current Selections Box* will show a numeric summary of the selections (i.e. 22 of 100) rather than a list of selected items. This is done to save space and can be adjusted in the *User Preferences* properties dialog (*Settings>User Preferences>General>Search Settings>Max Values in Current Selections*), but such settings are specific to the local environment will not follow the document when it is deployed. The *Current Selections Box* also allows users to clear selections for an individual field or (if you have version 10 or later), change settings for an individual field. Figure 7-3 shows a *Current Selections Box* with selections made on several fields.

FIGURE 7-3 CURRENT SELECTIONS BOX

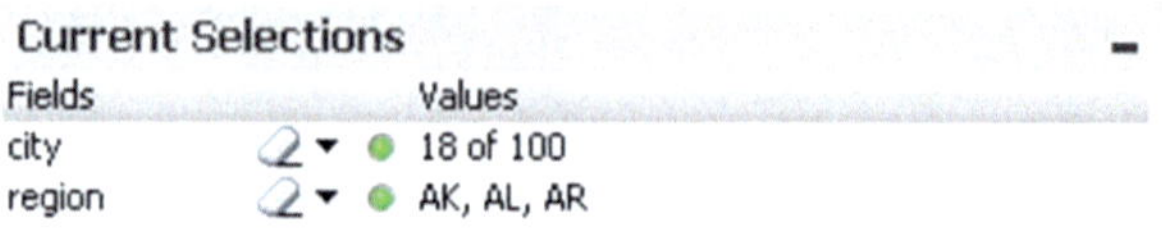

You can resize the columns in the current selections box by hovering over the border between two columns. A variety of properties also allow you to control what is shown (which columns). You can, for example, disallow the *Dropdown Select*

feature that allows users to change selections or deactivate the *Clear Icon* that allows users to clear selections for a given field. These and other features are found on the General tab of the object (*Properties>General*).

User selections may also be accessed and displayed using an expression. There are QlikView functions that return strings with values that have been selected for a given field. The following example of the *GETFIELDSELECTIONS* function shows how the field selections for the region field can be displayed with the words "Selected Regions:" prepended to the beginning of the selected values.

```
='Selected Regions: ' & GETFIELDSELECTIONS(region)
```

Other functions, such as the *GETCURRENTSELECTIONS* function which returns all selections, offer additional options for creating a custom presentation of user selections. Expressions using these functions can be leveraged in Text Box objects and formatted to meet desired standards. It is worth noting that within such expressions escape character syntax may be used to insert carriage returns, tabs and other formatting characters.

You should also be aware that current selections boxes do not allow you to apply a label to a field name. Therefore, it is highly advised that you alias fields appropriately in the load script so that they appear as desired within sheet objects such as the current selections box as-is.

Visualizing Data with Charts

Unquestionably, the ability to visualize data is among the top benefits associated with QlikView. Not only does QlikView produce appealing and robust data visualization, but it makes the creation of such visualizations quick and easy. In earlier chapters you were introduced to the basics of creating charts. In this section you will learn how to create and use more sophisticated chart objects. Additionally, you will learn which charts commonly make the most sense for certain situations. It is not our intent to cover every chart type and we certainly cannot cover all of the properties and features of the chart objects in QlikView. There are far too many capabilities and combinations. However, you will be introduced to several examples of more advanced charts and a variety of tips and tricks that make it easy to accomplish what we believe to be common goals in data visualization.

Before diving into chart creation and advanced data visualization techniques, it is important to understand some charting basics and to develop an approach as to how and when specific charts make sense. Charts always represent summarized data. That means you always need two things to create a chart in QlikView. First, you need one or more fields to represent the dimensions of the chart. Dimensions are categories of data the chart will represent visually. The most common example of this is a bar chart. Each bar is an item found in a field from the data model. Usually, fields that are used as dimensions are text fields with names of things such as regions, people, products, etc.... If the dimension for a chart is based on the region field, the bars in the chart each represent a single region. The second requirement for creating a QlikView chart is to create one or more expressions; also known as measures. Chart expressions represent a calculation that summarizes data for each dimension item. In a bar chart the expression determines the height of each bar. Chart expressions may be very complex, but they must return a numeric value that can be used by the chart to illustrate values for the dimension items.

Data Ink

While many BI tools include chart enhancements designed to make basic charts such as bar and pie charts more visually appealing, a school of thought in the BI community has begun to take hold that discourages excessive enhancement of data visualizations. In the book *The Visual Display of Quantitative Data*, Edward Tufte introduces the idea of the *Data Ink Ratio*. Understanding the data ink ratio, we believe, is important to developing an effective QlikView document. The basic concept is that any data visualization such as a chart in QlikView has a ratio of data and non-data ink. The presentation of the basic visualization such as the bars in a bar chart is considered data ink. However, such representations must be non-redundant to be considered data ink. When a bar in a bar chart is rendered in three dimensions (3D), the multidimensional effect results in redundant and unnecessary ink. In other words it isn't necessary to show a bar in a bar chart as a 3D pillar or column for the chart to illustrate the data. Other non-data ink elements of a chart may include such things as a background color, background pattern, grid lines, etc.... We don't suggest that you eliminate all non-data ink, but reducing unnecessary and redundant visual elements may make your document more readable and effective. There are notable exceptions to these general guidelines. For example, you may wish to include x-axis grid lines on a bar chart to make bar height relationships to values shown on the axis easier to read. However, as a general rule, reducing non-data ink is a good idea.

Chart Usage

Charts typically help users understand the data in one of several ways. It is a good idea to begin with this in mind and then determine which type of chart makes sense. In many cases a developer creates a set of charts without regard for the user's needs. Or equally problematic, the effort is based on a presumption of user needs. The idea of prototyping, discussed in earlier chapters, is a good one. However, you still need some framework to get started. Determining which charts are best for your users' needs should start with an understanding of the basic categories of data visualization. These include the following:

- Comparisons: Comparing values (showing distribution)
- Trends: Showing how values change over time
- Ratios: Showing values as part of the total
- Correlation: Showing how values relate to each other and to a scale

Each of these represents fundamentally different use cases. Understanding them and understanding which types of charts best fit a user's need helps you create meaningful and relevant content with QlikView. It also prevents lost time and effort, but more importantly it results in a meaningful result that encourages your users to adopt and leverage your work. Producing irrelevant visualizations in your QlikView document discourages users, and users are the people who determine relevance.

Comparisons: Showing distribution

Perhaps the most common use of charts is to compare two or more items. In the statistical world, the idea of comparison is often referred to as a "distribution" because it represents the need to see how a total is distributed across a variety of entities such as categories, people, places, things or timeframes. Such entities in QlikView charts are represented by the chart's dimension. The types of charts used to compare values or represent a distribution include bar charts, and Mekko charts. By far the most common comparison chart is the bar chart. The reason for this is that bar charts are very good at showing small differences in distribution and they lend themselves to showing groups of values as well as combinations. QlikView allows you to create bar charts that include separate measures represented as lines (combo charts). It also supports differing value ranges for different measures.

Bar Charts

Basic bar charts are easy to create in QlikView. In many cases, however, you will find that the default chart properties result in a cluttered look. With a few tweaks, you can make a basic bar chart more readable and force it to represent more meaningful information. In the following bar chart, a distribution of order counts is shown for each region. The dimension for the chart is based on the region field. The expression for the chart sums the quantity field from the order_information table. It is a simple example of a bar chart, but several properties have been changed to make it more presentable and easier to understand.

FIGURE 7-4 BAR CHART

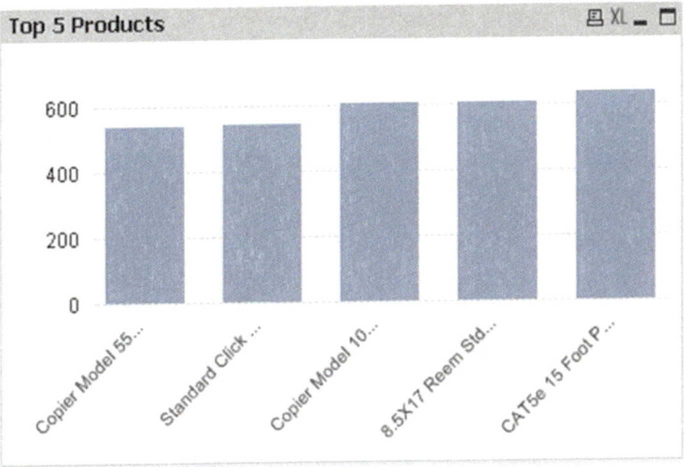

The adjustments to the properties in this bar chart represent basic things you should consider when creating all charts. Some of them are specific to bar charts, but similar considerations should be made for other chart types. They include the following (accessed by right-clicking on the chart and selecting the *Properties* dialog):

1. Give the chart a title (*General>Window Title*). It is a good idea to type in a title that will mean something to the user and describes the chart's contents.
2. Do not show the title in the chart (*General>Show Title in Chart*). If you are showing the caption of the chart, there is no need to show the title in the caption and in the chart.
3. If there are too many dimension values, limit them to the top or bottom of the range (*Dimension Limits> Restrict which values are displayed using the first expression*). Note: this feature is new to version 11. In earlier versions of QlikView this must be done by creating a calculated dimension and a combination of the *AGGR* and *RANK*

functions. Here is an example of the expression syntax used in the calculated dimensions:

```
=AGGR(IF(RANK(SUM(quantity))<5,
region,'Others'),region)
```

4. Do not show the dimension label if the chart title adequately describes the dimension or the dimension item names are obvious (*Dimensions>Label*).
5. Label the expression so the expression syntax is not used its label (*Expressions>Label*).
6. Display dimension item names at an angle (*Axes>Dimension Axis>Primary Dimension Label*).
7. Display dimension item names in a smaller font (*Axes>Dimension Axis>Font*).
8. Show the horizontal axis grid to make it easier to see the value of a bar (*Axes>Dimension Axis> Show Grid*)

Grouped Bar Charts

One of the features of bar charts is that they can illustrate data values for groupings. This can be helpful when you want to show more than one value for each dimension item. Consider the following example where unit cost and revenue are shown for each region.

FIGURE 7-5 GROUPED BAR CHART

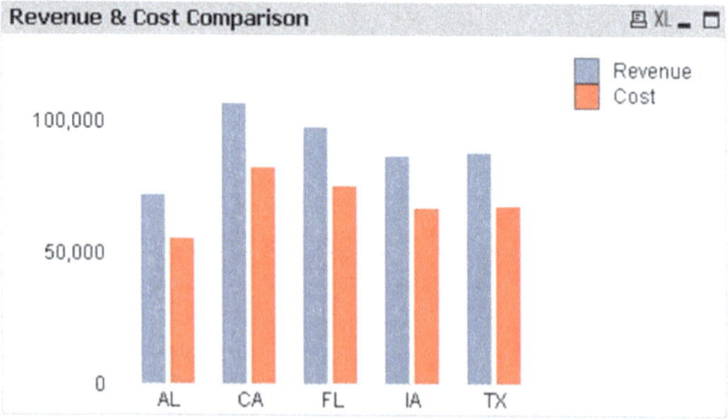

In the example above, the only thing that is needed to show two values as a grouping for each region is to add a second expression. The grouping is automatic in QlikView. Adjusting additional chart properties makes grouped bar charts easier to read. In this example, the Cluster Distance property (Presentation>Bar Settings>Cluster Distance) has been adjusted the maximum value of eight. This makes the groupings for each region more distinct and causes the bar' widths to reduce to allow for more room between the groupings. It is worth noting that if the value ranges for each of the expressions are significantly different, then the chart may not be effective. For example, if costs in this example ranged from zero to 10, and revenue ranged from zero to 100,000, the cost bars would be too small to see. This problem can be addressed with combo chart.

Combo Charts (Bars and Lines)

Combo charts begin as bar charts, but allow chart expressions to calculate at differing levels of aggregation. If you have a grouped bar chart such as the one shown previously that compares costs to revenue, and one of the expression values is significantly different than the other for each dimension item, then one set of bars may appear very small or not at all. This is because each expression needs its own scale for the vertical axis. You cannot compare values that are significantly out of range to each other visually. QlikView combo charts address this by allowing different expressions to render graphics against different ranges. For example, if you wanted to see revenue, which runs in the tens of thousands of dollars compared to order counts which run in the dozens, a combo chart is your best choice. Consider the combo chart below that does this.

FIGURE 7-6 COMBO CHART

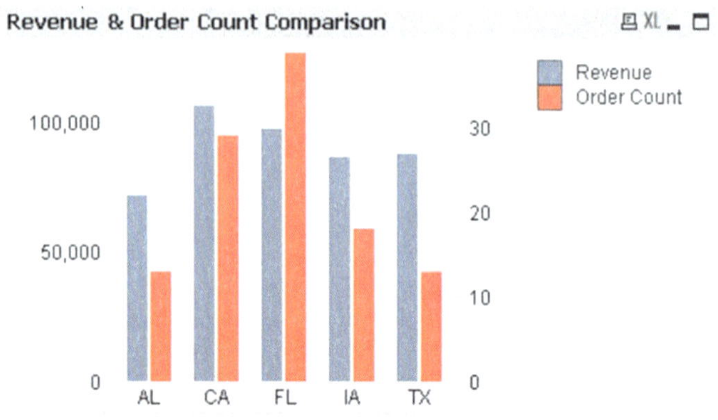

In the example of a combo chart above, there are two axes. The left axis represents the first expression (Revenue). Notice that the revenue bar is on the left side of the groupings. The right axis represents the second chart expression, order count. The order count bar is on the right side of the grouping. Notice that the axis on the right is a different scale than the left axis. To do this the following steps were taken:

1. Make sure the chart type is set to Combo Chart.
2. Create both expressions (first one *SUM* and second one *COUNT* in this case).
3. Make the axis for the second expression (order count) appear on the right (*Axes>Expression Axes>Position>Right Top*), and make sure the second expression is selected when you set this.

There are a number of other properties such as split axis that allow you to present both expression values in different ways. Another common way to show multiple values is to show one expression's value as a symbol or a line. This is done by changing the expression's *Display Options* (*Expression>Display Options*).

Mekko Charts

New to version 10, Mekko charts enhance conventional bar chart comparisons in two fundamental ways. First, they automatically adjust the width of the bars so that each bar represents the proportional amount of the chart total. This works in a manner similar to a pie or block chart. If a dimension item's bar value represents 25% of the chart total, the bar will be 25% of the chart width. Second, Mekko charts allow for a stacked bar presentation. This allows you to sub divide each bar to illustrate the relative amounts of the bar each subdivision represents of the bar total. Mekko charts in QlikView can represent bar heights in one of two ways depending on the *Style* (*Style>Look*) selected. The default style causes the height of each bar to be the same. In this case the bar heights all represent 100% of each dimension item's value, but the bar widths are automatically set to the dimension item's percentage of the chart total. If more than one expression is created in the chart, each bar will be subdivided for each expression value (stacked bar look). Consider the chart below where each bar is subdivided into three areas. It shows 2002, 2003 and all other years as a breakdown of each bar.

FIGURE 7-7 MEKKO CHART BLOCK STYLE

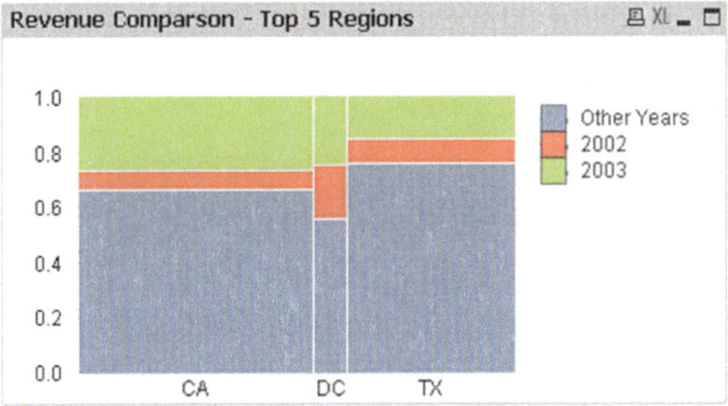

In Figure 7-7 the Mekko chart uses the default block style. Each region's bar shows a total height representing 100% of the region's revenue. Each bar is then subdivided and color coded to show the relative percentage for years defined in the chart's expressions. These values are shown as percentages, but the expression calculation is a straight summary of (*SUM*) dollar amounts. The chart automatically determines the proportions based on the expression values. The first expression in the chart is a general calculation that summarizes revenue for all regions. It is labeled "Other Years", and if no other expressions existed each bar would show a single blue block. The other two expressions use set analysis to force summarization of revenue for a specific year. The addition of these expressions causes the chart to subdivide the bars, taking value away from the first expression. The width of each bar is automatically determined by the chart based on the dimension item's percentage of the chart total.

Mekko charts in QlikView may also represent summarized total values that are not percentages for each dimension item. This is done by changing the chart's style (*Style>Look*) to the second option as shown in Figure 7-8.

FIGURE 7-8 MEKKO CHART STYLE SELECTION

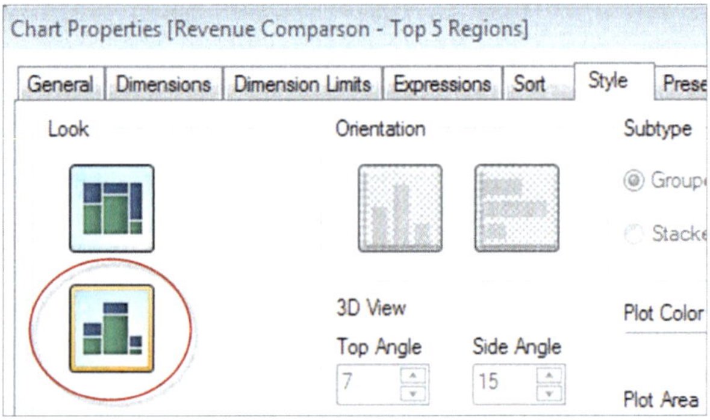

When a Mekko chart uses the bar style in place of the default block style, it returns the actual summarized values of each expression. This causes the second and third expressions, which summarize specific years, to determine the height of each bar relative to the first expression, which summarizes all years. In effect, the first expression determines the vertical scale for the chart and the other expressions determine the bar height. Figure 7-9 shows the result.

FIGURE 7-9 MEKKO CHART BAR STYLE

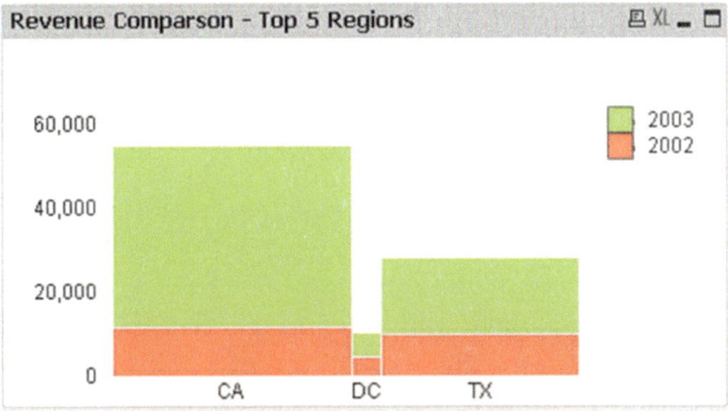

In this example the bars remain subdivided to show the relative value for each year, but the bar heights vary and are shown against a scale that represents the expression value, not a percentage. The bar widths remain representative of each bar's percentage of the chart total.

Trends: Showing changes over time

Unquestionably, you will encounter the need to show how values have changed over time. This type of visualization is typically referred to as a trend. Trends are most commonly shown with line charts. QlikView includes a line chart object that has a wide variety of formatting options. Lines can be shown as steps (plateaus), smooth or jagged (normal). You can display multiple lines by adding more than one expression to a QlikView line chart. In some cases bar charts may also be used to show changes in values over time, where each bar represents a point in time. However, this approach doesn't lend itself to trend analysis as much as a line chart. To create a meaningful line chart, the QlikView document's data model must include the appropriate field values for the date or time increments used in the chart. Alternately, you can create such increments with a calculated dimension. Using a date or date-time field as the chart's dimension is usually not a good idea because too many values exist to show on the dimension (horizontal) axis. To address this you will need to create fields in the load script to group date values. In most cases it is appropriate to group dates based on year-month or year-quarter combinations. Grouping on month alone may present a problem if the user hasn't selected a year or selects more than one year. The following is an example of script syntax for doing this in the load script.

```
year(date_placed) & '-' & month(date_placed) as
order_year_month,
```

In this script example, the date_placed field returns an order year and order month. These values are combined with a dash to produce a combination of year-month. Note that for these values to show up in the right order they should be ordered in chronological order while loading (in the load script) and then *load order* must be used as the sort option in the chart. This is because the new field cannot be sorted properly on text or numeric values. The new field can be used as a dimension in a line chart to show groupings of dates. When combined with one or more expressions the line chart will look similar to Figure 7-10.

FIGURE 7-10 LINE CHART

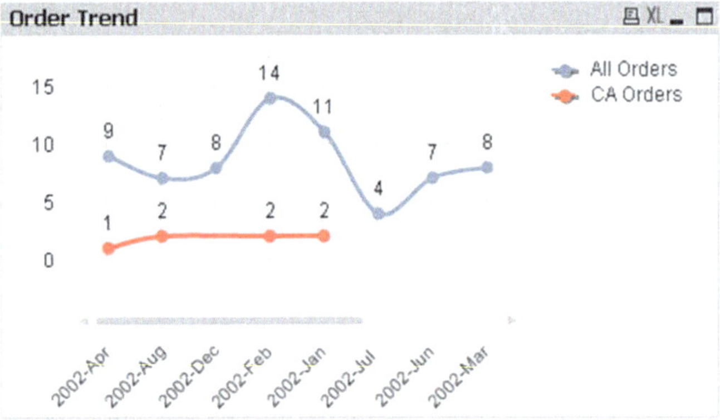

In the line chart above, several properties have been adjusted to make the chart easier to read. These include the following:

- Line smoothing: the Line property for each of the expressions has been set to show a smooth line. This eliminates the jagged spike normally associated with line charts (*Expressions>Display Options>Line*).

- Show data values: The values for each data point are shown (*Expressions>Display Options>Values on Data Points*). This makes it easier for users to see specific values, but be careful with this option. If you are showing a trend for large numbers it may crowd the chat and make it more difficult to understand.
- Grid Lines: Both horizontal (expression) and vertical (dimension) grid lines have been enabled (*Axes>Expression or Dimension Axes>Show Grid*). This is helpful with line charts for the vertical axis because it is sometimes difficult for users to see how data points align to date values at the bottom. The horizontal grid is less important in this case and may be unnecessary non-data ink.
- Symbols for Data Points: Data points have been highlighted using symbols (*Expressions>Display Options>Symbol*) for each expression. Note that the default symbol size may seem small, so small in fact you may not see the symbol show on the chart. To increase the symbol size adjust the Symbol Size property (*Presentation>Line/Symbol Setting>Symbol Size*).

Although the chart in Figure 7-10 uses a field that groups dates ranges into a combination of year and month, there may still be too many values to fit on the horizontal axis of the chart. For this reason the chart has be configured to allow for horizontal scrolling as shown in Figure 7-11.

FIGURE 7-11 LINE CHART SCROLLING

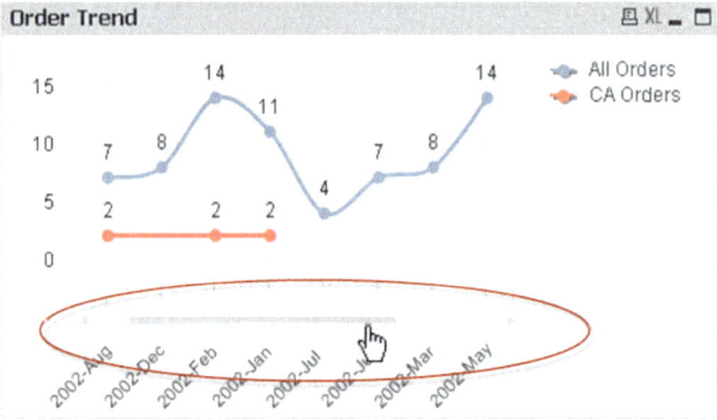

To activate horizontal scrolling in a QlikView chart, adjust the *X-Axis Scrollbar* property (*Presentation>Chart Scrolling>Enable X-Axis Scrollbar*) and set the corresponding value for the *When number of Items Exceeds* property. This makes the chart much more functional when you have to include a large quantity of dimension items. Note that this property can also help with other chart types such as bar charts.

Other options that may help make line charts more meaningful include such things as filling the plot area and adding trend lines. Filling in the area from the bottom of the plot area to the line makes the volume changes for the date grouping more profound. This is often used in publications because the line is sometimes difficult to see. Adding a trend line helps the user understand the overall trend based on one of the standard statistical methods for trending. QlikView supports several. In Figure 7-12 a line chart with the plot area filled in and a trend line added is shown.

FIGURE 7-12 LINE CHART WITH PLOT FILL AND TREND

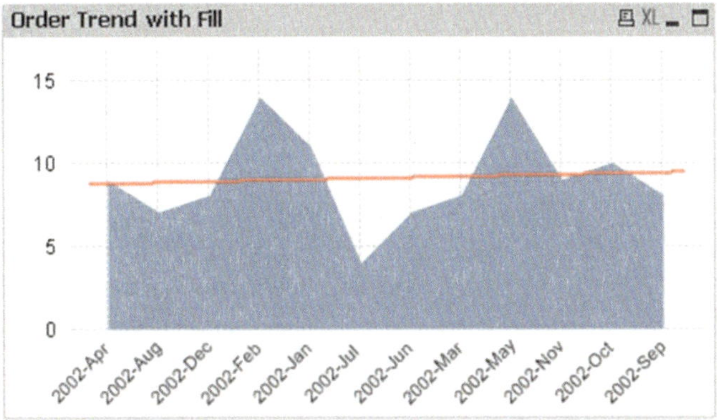

In this chart the chart style (*Style>Look*) has been changed so that the line area is filled in with a solid color. The fill style can also include a gradient by adjusting the Plot Color Style (*Style>Plot Color Style*). Also, a linear trend line has been added (*Expression>Trendlines*) to show the overall trend. Trend lines may also be created as separate expressions, but QlikView includes a number of common statistical trend line options. You can activate more than one at a time in a line chart.

Ratios: Showing values relative to a total

In some cases it is more important to show how much of the total each item represents in a chart. This type of visualization is designed to present ratios. Although somewhat less common than comparisons and trends; ratios are often a critical element to analyzing data. Including a chart that illustrates ratios can improve the overall value of your QlikView document. However, as with just about everything else you should be sure that presenting data ratios is what the users need. QlikView includes several types of charts aimed at showing ratios. The most common of these is the pie chart. Pie charts are well known and common to most users. An alternative to pie charts in QlikView is the block chart. Block charts are similar to Mekko charts, but are designed exclusively to illustrate ratios.

Pie Charts

Pie charts can be helpful in showing how values compare to each other. They work best when there are dramatic differences in the distribution of values. Many BI industry consultants discourage the use of pie charts because if the dimension values are similar, each slice in the pie chart will appear as the same size. This makes it difficult to determine subtle differences in the values. The pie chart in Figure 7-13 shows a breakdown of all orders by region. Because there are so many regions it is difficult to identify certain region values in the chart. This is partially because pie charts use color to distinguish one dimension item from another.

FIGURE 7-13 PIE CHART WITH MANY ITEMS

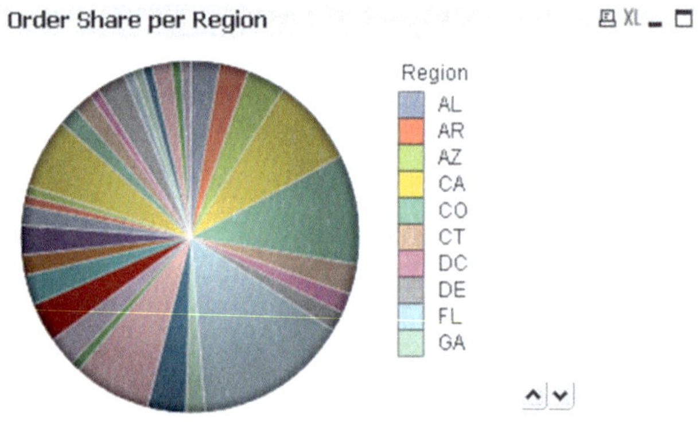

In the pie chart above, a simple expression that counts the number of orders is used. There is only one dimension, which is based on the region field. Notice in this pie chart that there are so many divisions (dimension items) that they cannot all fit into the legend list on the right. For this reason QlikView automatically creates scroll buttons. While this is a nice feature, a chart with this many divisions provides little value. Pie charts, and most ratio visualizations, work best when there are only a few divisions. In Figure 7-14 the previous pie chart has been changed to show fewer divisions and with a different style.

FIGURE 7-14 PIE CHART SHOWING TOP 5

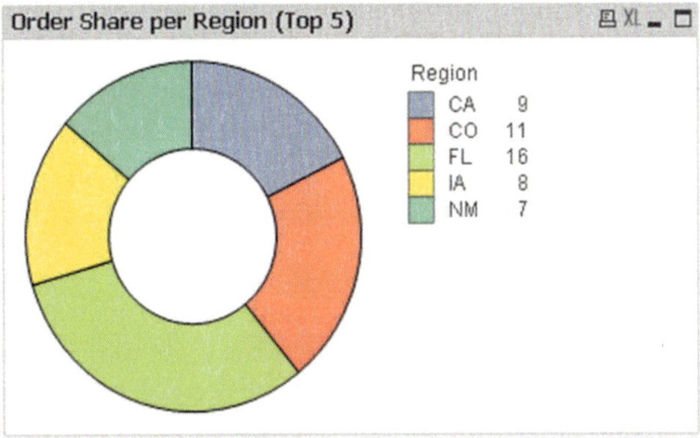

Notice in this second version of the pie chart several changes have been made that make the chart easier to read. Dimension limits (*Dimension Limits>Limits>Show Only*) have been set to show only the top 5 regions and not to show others. Note that dimension limits are new to version 11. As previously mentioned, to accomplish a similar effect you must create a calculated dimension based on an advanced aggregation expression. The chart style has also been changed to render as a doughnut chart (*Style>Look*). This is not necessarily better, but provided to show that pie charts in QlikView have a variety of styling options. Finally, the legend has been modified (*Presentation>Legend> Show Numbers in Legend*) to show the expression values (the number of orders for each region) next the region name. This helps in two ways. It provides actual values; and the numbers correspond to the size of the slices making it easier to relate a region to a slice. This can be helpful for situations where color alone is not adequate for identifying a slice.

Pie charts can make a disproportional distribution of values very clear. Consider, for example, a situation where two thirds of the sales for the country occur in a single region. Seeing a big slice in a pie chart immediately draws attention. Similarly, a very small slice may also illustrate an exception and make clear something that needs attention. To show both very large and very small slices you can use set analysis in the chart expression to select specific dimension items. For example you may want to compare three of four regions to each other where you know there is a significant difference in value. Of course a normal pie chart that includes all dimension items will automatically adjust when the user makes selections, but the default where all data is shown will not be very helpful.

Block Charts

Similar to bar charts, Block charts show values in rectangles that vary in size relative to the value for each dimension item. Unlike bar charts, block charts divide the total chart area into smaller areas representing data values by their sizes in both dimensions, not just height. Each block's size is representative of its percentage of the total value for the chart. This is what makes block charts a good candidate for showing ratios. Block charts make it very clear which items are larger (higher in value) than other items. Keep in mind that block charts, like pie charts, are only good at showing the differences between limited numbers of values (dimension items). They are not good at showing a large number of values. Under such circumstances, they tend to look busy and may not have room to show the legend information for each block. The block chart shown in Figure 7-15 shows the ratios of revenue for different regions.

FIGURE 7-15 BLOCK CHART

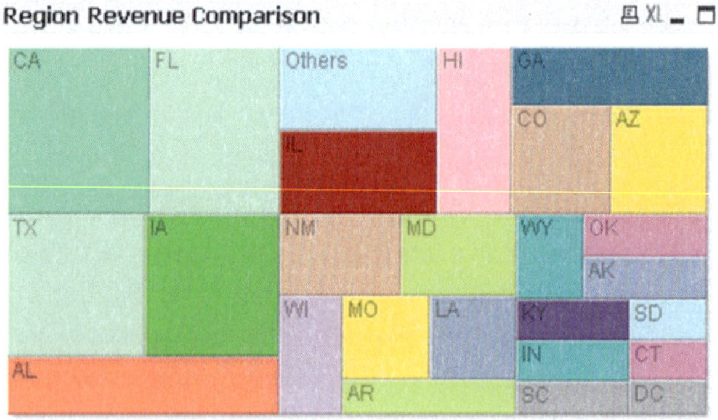

In this chart a single dimension (region) is used and a single expression that sums the quantity times the *unit_price* is used to return a revenue amount. Notice that in this block chart a region named "Others" appears. This is automatic with QlikView block charts. When the number of dimension items becomes too large to illustrate meaningful values, a number of the lower value items will be grouped and shown this way. This is similar to what you can do with dimension limits, but it is automatic. Block charts also support more than one dimension. For example, cities could be added to this chart and it would show a bigger block for each region and smaller sub-blocks for each city. This can be an interesting way to show multi-level ratios, but compounds the problem of having too many dimension items.

As with pie charts, it may be a good idea to use set analysis in the chart's expression to control the number of dimensions for which the chart calculates totals. For example: `SUM({$<region = {CA, CO}>}quantity*unit_price)`. An expression such as this will force the chart to only include the defined regions, even if the user selects all regions or many regions. Keep in mind that if you do this, you need to add language to the chart label, or somewhere on the screen, that indicates the chart's restrictions. Otherwise, users will be confused when they make selections that do not match the chart.

Correlation: Showing value proximity

In some cases you may wish to show how close values are to each other relative to a scale. This is a common statistical analysis scenario and is often applied to populations of data. While similar to a comparison, a correlation allows users to see a bigger picture of the data. Likewise, it should be noted that correlations are not meant to show cause and effect: A point that should be made clear to users of the QlikView document. Often correlation visualizations can work better than comparison charts for big picture scenarios.

Radar Charts

QlikView Radar Charts show expression values as points on a circular chart where the dimension items appear around the circumference of the circle, similar to a radar screen. The distance from the middle of the circle to the edge (the radius) represents the scale against which the values are plotted. A line is then created connecting each dimension item's relative value. The result is a high level view of how all of the values correlate to each other and to the center of the chart, which represents the lowest value or zero. Figure 7-16 shows a QlikView radar chart that correlates region order counts.

FIGURE 7-16 RADAR CHART

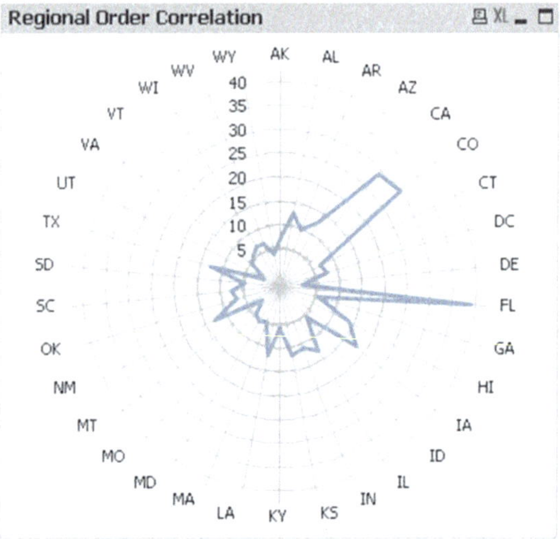

In this radar chart, a single dimension based on the region field is used. It also uses a single expression that counts the number of orders. The scale that appears at the top part of the chart calculates automatically. Notice how this chart makes it easy to see that FL, CO and CA are outperforming all other regions by a significant amount. While a comparison chart, such as a bar chart, would show this, if a high number of regions are included the user may have to scroll the chart to see how high values compare to low values. For this reason bar charts are not good at showing correlations. Radar charts allow the user to see all of the values and how they correlate at one time. This provides a meaningful high level picture. This can be especially meaningful when the document's data set is filtered on other dimensions. Imagine a user selecting different periods of time from a list box and watching the lines on this chart change. The user could toggle between two years, for example, to see how top performers correlate to low performers. Radar charts are not used as often as other types of charts because most developers don't understand where they can make a difference for users. Understanding that sometimes a correlation communicates better than a comparison opens the door to using radar charts.

Radar charts also tend to make a valuable choice of correlation charts when the dimension values can read similar to the way you read a clock. For example, imagine the dimension of month as the points around the radar chart and you can quickly see how reading in a clockwise fashion can also give the user a sense of time or movement across the values represented in the chart.

Scatter Charts

Scatter charts offer users the opportunity to visualize density. They allow users to see how dimension items correlate to each other relative to two scales. Scatter charts are different than radar charts in a few key ways. First, scatter charts use measures (expressions) to create x and y axes. That means the symbols in a scatter chart represent the dimension items and are plotted relative to two expression values. For example, the horizontal axis (x) might show something like order counts starting at zero and increasing in increments of 10. The vertical axis (y) might show cost in dollars. The symbols, which are scattered between the two axes, might represent regions. The location of the dots indicates two important things to the user. They show how a given region's orders correlate to cost. And, they show how regions compare to each other relative to orders placed and cost. The clustering of the symbols show how some regions are similar to each other. It also shows which regions are unusual. Scatter charts can tell a compelling story since understanding that a region may have a large number of orders but ranks low on the revenue scale could be an interesting deviation if other regions have a different set of values.

Consider the scatter chart in figure 7-17, which illustrates this scenario. Notice that the majority of regions show order counts of 1 to 15, and costs ranging from a few hundred dollars to 40K. However there are some exceptions such as FL.

FIGURE 7-17 SCATTER CHART

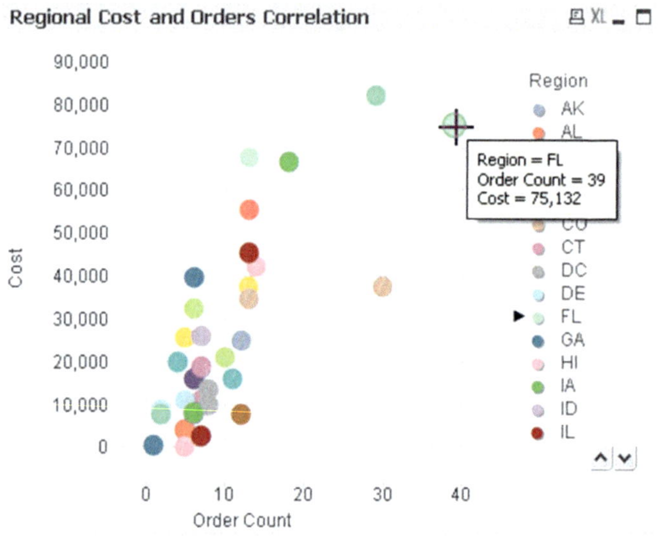

In the scatter chart above, each region is represented by a colored symbol. By hovering the mouse pointer over a symbol a hint window appears that shows the region's name and the values from the two expressions in the chart (see Figure 7-17). This is automatic in QlikView, but it can be disabled by changing a chart property (*Presentation>Labels in Chart> Pop-up Labels).* Hovering works in both the Windows and Web clients, but keep in mind that mouse-over effects are not available in mobile devices where a touch-screen is used. This is helpful because the colors can be a poor differentiator for the regions. It is a good idea to add a text box or other object that instructs the user to hover.

In this chart, there is one dimension (region) and two expressions in the chart. It is important to base a scatter chart on expressions of differing value ranges. In this example, the cost expression has a range of zero to ninety thousand, while the order count range is from zero to 40. If the ranges for both expressions were similar, the symbol may line up in a straight line or arch. While this may be accurate, it may not illustrate anything meaningful because no clustering occurs. For example, if this chart used cost and price for the expressions it would look different. See figure 7-18.

FIGURE 7-18 SCATTER CHART SIMILAR EXPRESSIONS

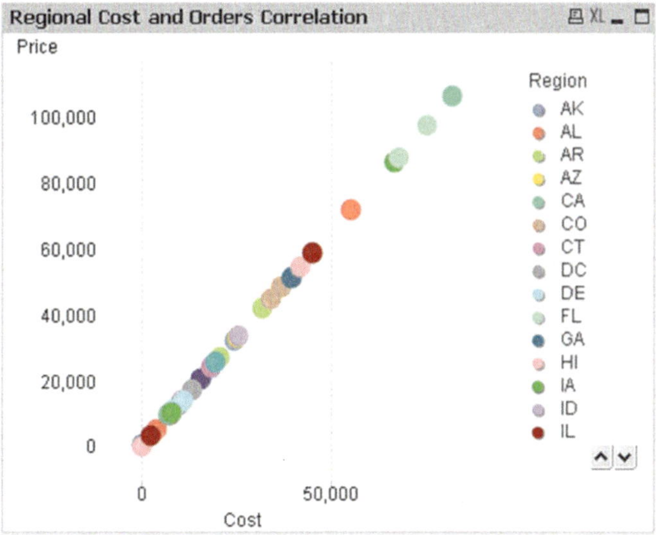

The chart in Figure 7-17 includes adjustments to a number of property settings that make it more presentable. Consider the following when creating a QlikView scatter chart:

- Show the grid on both axes (*Axes>X (or Y)-Axis>Show Grid*): This makes it easier for the user to see how a dimension item aligns to a value.

- Increase the Symbol Size (*Presentation>Representation> Symbol Size*): The default symbol size is set to 2 pt. This is quite small. Consider increasing it to 8 or more and your chart will be much easier to read.
- Use a simple look (*Style>Look*): You can select from a variety of looks for your chart. Some have bubbles or other symbols. A good choice is the simple solid circle look. It reduces non-data ink and makes it easier to see the color of the symbols on the chart.
- Log scaling: Sometimes QlikView automatically enables a Log scale for one of the axes (Axes>Y Axis>Log Scale) because of a difference in the scaling of the two expressions. The idea of using a Log Scale is that rather than showing the actual value, which may be very high, you want the axis to show increments that are exponents of the original values. For example, rather than showing 1,2,3,4, you show 1,20,100,1000. You may not want this, so consider disabling it to see if the symbol locations on the chart make more sense. Also, keep in mind that if you've already applied a log to your figures, on a log-log plot, everything is a straight line.

Gauges

In some cases conventional charts fail to illustrate values and correlations well. This is because conventional charts expect to plot values relative to two axes. A common use case for other correlation techniques is a dashboard. Consider an automobile's dashboard. The two largest indicators display the speed and the tachometer. The speed represents the rate at which the vehicle is traveling forward; the tachometer represents the relative use of the engine to propel the vehicle in revolutions per minute. Most drivers develop an understanding of the appropriate RPM's needed to move at a particular speed for a given vehicle. Correlating the speed to the RPM's allows the driver to know if something is unusual. For example, if the speed is lower than what the RPM's suggest it should be, there may be a problem with the drive train or transmission. Correlating these two instruments also allows the driver to optimize fuel economy on highways. It may also allow the driver to compare the relative gear ratios of different vehicles based on these two measurements. While such a correlation could be shown in a chart, having separate gauges seems to be universally accepted as a better approach. Similar scenarios may become clear to you while designing your QlikView document. QlikView, therefore, includes a gauge chart type. Gauges are good at showing a single value relative to a range or set of ranges.

It is important to keep a few things in mind when considering gauges for use in your document. First, gauges are commonly overused. A gauge is helpful only when you want to show a value relative to scale. If all you need is to show a value, a text box with an expression is the better choice. It reduces non-data ink and increases the amount of screen real estate available for other, more meaningful objects. In our experience we often see QlikView documents with dozens of gauges. They frequently appear cluttered and hard to use. Developers use gauges because they think the gauges look nice and are an inherent part of a conventional dashboard. However, it is more important to produce a QlikView document that meets the needs of your users than it is to have something that at first glance looks good. Ease of use and clarity should be paramount. Another challenge with using gauge charts is that it is still important to include a comparison on the chart. This is a little more difficult with gauges because they only show a single value. Therefore, thresholds, ranges, or colors must be employed to assist a user with understanding if what they see is good, bad, or to be expected.

When creating a gauge with QlikView, you begin by adding a chart to a tab sheet. A gauge in QlikView is nothing more than a type of chart. You may select the gauge icon on the *General* tab of the chart properties (*General>Chart Type*) to get started. Even though the chart wizard prompts you for a dimension when first creating a gauge, it does not use dimensions. You can ignore the dimension tab and properties. Even if you enter a field to be used as a dimension, it is ignored. You are also prompted for an expression, which must be created. The chart expression determines the value depicted in the gauge. For example, in a conventional gauge, the expression determines where the needle points. Sorting is not relevant because there are no dimensions associated with a gauge. There are several gauge styles available. The default in QlikView is a dial type gauge shown as a circle with a needle indicating the expression value. However, there are other styles such as the progress (sometimes called a thermometer) style. You will also see that for some of the gauge styles there are flatter versions as well as 3D versions. In keeping with the concept of limiting non-data ink, you may want to consider the flatter gauge styles. But, it is more important to maintain the overall theme of the document. If you used 3D style charts, you should consider keeping gauges consistent with that style.

When setting the presentation properties of the gauge, you will see that there are options for controlling the minimum and maximum values of the gauge (Presentation>Gauge Settings). These properties are important, especially the *Max* property because they affect the relative position of the gauge indicator (needle). If your expression returns a value of 1000 and the maximum gauge value is 100, the gauge will be pegged at maximum all of the time. It is often necessary to create an expression for the minimum and maximum values so that they correlate appropriately to the range in which the gauge is expected to work. For example, you may want the gauge to show a value relative to a predetermined maximum. This would result in the gauge indicator changing as the user makes selections in list boxes or charts because the gauge expression would result in a number lower than the corresponding maximum value expression. Creating an expression to control the gauge's maximum value can be tricky because the main expression is usually an aggregation such as *SUM*, which is subject to user selections. That means the expression that controls the gauge's maximum value must be also be an aggregate, but must not be subject to user selections. For example:

- Main Expression: `SUM(quantity)`
- This is simple enough; it sums the quantity field to drive the needle in the gauge.
- Max Property Expression: This cannot be a simple *SUM* function expression because that will return the same relative value as the main expression. The expression must summarize the quantity field irrespective of user selections. To do this you may use set analysis: `=SUM({1} quantity)`
- By adding a set identifier of "1" you force the expression to operate on the entire data set without regard for user selections. You could also accomplish this using the *ALL* qualifier: `=SUM(ALL quantity)`. However, if you wanted the gauge to only account for a predefined set of dimension values such as a given set of years, you would need to use set analysis set modifiers to force both expressions to operate within the given data set bounds. See the chapter covering advanced expressions and set analysis for more on how to use set analysis.

Another common consideration with gauges is how to show value qualifications. This is referred to as segmentation in QlikView charts. Its purpose is to show how certain value ranges should be interpreted by the user. For example, a low value may be shown in red and a high value in green to indicate that low values are bad and high ones are good. It is important to keep in mind the grain of the measure when setting values for colors, as sometimes a low value may actually indicate a favorable outcome. By segmenting the chart the user can easily understand at which point a value is considered good. This is done in QlikView using *Segment Setup* (*Presentation>Segment Setup*). By default, QlikView creates two segments in a gauge chart. You can delete and add segments using the corresponding buttons in *Segment Setup*. You can also set the colors for the selected segment by clicking on the color rectangle to the right in the *Segment Setup* Area. This will pop up a *Color Area* dialog from which you can change the *Base Color* (click on the fixed color rectangle to change it). When you close the dialog the color of the highlighted segment will be changed. At the bottom of the *Presentation* tab for the chart properties you will see a checkbox labeled *Autowidth Segments*. It is checked by default, resulting in the *Lower Bound* field in the *Segment Setup* area being disabled. This means the segments represent percentages of the gauge total and will automatically be calculated. If you uncheck it, the *Lower Bound* field will be enabled and you can write an expression or enter a value to control where the segment begins on the gauge. The way in which segments are drawn on the gauge is based on the lower bound setting. It determines where the segment color begins. It ends at the maximum value for the gauge. For example, if the lower bound of a segment is zero, the entire background of the gauge shows that segment's color unless a higher level segment has a higher value for its lower bound. Note that you can change the segment order by promoting or demoting segments.

The chart displayed in Figure 7-19 shows a gauge using set analysis to control the maximum value and has segments that highlight value ranges. It also has a variety of properties configured to make it presentable.

FIGURE 19 – A QLIKVIEW GAUGE

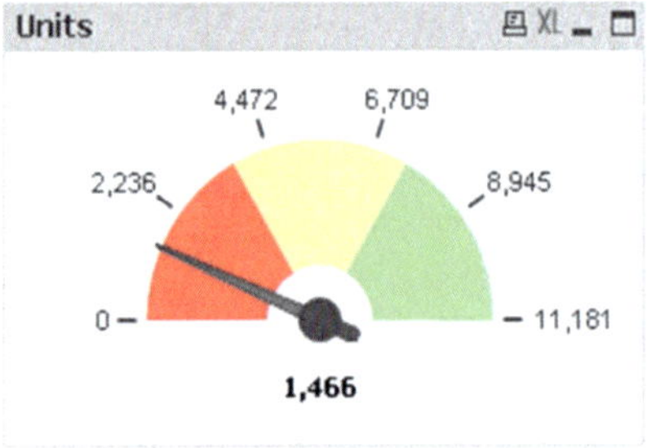

The gauge above has a number of properties modified to make it appear more presentable. The default settings for QlikView gauges may not be best for your document. Consider what's been done here:

- Three segments have been set with the lowest showing red, middle showing yellow and highest showing green. The segment bounds are automatically set (*Presentation>Autowidth Segments).*
- A scale is shown (*Presentation>Show Scale*) with six major units. It is also set up to show labels for each major unit (*Presentation>Show Scale>Show Labels on Every X Major Unit*).
- The numeric format has been set to show thousands separators and no decimal places (*Number>Fixed*). Decimals have been set to zero.
- The thickness of the gauge area is wider (*Presentation>Circular Gauge Settings>Cylinder Thickness*). It is set to 70%.
- The angle of the gauge area has been changed to take up less space (*Presentation>Circular Gauge Settings>Angle Span*). It has been set to 180 degrees.
- Text has been added to show the indicator value (*Presentation>Text in Chart*). An expression matching the main chart expression was added, but a formatting function was used to make the value format the same as other chart values:

```
=Num(SUM(quantity), '###,###.')
```

- The font for this text was also set to bold and it was centered. By using the *Ctrl+Shift* keys this text was relocated from the default location in the upper-left of the chart to the center of the bottom.

Gauges can add an effective way to present single values graphically. The example in this section is designed to introduce a reasonably complete use of a QlikView gauge. Hopefully, you now understand how and when to use gauges and feel comfortable exploring other gauge styles and properties.

Chart Tips and Tricks

The default settings for QlikView charts are often not ideal. There's no way that QlikView can anticipate the needs and preferences of everyone, so a default set of property values for each chart is provided. Changing properties for charts is easy and something you can explore. Experimentation with property values is often the best way to determine which settings are best for your document. For this reason QlikView includes an *Apply* button on the *Properties* dialog. This allows you to change properties and see the resulting effect without closing the dialog. However, there are some things that basic property value manipulation cannot do. Among such needs are three that we have found stand out with some of our customers. First, sometimes data brought into QlikView is improperly populated to show zero values. Second, large numbers often create problems with presentation on charts. And third, sometimes you need to manually adjust the way in which a chart is laid out.

Forcing Zero Values

QlikView charts use field values as dimension items to illustrate data graphically. That means in order for a graphical representation of a value to occur there must be an actual value. In other words, if the underlying data has NULL values, then the chart cannot represent the corresponding dimension items. The result is that such items are not included in the chart. This can be a problem if you want to include dimension items that have zero values. For example, you may want to show sales performance for all regions, but some regions may not have sold anything. Therefore their sales values may be zero or NULL. If the data has zero as a value QlikView can show the dimension item (region) in the chart. There is a property that allows this to happen (Presentation>Suppress Zero-Values). By unchecking this property zero values are honored. However, if the data includes NULLs rather than zeros for some of the dimension items, there is no way for QlikView to include these items in the chart. You can address this by changing the chart expression. You can add a fractional amount to the numeric value of the chart (i.e. .00001) and then set the decimal places to less than the value. The calculation will return a true zero, rather than a NULL value. This is a value that can be included in the chart. You will also have to uncheck the *Suppress Zero-Values* property (*Presentation> Suppress Zero-Values*) so the chart can include zero values.

Displaying Large Numbers (Using Numeric Symbols)

When presenting data visually, screen real estate is always a concern. It is difficult to show all of the information in the available space on the screen. This is especially true with mobile applications of QlikView. This problem is compounded by very large numbers. For example, when numeric values are in the millions or billions, showing them in a chart becomes a problem. This is because the horizontal space needed to display the entire number is considerable and competes with the visual aspects of the chart. There are several ways to address this in QlikView. You could use expression syntax to summarize the numbers. However, QlikView includes some properties that performs this automatically for you.

To reduce the space taken by large numbers, you can format the number to use a thousand's indicator. You do not need to write an expression to convert the values into thousands. By adding the indicator to the number formatting (Number>Thousands Symbol), QlikView will automatically convert the value in the increments of one thousand and the symbol you enter will appear on the appropriate axis of the chart. If you don't want the symbol to appear, place a space in the field. Other fields for millions and billions are also provided.

Customizing Layout Manually (Ctrl+Shift)

QlikView automatically organizes charts. It places legends, chart areas, axes and text in default locations and sizes these items appropriately. However, in some cases the way in which QlikView organizes the presentation of these chart items isn't desirable. For example, you may want to adjust the size or position of the legend. Or, you may want resize the chart area to accommodate larger axis values. QlikView for Windows include a little known feature that allows you to manually resize and move some chart items. It varies in functionality from one type of chart to the next. But, it is a helpful utility. To use it you must first select the chart and then hold the *Ctrl* and *Shift* keys down (*Ctrl+Shift*). The items within the chart that can be adjusted will appear with a red outline. You can then move the mouse pointer over the edge (red line) to resize the item or hover over the center of the item to move it.

Chart Changing

Most charts are created based on a given chart type such as a pie, bar or line. However, in most cases QlikView can be configured to allow the user to change the chart type without modifying the properties of the chart. This feature is known as *Fast Change*. *Fast Change* is enabled in the chart properties (*General>Fast Type Change*) by selecting two or more *Allowed Types*. You can also control where the *Fast Change* icon, which allows the user to cycle through the chart types, appears (*General>Fast Type Change>Preferred Icon Position*). Once two or more chart types are selected the Fast Change icon will appear. As the user clicks on it, the chart type will change. It is worth noting that if the chart started out as a particular type such as *bar* and that type is not selected, it won't be available and will not be able to return to the original chart type.

Data Tables & Detail Level Data

QlikView offers great visualization options through its robust and graphically rich set of charts. Showing data graphically is a key feature, but it is not the only way in which users want to see and interact with data. Among the many advantages QlikView offers over other BI tools is its ability to load and make available vast amounts of data. The in-memory compression capabilities in QlikView are legendary and allow billions of rows across hundreds of columns of data to be made instantly available to users. This means that your QlikView document can provide both summarized and detail level data to users. The most common, and effective, way to provide detail level data is through tables. Tabular data is the most common paradigm for how users interact with larger volumes of data. Excel and other spreadsheet tools drove the PC revolution because they provided an interface that allowed user to sort, subtotal and browse thousands of rows of data. This same functionality exists within QlikView though the user of several sheet objects that present data in a tabular format. The two most powerful and common of these are the *Straight Table* and *Pivot Table.*

Tables in QlikView are technically considered types of charts even though they don't present data graphically. To add either a *Straight Table* or *Pivot Table* to your QlikView document you begin by adding a chart sheet object (right click and select *New Sheet Objects>Chart.*

Using Straight Tables

Straight Tables in QlikView are simple two dimensional tables that resemble a worksheet in an Excel workbook. A Straight Table presents columns of data that are based either on a field (dimension) or on an expression. You cannot create a Straight Table without including an expression. This is largely because a Straight Table is a chart type and all chart types must have an expression. The expression doesn't have to perform an aggregation or calculation, but it must exist. However, an expression in a table may be very important as it can show calculated values similar to a formula in Excel. If all you need is to list fields of data, and you have no desire to calculate one or more columns, a Table Box object (New Sheet Object>Table Box) may be preferable. Table boxes provide lists of field data with column headers and sort capabilities, but cannot perform calculations.

To create a *Straight Table,* begin by adding a chart to a tab sheet as you would with any other chart type. On the General tab of the chart wizard select the *Straight Table* icon under *Chart Type* as shown in Figure 7-20.

FIGURE 7-20 CREATING A STRAIGHT TABLE

As with other chart types, your first task is to select one or more dimensions to use in the table. Unlike some chart types, you will likely select more than one field as a dimension because you will likely want your table to have more than one column. It is also a good idea to enter a label name for each dimension if your field names are cryptic. The label name will be used as the column header in the table. Note that it is always best to alias the column names in the load script, but if this has not been performed, providing a label is a suitable remedy. Do not select fields that would represent numeric values for rows in your table. That should be done as an expression because if you select them as a dimension, there will be no way to create totals. Also, remember you must have at least one expression in the table or no data will be presented. For example, if there is a quantity field in the data set you should not select it as a dimension for the combination of columns (for each row). This could result in other dimension values being shown over and over again for different quantity amounts. If you display quantity as a dimension and region as the only other dimension, the region will be repeated for each unique quantity value for each region. The better approach is to add the quantity field as an expression with an appropriate aggregate command such as *SUM*. This will still show the proper amount on each row, but will also sum all the rows and show the total for the whole table. Figure 7-21 shows a simple Straight Table with an expression that sums the quantity field.

FIGURE 7-21 STRAIGHT TABLE

Item Quantities by Year-Month-Region

Year	Month	region	Items
			11181
2001-Apr-Jun 20...	2001-Apr	AK	176
2001-Apr-Jun 20...	2001-Apr	CA	98
2001-Apr-Jun 20...	2001-Apr	MA	37
2001-Apr-Jun 20...	2001-Apr	WV	22
2001-Apr-Jun 20...	2001-Jun	AR	32
2001-Apr-Jun 20...	2001-Jun	IL	86
2001-Apr-Jun 20...	2001-Jun	TX	82
2001-Apr-Jun 20...	2001-May	AL	33
2001-Apr-Jun 20...	2001-May	FL	166

In the straight table above, notice that the default sort order is shown in the first column header. Also, notice the scroll bar on the right. All of the data is available in this table. If there are ten million rows of year-month-region combinations, all of them are in this table. The user can sort (by clicking on column header) and scroll (by using the scroll bar on the right) the data. Clicking twice on a column header reverses the sort order by that column. Interaction with the data is fast even though there may be a lot of data. This is because all of the data is loaded into memory. In a QlikView server environment, this table works using the server's memory. The Web user is provided with chunks of the data (segments) from the server based on user actions. If the user scrolls every few hundred records will be passed to the user's browser as the scrolling occurs. The user may also change the column order by dragging the column header from side to side as shown in Figure 7-22. The final location is shown by a blue line and arrow which moves as you drag.

FIGURE 7-22 CHANGING TABLE COLUMN ORDER

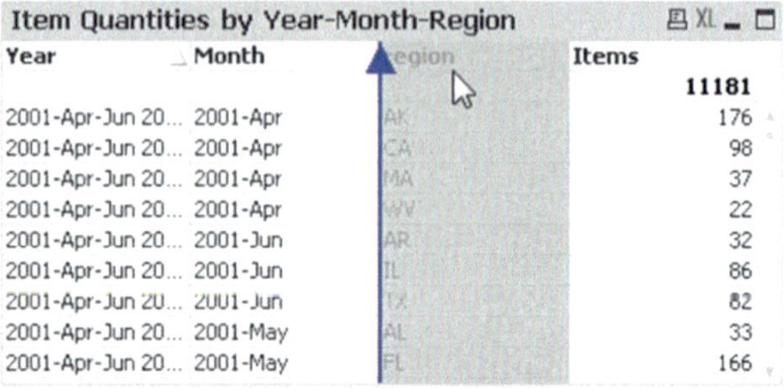
Item Quantities by Year-Month-Region

Year	Month	Region	Items
			11181
2001-Apr-Jun 20...	2001-Apr	AK	176
2001-Apr-Jun 20...	2001-Apr	CA	98
2001-Apr-Jun 20...	2001-Apr	MA	37
2001-Apr-Jun 20...	2001-Apr	WV	22
2001-Apr-Jun 20...	2001-Jun	AR	32
2001-Apr-Jun 20...	2001-Jun	IL	86
2001-Apr-Jun 20...	2001-Jun	TX	82
2001-Apr-Jun 20...	2001-May	AL	33
2001-Apr-Jun 20...	2001-May	FL	166

You can also rearrange the columns in a straight table by demoting and promoting the dimensions used in the chart properties (*Dimensions>Used Dimensions*). There are a variety of properties that affect how straight tables look and behave. Among the more common for your consideration are the following:

- User Sorting: You can disable the end user's ability to sort the table (*Sort>Allow Interactive Sort*).
- Show and Control Totals: You can determine if the table includes totals for the expressions. (*Expressions>Total Mode*). Totals appear at the top by default. You can force them to appear at the bottom as well (*Presentation>Totals>Totals on Last Row*). And, you can create a label (column header) for the totals column (*Expressions>Totals>Use Label*).
- Column Alignment: You can control the column alignment as well as alignment of column headers (*Presentation> Alignment*).
- Drop Downs: You can make column headers function as a drop down selection list (*Presentation>Dropdown Select*).

Dynamic Column Rendering

It is possible, using a straight table, to dynamically affect the labels and data in a column. This is somewhat obvious since columns are based on expressions, but creative use of this capability is often overlooked. A common example of dynamic column rendering is best illustrated in a previous period comparison scenario. For example, you may want to compare an aggregated value from this year to the value from last year. An enhanced version of this scenario would allow the user to select a year from a list box and show that year and previous year based on the users selection. Critical to this scenario is the need to show the selected and previous years in the column headers.

FIGURE 7-23 STRAIGHT TABLE DYNAMIC COLUMNS

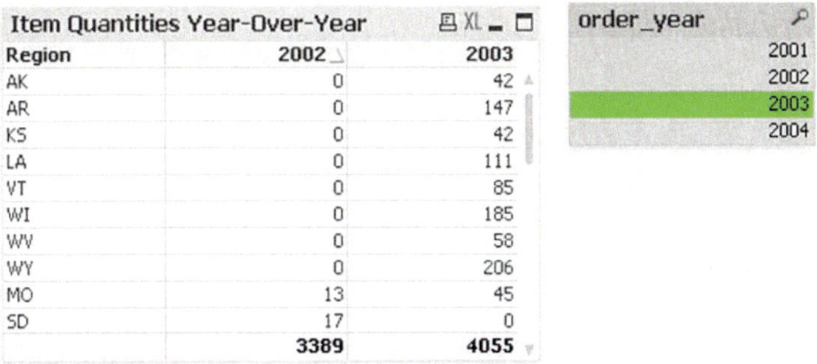

Item Quantities Year-Over-Year

Region	2002	2003
AK	0	42
AR	0	147
KS	0	42
LA	0	111
VT	0	85
WI	0	185
WV	0	58
WY	0	206
MO	13	45
SD	17	0
	3389	**4055**

order_year
2001
2002
2003
2004

In the Straight Table above, the last two columns are expressions that sum the quantity field. The first column performs this operation based on the user selected *order_year* (shown in the list box to the right) minus one year. It shows the previous year calculation. As the user selects different years the expression renders a different result based on the user's selection minus one year. The expression uses a set analysis modifier and dollar sign expansion to force the *SUM* function to operate on a specified year value.

```
=SUM({$<order_year={$(=order_year-1)}>}quantity)
```

The last column uses an expression that is almost the same, but does not subtract one from the selected *order_year* value. This column represents the "selected year." Each of these has an expression rendering the column label as well. These expressions force each column label to render the corresponding year value. Here is the syntax for the first expression label:

```
=order_year-1
```

Other settings used in the table in Figure 7-23 have been adjusted to make the table more presentable. Consider the following for how to further customize straight tables in QlikView:

- Column Headings for expressions are right aligned (*Presentation>Alignment>Label*). Do this for each of the expressions by selecting them in the *Columns* grouping on the left.
- Totals have been moved to the bottom of the table (*Presentation>Totals>Totals on Last Row*).
- Columns have been resized. It is worth noting that the last column is difficult to resize because as you drag the mouse pointer over the right side of it, it is easy to miss. The result is often that you are resizing the table and not the last column. The mouse pointer will change when you hover over the right side of a column. With the last column the right side is very close the right side of the table, but you can resize the column without resizing the table.

Drilling and Cycle Groups

Straight tables also support the use of groups. Groups are collections of fields that can be used as dimension values in the table. When a group of fields is created, it is used within a straight table to provide two different features. A group is created that represents a hierarchy and then used to provide the user with a drill-down experience. For example, the user might click on a year in the table and the values would recalculate to show the months within that year. Another option is to cycle through the fields making the table calculate for different fields. This “cycle group” approach allows one table to provide several views of the data where the same expressions (calculations) apply to different fields. It can be helpful in saving screen real estate.

To create a group, you begin by adding a dimension to a straight table. However, rather than selecting a field, you click on the Edit Groups... button at the bottom of the tab (*Dimensions>Edit Groups...*). This produces a dialog from which you may select one or more fields for the group. The dialog requires a name for the group and allows you to determine if the group is a *Drill-down Group* or *Cyclic Group* (radio buttons at the top). After naming the group and adding fields and then closing the dialog, the group appears in the field list and becomes available for selection as a dimension in a table.

FIGURE 2-14 STRAIGHT TABLE USING A DRILL-DOWN GROUP

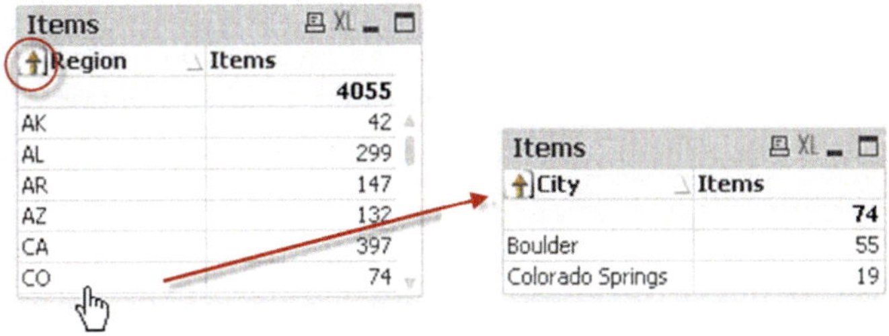

In the table above, the user can click on a *region* value (i.e. CO in this case) and the table will repopulate with a list of cities for the selected region. The item counts update to show the values for each city in the selected region. The up-arrow icon shows that a drill-down group is used as the dimension in the table. Once a drill-down has been performed by the user, the icon can be clicked on to drill back up to the original state. The drill-down group can include a large number of fields that represents levels in the drill path. It is important to note that when the user drills down on the table, a selection is made affecting other tab sheet objects. If the group was a cyclic group rather than a drill down group, then the icon would cycle through the fields rather than drilling down. With a cyclic group the user may click on the icon (which looks like a curved arrow) to see a list of fields. By selecting one of the fields the table repopulates. Cyclic groups do not provide drill-down capabilities, so if the user clicks on a region in the table a selection in the field is made, but no drilling to the next field occurs.

IMPORTANT: Cyclic groups may be used in other objects such as list boxes. They are not limited in use to charts or tables.

Using Pivot Tables

QlikView *Pivot Tables* have a great deal of functionality and a large number of properties associated with them. We cannot cover all of the features of pivot tables here, but we hope that we provide enough information to get you started so that you may explore them in more detail on your own.

Pivot Tables add functionality to what a *Straight Table* does to present data. Pivot tables have rows and columns similar to straight tables, but they allow for two fundamental enhancements. First, pivot tables may have row and column values stacked on top of each other to illustrate hierarchies. For example, if the first column is based on the region, and there are other dimensions added after region, such as city and year, the other dimensions are stacked under region. The QlikView pivot table reflects this hierarchy by creating a tree type presentation of the dimension values. Each higher level value has a plus-sign icon allowing the user to expand the dimension, which exposes the next level's values. Any expressions added to the pivot table appear as columns to the right and calculate relative to each level in the hierarchy. Figure 7-25 shows this basic functionality.

FIGURE 7-25 PIVOT TABLE BASIC HIERARCHY

Regional Pivot Table Analysis

region	city	order_year	Items
AK	Anchorage	2003	15
	Des Plaines		284
AL			631
AR			179
AZ	Phoenix	2001	59
	Prince Williams	2002	102
	Tucson	2002	98
		2003	132
CA			953
CO			282

In the pivot table above, three dimension fields are selected in a specified order (*region*, then *city*, then *order_year*). This automatically creates a hierarchy in a pivot table. The result is what's shown in Figure 7-25. Users may click on the plus-sign icons to expand the hierarchy. The expression (in this case just one expression is included, but more could be) is created as a column to the right of the last dimension column. Most of the same features and settings associated with *Straight Tables* also apply to pivot tables. There are also additional features that are specific to pivot tables. For example, you can show sub-totals for each dimension level (*Presentation>Show Partial Sums*). To do this you must enable this property for the desired dimensions by selecting each dimension and then clicking the checkbox. The result is that totals will show for each level selected. It is worth noting that selecting this property for the highest level (first) dimension won't do anything because the expression values are already summarized at that level.

The second fundamental feature of QlikView pivot tables is the ability for users to "pivot", or swap, the dimensions between the row and column orientations. By default all dimension values appear as part of a hierarchy based on the first column in the pivot table. That means the dimension values appear along the left side of the table vertically. While the user may expand or collapse the hierarchy, the only values shown to the right of the dimensions are those from the expressions. To change this you can drag a dimension to the right and up to force its values to appear across the top of the table. The user may do the same provided you don't disable pivoting. However, it is important that you modify the pivoting to properly address the preferred initial state of the pivot table while you are designing the document. Figure 7-26 shows how blue arrows illustrate to where the dimension will be moved when you finish dragging.

FIGURE 7-26 PIVOT TABLE PIVOTING

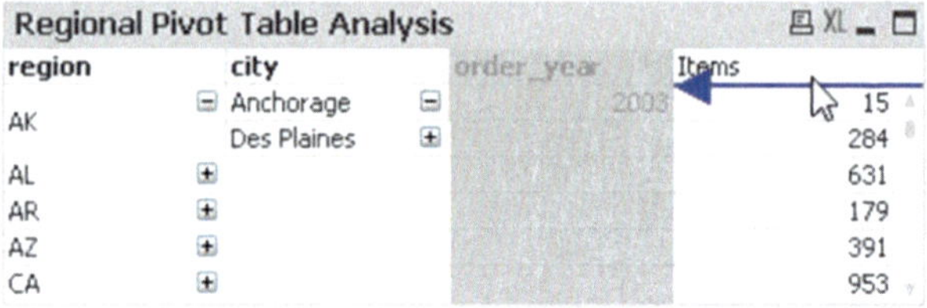

In the pivot table above the user drags the *order_year* column to the right and places it at the top (under the expression named items). This forces the *order_year* values to appear across the top and to the right of the other dimensions. The result is a presentation of item values at the intersection of *order_year* and the other dimensions shown in Figure 7-27.

FIGURE 7-27 PIVOT TABLE PIVOTED

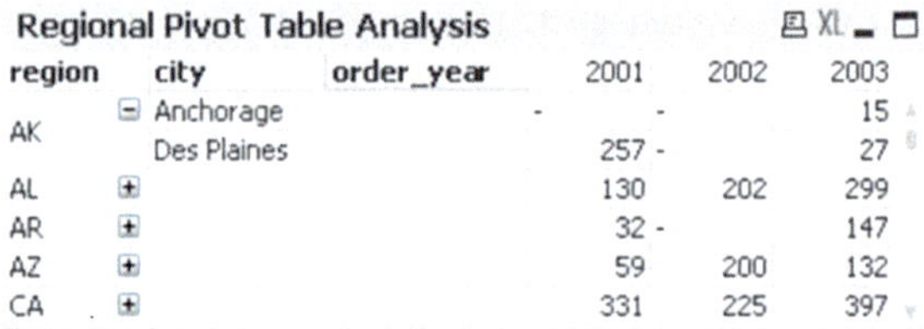

Creating Search Capabilities

Conventional reporting and BI software tools have traditionally provided limited data searching functionality. In most cases these tools allowed you to search within a predefined context, but failed to provide the robust searching features that are now popular on the Web. QlikView offers exceptional searching because it is engineered to make all of the data available in-memory. This opens the door to allow users to search data without being required to take a trip back to disk to retrieve new data. The associative nature of QlikView also enhances its ability to provide advanced searching.

Understanding Associative Searching

Associative data lends itself to the demands found in search features. This is perhaps one of QlikView's strongest features and one that is underutilized in most QlikView applications. Because all field values in your QlikView document are cross-associated automatically, searching all data is automatically available. For example, because region values are already associated with city values, it is possible to search both at once. A user could begin by searching the region field, and then expand the search to include other fields without having to perform multiple searches. As you will see, this capability is powerful yet simple. Additionally, because everything is already associated it is possible to use the results of a search to make selections. This makes the search experience a logical first step to selecting data and seeing results. The continuity of this experience is something not found in most other tools, and it resonates with users who become excited when they see it or use it for the first time.

Searching from List Boxes

Search capabilities are built into every list box in your QlikView document. There's nothing you have to do to enable searching, but there are a number of things you can do to enhance it and make more obvious to your users. To begin, you should understand that to perform a search in a list box all you or the user must do is click on the caption (header) and begin typing. This results in a text box popping up above the caption. It collects your text and immediately performs the search as you type. The search results are shown by filtering the values in the text box and highlighting the matches. The default search method performs a "contains" search. A contains search is considered to be a "normal" search in QlikView. The results are organized to show the items that begin with your search criteria at the top, followed by other matches. Figure 7-28 shows this process in action.

FIGURE 7-28 LIST BOX SEARCH

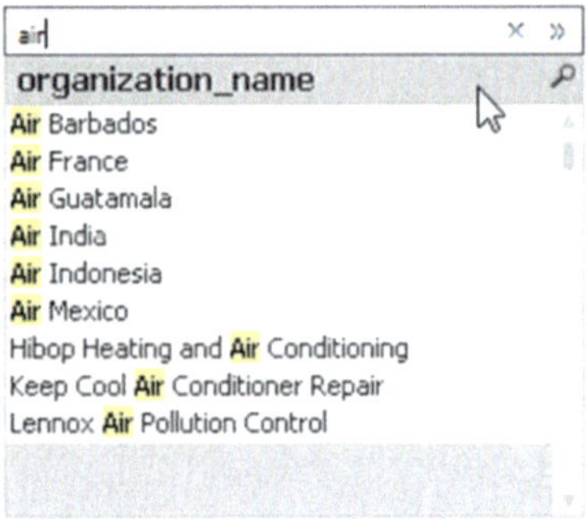

Notice in Figure 7-28 that a search icon appears in the caption area denoted by a magnifying glass icon. This is included by default when a list box is created. It can be disabled (*Caption>Special Icons>Search*), but searching will still work even if the icon is not displayed. Clicking on it shows the text box for entering search criteria. It is helpful to let the user know that searching is available. The results of the search can be used as selection criteria by pressing the Enter key. This action highlights all items in the results listing and makes them selected. It immediately affects the rest of the document as though you selected them manually. You may also select any of the items individually. This functionality is automatically exposed to the user as well.

The default search scope for list boxes is based on the field used in the list box. However, you can configure the search properties of the list box to use a different field or a set of fields (*General>Search>More Search Settings*). Additionally, users may expand the search to include other fields. If you haven't limited the search to specific fields, expanding the search includes all fields in the document's data model. This is done by clicking on the double-arrow icon (chevron) on the right of the search criteria text box. The result, shown in Figure 7-29, is a list of fields and matches that spans the entire data model.

FIGURE 7-29 EXPANDED SEARCH

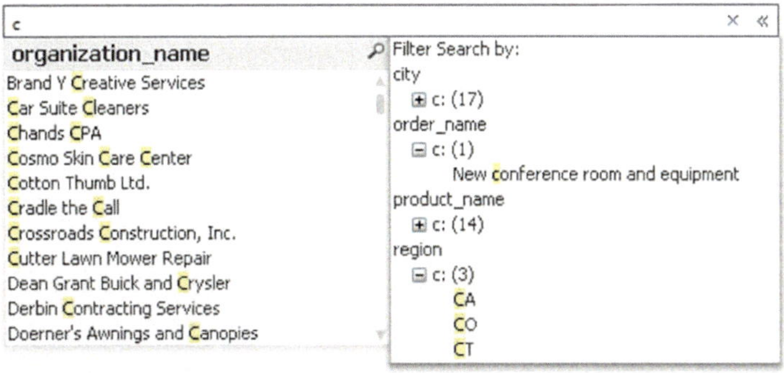

Types of Searches

There are several types of searches that can be performed in QlikView. The default is known as a "normal" search, which is based on the values in the data model containing a match to the search criteria typed in by the user. Other types offer different capabilities. The following is a list that explains each search type. This can be used by including qualifier characters in the search criteria or as the default search for list boxes (*General>Search>Default Search Mode*).

- Normal Search: The default search is a normal search which performs a "contains" search on the data. This search requires no special characters in the search criteria, but defaults to using an asterisk (*) before and after the text that is typed.
- Wildcard Search: A wildcard search uses special characters to control what is matched. For example, the asterisk character can be placed at the beginning or end of the search criteria to perform a "begins with" or "ends with" search (i.e. *com returns matches that end with com).
- Fuzzy Search: A fuzzy search attempts to find similar values to the search criteria based on a soundex type

search. It is initiated by prefixing the search criteria with a tilde character. For example, the string ~san returns matches that sound similar such as "hand" or "bland." It is helpful with spelling problems and names.

- Associative Search: An associative search is based on one of the other searches but expands the search to show matches across all of the fields in the data model.

Searching Using an Expression

While searching a field or all fields from within a list box is easy to do and automatically available, more advanced searching is also built in to QlikView. Advanced searching allows you to create expression syntax that is used to match values. This is possible because the QlikView expression engine is always present and available. To use an expression for searching the user simply types in the expression syntax as search criteria. The expression must begin with an equal sign to indicate that the criteria entered are to be processed as an expression. The result is a list of matches for the expression. Figure 7-30 shows an expression being used to return a list of organizations that have ordered more than one-hundred ninety items in the year 2003.

FIGURE 7-30 ADVANCED SEARCH EXAMPLE

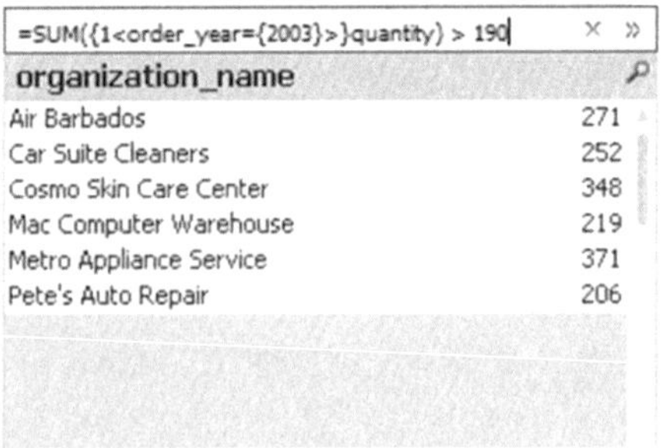

Notice in the example above that the expression begins with an equal sign and includes set analysis syntax to control which year is used to perform the evaluation. The result is a list of organizations (based on the list box field) that have ordered more than 190 units in the year 2003.

Creating a Search Object

Searching based on list boxes is a good feature and often adequate. However, in some cases you may wish to make the search capabilities of your QlikView document more obvious to users. You may also wish to control the searching at a more granular level. For this reason, QlikView includes a sheet object specifically for providing search functionality to users. Using the search object requires you to determine various aspects of how the search will function. To create a search object you simply add it to a tab sheet in the same manner as any other sheet object by right-clicking on the sheet and selecting *New Sheet Object>Search Object* which creates the object on the sheet.

The properties of a search object include selecting which fields you want it to search (*General>Selected Fields*) and if it should include excluded values (*Presentation>Search Results>Include Excluded*), which assumes other selections have been made in the document) in the results. The search object is a user friendly way of implementing searching. It is similar to search objects found on popular Web sites. Figure 7-31 shows a search object being used.

FIGURE 7-31 QLIKVIEW SEARCH OBJECT

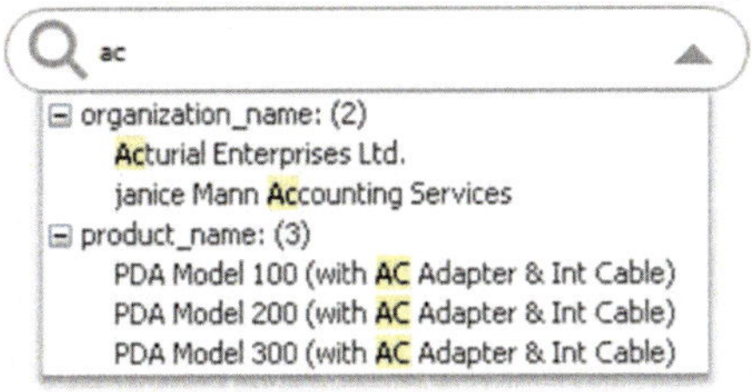

QlikView search objects do not include an option for associative search the way list boxes do. This is because the associative searching is controlled by the options you choose when you create the object. You select which fields the search object will use. In the example above, the *organization_name* and *product_name* fields have been configured in the search object's properties. This limits the search to those fields. You could select all fields making the search object fully associative, but in most cases that won't make sense. A few properties to consider when using search objects include the following:

- Including Excluded Values (*Presentation>Search Results>Include Excluded*): Searching can be performed with respect to other selections the user has made in list boxes, charts or other objects. However, the default behavior is to search all values (selected, possible and excluded). You can force the search object to ignore the excluded values using this property.
- Collapse Setting (*Presentation>Search Results>Collapse when results field exceeds*): This property allows you to control how many results to show for each of the search object fields before the object collapses the field and shows a plus-sign for manual expansion.
- Highlighting (*Presentation>Search Results>Highlight Search Substring*): This property allows you to disable the search highlighting. It is enabled by default.

Layout and Object Management

QlikView would not be complete without a variety of features that allow you to manage the way in which your document presents data and objects. Providing a clean, understandable layout and good use of screen real estate is very important. Many developers of QlikView and other BI content fail to fully understand the importance of managing the content layout. This often results in BI content that is not used or viewed as poorly designed. QlikView includes a variety of features to give you significant versatility in how you organize and present data and objects. These range from dividing things into different tab sheets to managing object visibility. QlikView also provides some mechanisms for making it easier to maintain the objects in your QlikView document.

Leveraging Tab Sheets

Tab sheets are a core component of a QlikView document. All documents must have at least one tab sheet. When you create a document the first tab sheet is automatically created and named "Main." You can add other tab sheets by using the Layout pull down menu in QlikView for Windows (*Layout>Add Sheet...).* This produces the tab sheet properties dialog from which you control many aspects of the tab sheet. After the tab sheet is created you access its properties by right-clicking on the sheet (not over an object on the sheet, but over a blank canvas area). You need to right-click below the tab row at the top and on the sheet itself. The first property to consider is the sheet Title property (*General>Title*). You enter a title as you would for any object, but note that you can also use an expression to determine the name. Another feature is the ability to set the sheet's background to a specified color or image (*General>Background*). If you use an image for the sheet's background, consider how this will affect the way the document looks as the user navigates from sheet to sheet. You may want to consider using the same image for all sheets. If you use a background image, there are several properties for selecting and importing the image and for adjusting it. The image is embedded in the QlikView document (.QWV) file.

Tab sheet properties also include the ability to control various security attributes of the sheet (*Security>User Privileges*). These work in conjunction with Section Access functionality (see the chapter covering *Sharing and Securing QlikView Documents*). There is also a tab in the dialog that lists all of the objects that reside on the sheet (*Objects*). This tab can be useful for finding and managing objects that may not be visible by default because it allows you to access object properties from within the *Sheet Properties* dialog. You can also control whether or not the sheet is visible (*General>Show Sheet*). This property can be set using an expression. When used in conjunction with a variable, the visibility of the sheet can be controlled by a button or event in the document giving you a great deal of control over how and when the sheet appears. When the *Show Sheet* property is set to Conditional, the value must contain something other than zero (0) for the sheet to appear. It can be set to any non-zero numeric value. When set to zero the sheet will disappear. If the sheet is hidden, you can access its properties from the *Document Properties* dialog, which is always available from the *Settings* pull down menu (*Settings>Document Properties>Sheets*). Note that the first sheet will always appear if all other sheets are hidden. If you show a different sheet and set the first sheet's visibility to zero, then only the sheet you want to show will appear, but there is always one sheet shown at a minimum. The following steps walk you through a simple example of how to use a button to show or hide a tab sheet. This example assumes you have a QlikView document with two tab sheets named "Main" and "Sheet1" respectively.

1. Create a variable for controlling tab visibility (*Settings>Variable Overview*). You create a variable by clicking *Add* and then give it a name and definition. Make the name of the variable "v_tab_to_show." Set the definition of the variable to zero (0). Click OK to save the variable.
2. Go the Main tab sheet and create a button object on it (right-click to add a sheet object). Set the name of the button object to "Show Sheet 1".
3. While in the properties of the button object add an action to set the variable (*Actions>Add>External>Set Variable*).
4. Make the variable name "v_tab_to_show" and set the value to 1.
5. Click on the Sheet1 tab and right-click on the sheet to bring up its properties.
6. Set the visibility to *Conditional* and use the variable (*General>Conditional*). Enter the variable name with an equal sign in front of it (=v_tab_to_show). The tab sheet will disappear when you click OK because the variable

value is set to zero. You should be returned to the *Main* tab sheet because it is the only one that is visible.

7. Now click on the button and Sheet1 should appear.

These instructions, while not exhaustive, provide a basic introduction for how to use variables and buttons to control tab sheet visibility.

IMPORTANT: Controlling visibility is not limited to tab sheets. Sheet objects may also be controlled in the same way.

Another consideration might be to hide the tab row at the top, which can be done using the Document Properties dialog from the Settings pull down menu (*Settings>Document Properties>General>Hide Tabrow*). In some cases, if you display the tab row, it may be desirable to change the font attributes used for the tabs at the top of sheets. This area is known as the *Tab Row*. It has its own set of properties that can be accessed by right-clicking on any of the tabs at the top.

Container Objects

Beginning with QlikView version 10 a new object known as a *Container Object* was added. The container object allows you to combine several other objects such as charts, list boxes and tables into one area on the screen. It provides a navigation mechanism for toggling between them by showing tabs along the top, bottom or side of the container. The result is that the user may click on the appropriate tab to switch the contents of the container object from one object another. In version 10 the container object supported one object per tab, but in version 11 a grid capability was added, allowing the container to either work in the same mode as before or as a single tab with a grid into which several objects can be displayed at one time. By nesting one version 11 container object in grid mode inside of another in tab mode you can create a variety of combinations.

To use a container object you add it to a tab sheet in your document the same way you add other objects, by right-clicking. When the properties dialog appears you select objects from the tab sheet and add them to the container object from within the properties dialog box. You can also save the object (close the properties dialog) and drag objects into the container object as shown in figure 7-32.

FIGURE 7-32 CONTAINER OBJECT – ADDING OBJECTS

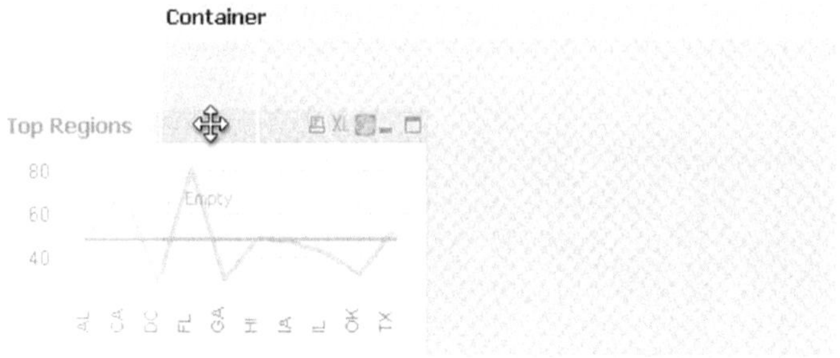

In Figure 7-32, a line chart is dragged over the “Empty” area of a container object. This adds the chart to the container and the chart’s title will appear in a tab on the left. The chart appears on the right and is sized to fit into the full space. Other objects can be dragged into the tab area and the same will occur for them. In this case, the container object is set to its default type which is a Single Object Container (*Presentation>Container Type*). This allows one object to be shown for each tab. Figure 7-33 shows the completed container with two objects, one chart and one table added.

FIGURE 7-33 CONTAINER WITH TWO OBJECTS

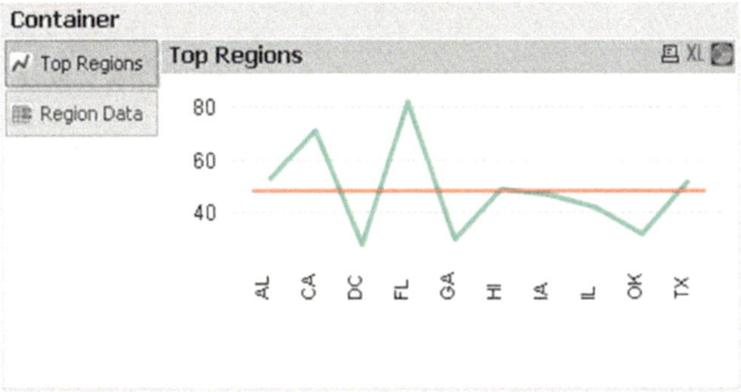

With the container control in version 11 you can change the control's type to *Grid* (*Presentation>Container Type*). This allows you to determine how many rows and columns appear in the control. In this mode the tabs are eliminated and all objects appear at once in their respective grid cells. Figure 7-34 shows a container control with two columns and one row where two objects have been added.

FIGURE 7-34 CONTAINER WITH GRID

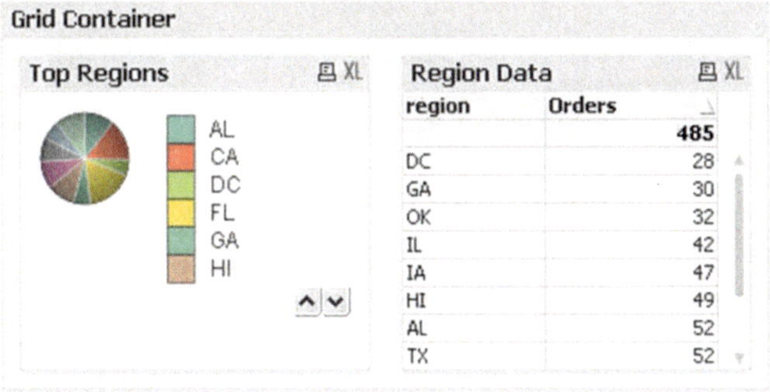

When we first began working with version 11 it appeared that the grid mode for the container control had little value since it is easy to size and position objects next to each other without it. However, with a little experimentation we quickly discovered that you can embed one container control inside of another. That means the main container control can be in single object mode allowing tabs for each object. The embedded container control can be in grid mode showing two objects side by side as one of the object tabs in the main container. This makes the container control very versatile.

Object Linking

QlikView offers a great deal of functionality and versatility, but it comes with a price. You quickly find yourself spending time managing property settings across a large number of objects and tab sheets. During the initial development of your QlikView document this is not a major concern because you must address certain properties to create objects. However, after you have created the first version of your document it can be tedious to make changes. This is especially true if you need to make the same change to many objects. The effort to do this requires a great deal of repetition. To make matters worse, if you skip one or more objects, the document may appear or function poorly. For this reason beginning with version 10, QlikView includes a feature that allows sheet objects to be linked to each other. Linking two objects in QlikView is simple, but they both must be the same type of object. For example, you cannot link a list box and a chart. If you do you may notice strange results when modifying common properties, but in our experience it appears that this feature is intended for use in linking multiple objects of the same type only. To link two objects in your QlikView document you only need to make sure they have the same object ID (*General>Object ID*). This can be done manually after copying an object.

NOTE: You can use *Ctrl+C* and *Ctrl+V* to copy and paste objects in QlikView, but this will not link the new (copied) object to the original object. You will still have to set the object ID to match that of the original object.

You can also use a right-click or the Object pull down menu to copy and paste objects. These menus offer a *Paste as Link* option which creates the pasted object as a linked object (sets the Object ID to that of the original object automatically). If several objects are linked, all of the properties except for size, position and display state (minimized, normal, and maximized) are linked. Changing a property on one object causes the corresponding property on other linked objects change. You can have linked objects on the same sheet or on different sheets. If you want all objects that are linked to your current object to share size and position, you can right click on the object and select Linked *Objects>Adjust Position of Linked Objects*. This forces the linked objects to synchronize. This option may also help if the linking isn't working properly.

Comparative Analysis (Alternate States)

In many cases it is necessary to compare data based on differing criteria. Perhaps the most common example of this is a year-over-year comparison where users wish to see how the current year compares to the previous year. This type of functionality is easily accomplished using set analysis syntax as shown in the data-tables examples earlier in this chapter. However, a more powerful comparison involves allowing users to make different selections on the same dimension. For example, a user may wish to see order volumes for different groups of regions and have two different charts illustrating values of each of the groups. One way to accomplish this might be to engineer your QlikView document's load script to organize data into the appropriate groupings, but this would not allow the user to randomly decide how regions are grouped. Beginning with QlikView version 11 a new feature known as *Alternate States* is available. This feature allows you to create and name states that can operate independently of each other. You may then associate sheet objects with one of the states allowing different objects to affect and be affected by different states. Essentially, alternate states functionality allows you to segment the list boxes, charts and other controls in your document so that they don't all tie to one set of user selections.

Creating states in your document is done using the *Document Properties*. This is a simple task that only requires you to add a state and give it a name. There are two states that always exist in a QlikView document. They are:

- Default State: This is represented in expression syntax by a dollar sign ($). It refers to the main condition of the document. All document objects are in the default state when they are created and therefore they all interrelate.
- Inherited State: Because a state may be applied to virtually any type of object, it is possible to apply a state to an entire tab sheet or to a container control. If the objects within such containers have their state set to “inherited”, then they inherit the state of the parent object. This makes it easy to create entire tab sheets or areas that are controlled by a predefined state.

Alternate state properties do not appear in the properties dialog for sheets or sheet objects until you define one or more states at the document level. If you are looking for where to assign a given object, such as a list box, to a state, you first must create the state in the Document Properties. To do this open the Document Properties dialog from the pull down menu (*Settings>Document Properties*) and look for the *Alternate States* button on the *General* tab. This launches a simple dialog that allows you to add or remove states. A state is nothing more than a name. Once you have created one or more states, tab sheets and sheet objects display a new property in the properties dialog. It is located on the *General* tab and called *Alternate State*. This property allows you to select a state from the list. The list includes default and inherited states. When you assign two or more objects to the same state they work together, but ignore selections from objects in the main document or other states made by the user. Figure 7-35 shows two sets of objects that are associated with two separate states.

FIGURE 7-35 ALTERNATE STATES EXAMPLE

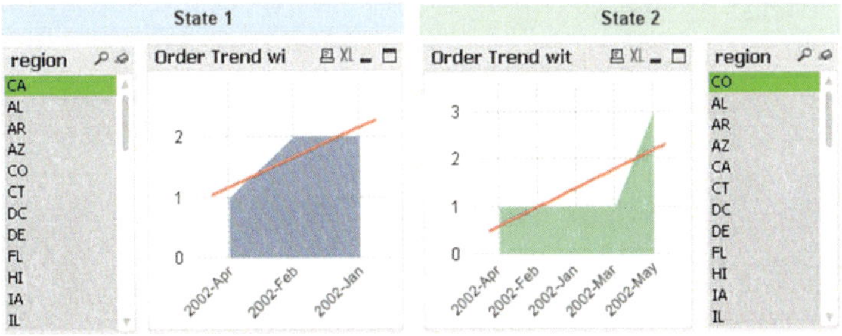

In the example above, notice that the list box and chart on the left are associated with State 1 and the objects on the right are associated with State 2. Each list box has a different region selected and each chart shows a different order trend.

When alternate states are used there are some important considerations that affect the user experience. The most important consideration is that there is nothing built into QlikView to notify the user that a set of objects is assigned to a given state. This can be disconcerting and may result in confusion. Therefore, it is important that you include information using text boxes or other objects in your document to make it clear how the objects will behave. Other considerations include the following:

- The Clear button at the top of the viewer clears all states by default, but there is a drop down menu built into the button that allows the user to clear selections for a given state.
- Other selection features such as previous/next and locking will affect all states.

You can also affect states using buttons and actions. There are two button actions designed to work with states: Swap State Contents and Copy State Contents. Both of these actions allow a button to manipulate one state's selections by using another state's selection. You access these actions by creating a button object (*Add Sheet Objects>Button...*) and then adding an action in the properties dialog (*Actions>Add*). At the bottom of the actions list you will see these two actions as shown in Figure 7-36.

FIGURE 7-36 CONTROLLING STATES WITH ACTIONS

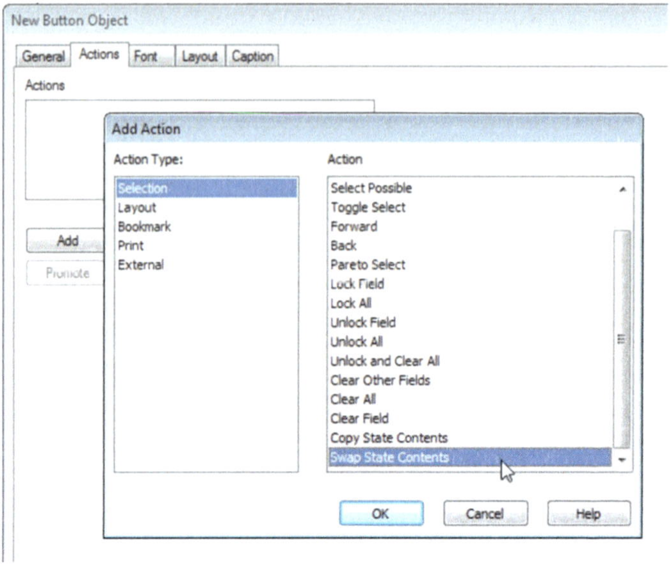

Once you have added one of these actions, two text boxes appear to the right of the Actions list. Type in the name of the states you wish to use in these text boxes. In the case of swapping, it doesn't matter what order you use; the action swaps the selections from one state to the other. In the case of copying, you must enter the state from which you want to copy as the source (first) state.

States may also be used in set analysis expressions. For example, you may want a column in a table to show the results from a desired state. The state name may be used as a set analysis identifier. The following example shows a set analysis expression that counts the orders placed based on the selections associated with State 1.

```
COUNT({[State 1]} order_name)
```

The Alternate States feature is relatively easy to use, but powerful. It may significantly enhance the users' experience. Keep in mind that it is not available in versions of QlikView preceding version 11.

Working with Data from Users

While QlikView documents are fundamentally based on providing users with the opportunity to interact with data, most user activity is oriented toward selecting values. In some cases however, it may be necessary for users to enter their own values or select a range of values that are not part of the data in the document. For this reason, QlikView includes a set of user input objects that allow you to collect and use data created by the user. While the intent of these objects is to allow user input to affect expressions and ultimately data visualizations, in some cases these values can be sent to other systems or databases. However, we do not recommend using QlikView as a data input system. Doing this may not work when you deploy your document to a QlikView server environment and it opens the door to creating problems with data integrity.

The most common example of user input is through the use of an *Input Box*. *Input Box* objects appear as text boxes that users may enter text into. The user text may then be assigned to a QlikView variable (see the chapter covering expressions). QlikView variable values can be used in any QlikView expression, so that means that the user's input may affect how charts display data. The example in Figure 7-37 shows a chart that compares the cost and price of two products. It also includes a symbol (a square) indicating the sales goal for each product. Above the chart are two input controls shown with yellow backgrounds. One is an input box that allows users to type values directly; the other is a slider control that allows users to determine a value by dragging the slider token. Both of these controls are tied to a variable representing a numeric value for a markup percentage. You add these controls to a tab sheet in your document using the right-click menu (*New Sheet Object...*) in the same way you add list boxes, charts and other objects. The variable that these controls update is used to calculate the price value in the chart.

FIGURE 7-37 USER INPUT CONTROLS

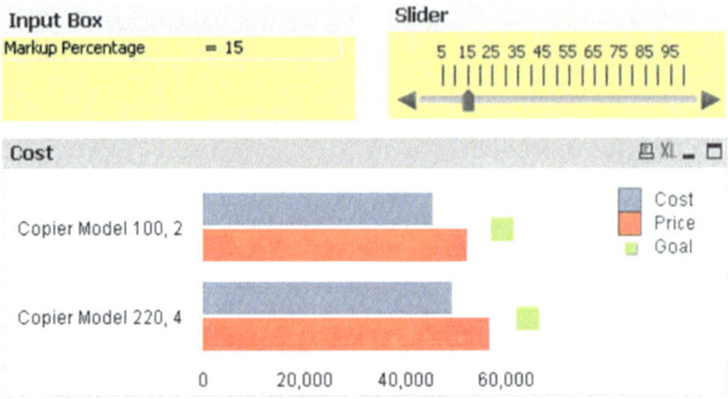

In the example above, a variable named "Markup Percentage" is used to collect the user data and make it available for use in expressions. As the user changes the value in one object, the value in the other is updated immediately and the chart values change. Each of the controls has properties for selecting a variable:

- Input Box: There is a feature that allows you to select one or more variables on the *General* tab (*General>Available Variables* and *General>Displayed Variables*). You can also create new variables from the properties dialog (*General>New Variable*).
- Slider Control: There is a dropdown box that allows selection of a variable on the *General* tab (*General>Data>Variables(s)).*

There are many properties in each of these objects that affect presentation and how data is stored in the associated variable. For example, the Input Box object properties dialog includes a *Constraints* tab from which you can constrain input values to ensure that they match certain conditions such as whole numbers (integers). You can also force users to select from a predefined list of options. Input Box objects may also have more than one variable assigned to them so that one sheet object may receive user input for multiple purposes. Slider objects also have a variety of options including the ability to support a range rather than a single value.

Hopefully, this introduction to input controls provides you with enough of an understanding to explore them further. There are a number of properties for these objects that are worthy of your time as they may address specific needs, or inspire ideas for how to enhance your document.

Other Topics

Actions

QlikView documents include a series of actions that may be invoked by users to cause certain things to happen. The most common way for one of these actions to be used is through a button object. When the user clicks the button, one or more actions occur based on which actions you associated with the button. There are also triggers that are invoked automatically when certain activities occur within the document. These triggers may invoke actions. Common actions include such things as activating a specific tab sheet, maximizing an object, setting a variable value, navigating the user's selection history, locking or unlocking selections, activating a bookmark, printing or executing an external command, etc... . Adding an action to a button or trigger event is done in the object properties. In the case of a button object, you will see an *Actions* tab in the properties dialog where you can add one or more actions (*Actions>Actions>Add*). You may also associate the action with an Alternate State if you have set up alternate states in the document properties.

Once an action has been added to a button object, additional property fields appear to the right of the action list if the selected action is designed to operate with parameter values. For example, actions associated with managing selections may require a specific field to be chosen as shown in Figure 7-38.

FIGURE 7-38 ACTION PROPERTIES

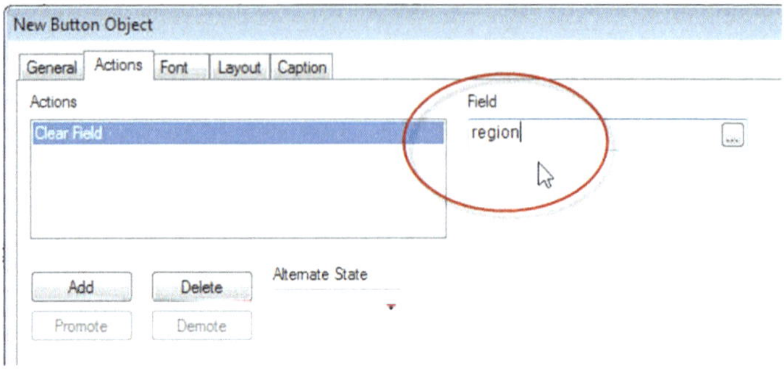

Actions are relatively straight forward in their use, however they can create problems. Some actions, for example, are not supported on a QlikView server. Of particular concern are some the *External* actions. For example, you can create an action that executes an operating system command or calls an external program. If you deploy your document to a QlikView server, the service account running the QlikView server services must have the appropriate rights and access to such external commands. In some cases the QlikView server may not allow certain actions to execute. Before making a decision to use QlikView to do such things, you should test the desired functionality on the server. Most common actions however, such as selection, setting variables etc., will work fine in a server deployment.

Triggers

Triggers represent events that are built into the QlikView document processing model. That means they occur automatically. Examples of triggers include such things as when the document is opened by a user, or when a tab sheet is selected. There are several types of triggers that occur in association with events that occur in different parts of the document.

- Document Event Triggers: These occur when general events pertaining to the document occur. Examples include when the user makes any selection, when the document is opened, when data is reloaded or when data is reduced by the user. These triggers are found in *Document Properties>Triggers>Document Event Triggers*.

- Field Event Triggers: These occur when an event occurs in association with a specific field in the document. Examples include the field being selected, locked, unlocked or when an associated field is selected causing the field to be deselected or excluded. These triggers are found in *Document Properties>Triggers>Field Event Triggers*.
- Variable Event Triggers: This occurs when a variable in the document is changed or receives input from an input object. These triggers are found in *Document Properties>Triggers>Variable Event Triggers*.

For each of these triggers you can add one or more actions by clicking on the appropriate *Add Action(s)* button. Examples of how triggers might be used include things such as clearing all selections and setting a default tab sheet when the document opens.

IMPORTANT: Triggers are sometimes not automatically activated in QlikView when you think they should be. For example, if you use a button action to force the changes of tab sheets then the sheet triggers do not activate. In such cases you may need to add several actions to the button and none to the sheet trigger.

Chapter 8: Reporting, Printing and Exporting

Analyzing and interacting with data is the primary reason for using QlikView. However, there will be times when your users need to share the results of their analysis. In these cases it may not be practical to distribute the QlikView document. For this reason QlikView includes several features that enable you to share data in both formatted and raw form. This is done through three separate features found within a QlikView document. The reporting feature allows you to create one or more formatted, single or multi page reports as part of your document. The data and charts in the reports are created from tables, charts and other objects found with the document.

Object Printing and Exporting

QlikView documents have built-in features that provide basic exporting and printing capabilities at the sheet object level. This means that users, if you as the developer allow it, can print or export data and format it from given sheet objects. This is done by enabling certain caption icons for the sheet object from its properties dialog (*Captions>Special Icons*). It is important to note that many of these icons/features are not available in the Web Client (the AJAX ZFC client), which means that if you intend to deploy your document to a QlikView server, and if your users are not using QlikView for Windows or the IE plugin client, then these features won't be available. Some of these same features are also available to the user by right clicking on the object.

Object Printing

Most of the sheet objects on a QlikView document can be sent directly to a printer or PDF print driver. If you have QlikView 11 a new feature includes the ability to send the print output of an object directly to the locally installed PDF driver, which results in the creation of a PDF file with the rendering of the object included. This can be done by right clicking and selecting *Print as PDF*. If the user right clicks on a list box there is an option to print the possible (associated) values to PDF. However, keep in mind this option requires the use of QlikView for Windows as the QlikView client and that a locally installed PDF printer driver exists. Alternately, users may send the selected object directly to a locally attached or network printer. There are settings in the object properties dialog that affect how the object will behave when printed (*General>Print Settings*). These settings allow you to control header and footer information and provide some control over layout on the page when the object prints. Keep in mind that this feature also is not available in the Web client.

Object Exporting

Users may also export the object or object data to various formats. If the object is a chart and the user is using the Windows or IE plugin client, then the object can be exported as an image. This can be done by right clicking on the object and selecting *Export*, or via and export icon you activate on the caption named *Copy Image to Clipboard*, in which case the image of the chart can be pasted into another application such as PowerPoint. Data can be exported to Excel from the Windows clients as well as the Web client. If you enable the caption icon named *Send to Excel*, an icon will appear in the caption that allows the user to do this. It can also be done by right clicking on the object in either the Windows or Web clients.

QlikView Reporting

QlikView documents can include one or more reports that use the document's data and objects. These reports can be printed or previewed from within QlikView for Windows, or they can be processed and distributed via email by a QlikView server with additional options for publishing and PDF distribution. For many QlikView developers the reporting mechanism in QlikView for

Windows is challenging because it does not appear to offer the versatility and feature richness found in conventional reporting solutions. At first glance it is easy to see why QlikView developers sometimes become frustrated with the QlikView reporting functionality. It is different in concept, ergonomics and aesthetics than other tools. However, while not directly comparable to some reporting tools, the QlikView functionality is more complete and capable than many believe. It does require some special knowledge and extra effort, but a reasonably well engineered set of reports can be created and accessed from within a QlikView document. This chapter will provide you with the necessary information to enable you to become proficient at leveraging QlikView to produce quality printable and distributable report content.

Types of Reports

All reporting solutions provide features that allow you to create different types of reports. One of the first things a good report developer must do is determine which type of report best suits the needs of the report's audience. This, of course, requires you to first define the audience, but we will assume you have done this, and you have a good handle on what your users require in terms of printable reports. There are four primary types of reports. Each addresses specific needs. They are *dashboard reports*, *listing reports*, *grouped reports* and *data sheet reports*. Each of these report types represents a different way of organizing and presenting data to the user of the report. It is worth noting that these categories of reports are not imposed by QlikView. We have defined them to help you see how different types of reports can be created.

Dashboard Reports

Dashboard reports are among the simplest and easiest QlikView reports to create. This is because QlikView lends itself to dashboard type presentation of data with its rich set of charts and visualizations. A dashboard report is usually targeted at users who prefer to see highly summarized data in a graphical format. They often include substantial narrative as well. These reports rarely include more than a few pages of content unless they are combined with other types of reports. Such reports represent the best way to address the need to print multiple parts of a QlikView document in one, presentation quality report. With some effort this report can be reprinted at any time or, as with all reports, it can be automated and sent as a PDF to specified users if you have QlikView server and publisher products installed on a server. While the report version of a dashboard is not interactive, it allows a nicely formatted view of data to be distributed to users who don't possess a QlikView license or have access to your QlikView server. Figure 8-1 shows a sample dashboard report created within a QlikView document.

FIGURE 8-1 DASHBOARD REPORT

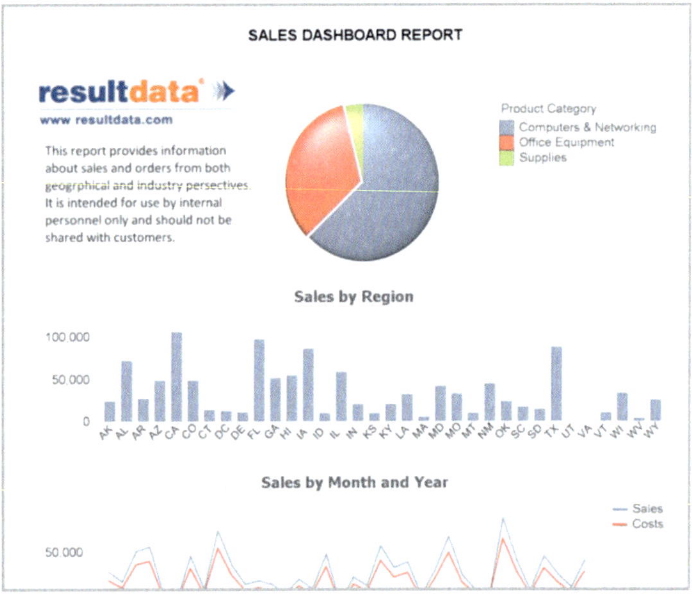

Listing Reports

In many cases users need lists of information without any sophisticated calculations, summaries or visualizations. Examples of listing reports include things such as student rosters, registration lists, inventory pick lists, contact and address lists and similar content. A listing report is usually organized in a columnar format. It can span a large number of pages and sometimes includes grand totals at the end or beginning of the report.

FIGURE 8-2 LISTING REPORT

ORDER LISTING REPORT

Customer	Order Date	Order Description	Total Sales
Dependable Plumbing and...	6/9/2002 4:20:00 PM	Re-outfitting facilities	$613.08
Dependable Plumbing and...	1/1/2002 7:14:35 AM	Re-outfitting facilities	$442.85
Ebert Music Center	12/23/2003 12:19:59 PM	Re-outfitting facilities	$423.46
Ebert Music Center	10/25/2003 7:28:06 AM	Re-outfitting facilities	$525.93
Ebert Music Center	7/13/2003 8:06:26 AM	Improving offices and reception	$756.22
Ebert Music Center	3/20/2003 5:06:26 PM	Upgrading	$330.10
Ebert Music Center	6/17/2001 1:13:06 PM	Upgrading	$505.96
Elm Place Business Supplies	1/9/2002 8:59:41 PM	Improving offices and reception	$451.62
Elm Place Business Supplies	2/4/2001 7:34:34 PM	Improving administrative systems	$1,042.74
Energy Source Diet Centers	11/2/2002 6:19:43 AM	Upgrading	$1,563.54

Grouped Reports

Grouped reports are similar to listing reports, but present the columnar data in a hierarchical manner where grouping levels often represent subtotals. When a listing report has repeated data in a column it is often a candidate to become a grouped report. Grouped Reports are very common. They address the need to show data at multiple levels based on things such as industry, region, or product category. Grouped reports usually include indenting of subgroupings and details to make the hierarchy of data clear to the user. Groups and subgroups often span multiple pages and the total number of pages can be high.

FIGURE 8-3 GROUPED REPORT

SALES BY REGION REPORT

Industry Category	Cost	Price
All Other Business Support Services	$1,259.83	$1,637.78
All Other Support Services	$1,686.88	$2,192.94
Employment Placement Agencies	$1,171.42	$1,522.85
Other Services to Buildings and Dwellings	$654.52	$850.88
Administrative and Support and Waste Management an	**$2,018.19**	**$2,623.65**
Crop Harvesting, Primarily by Machine	$1,382.85	$1,797.70
Agriculture, Forestry, Fishing and Hunting	**$1,382.85**	**$1,797.70**
Amusement and Theme Parks	$356.20	$463.06

Data Sheet or Record Oriented Reports

In some cases a highly detailed view of a given row (or record) of data is desired. The type of report that addresses this need is a data sheet report. Data sheet reports are designed in a manner similar to a form where various details appear at different horizontal and vertical locations on the page. Common examples of data sheet reports might include a real estate listing, personnel record, account profile or tax form. Within data sheet reports are data elements (fields) that have labels describing them. In some cases a data sheet report produces a form for a number of entities such as properties, employees, customers or vendors, where each entity has its own data sheet.

FIGURE 8-4 DATA SHEET REPORT

resultdata
www.resultdata.com

Customer Name: **Air India**

Industry Category: Transportation and Warehousing

Industry: Nonscheduled Chartered Passenger Air Transportation

Region: IA

Product Purchases (7 purchased)

8.5X11 Legal Pad (yellow)
8.5X11 Reem Recycled Office Paper
8.5X11 Reem Std. Office Paper
8.5X17 Reem Std. Office Paper
10/100 Base-T 8 Port Switch
10/100 Base-T 16 Port Switch
10X14 Poster Board (foam)

Purchase Trend

2.0

Creating a QlikView Report

Since QlikView reports are part of a QlikView document, they are created with QlikView for Windows while editing the document. The data for QlikView reports is derived from the document's data set. This means the QlikView load script will directly affect what a report can present.

To create a QlikView report you begin by clicking on the *Report* pull down menu at the top. This presumes you already have a QlikView document opened and data is loaded. To create a new report, select the *Edit Reports...* option. The *Report Editor* window appears on top as shown in Figure 8-5. The report editor appears as a non-modal window, which means you can click on the underlying windows and interact with the QlikView document while the report editor is open. The default view in the report editor shows a listing of existing reports. To create a new report you must click the *Add...* button. You will be prompted for a report name and provided with an option to copy the pages from an existing report into your new report. Once you have provided a report name the new report will be added to the list and it will be highlighted.

FIGURE 8-5 REPORT EDITOR

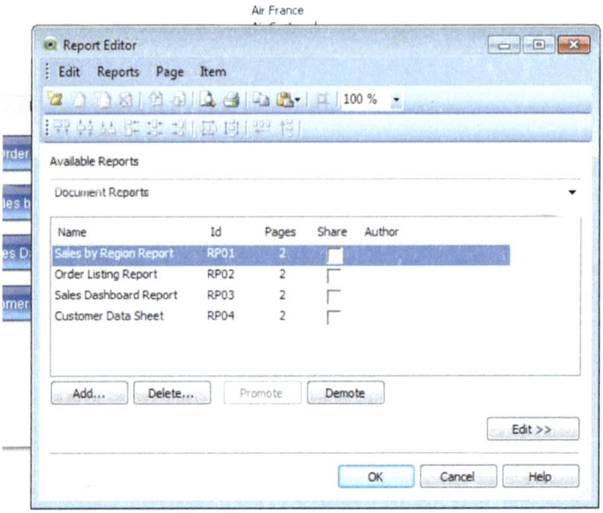

Next, you can begin editing the report by clicking the *Edit >>* button in the lower right corner of the report editor window. This changes the view in the report editor to show the report and a default page is created. You should note that the button in the lower right corner now reads *Report List >>*. This button now has a different function. It returns you to the view to the list of reports.

To add information to your report you drag an object from the underlying document on to the page of the report. The page is represented by a white rectangle in the report editor. As you drag a chart, list box or other sheet object from your QlikView document to the page it appears as a dashed rectangle allowing you to decide where to place. This is shown in Figure 8-6.

FIGURE 8-6 ADDING AN OBJECT TO A REPORT

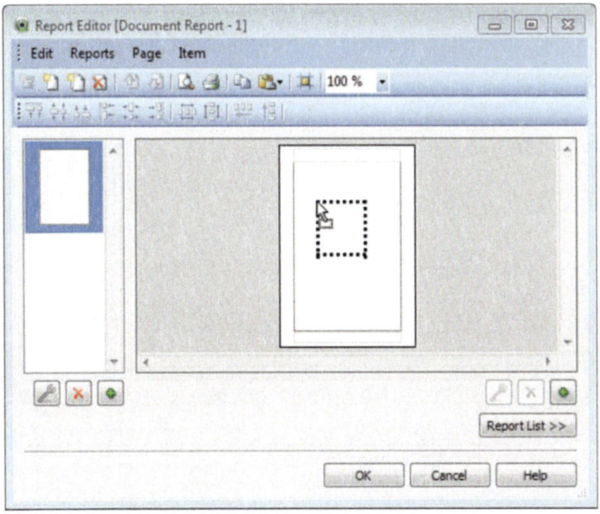

Once an object is on a page in the report you can right click on it and select *Item Settings...* which allows you to adjust how the object appears and behaves within the report. The item settings dialog allows you to create a border around the item. The border setting on the *Layout* tab of the object properties is ignored in reporting. It also allows you to change how the object appears when you resize it in the report. This is controlled by the *Stretch* dropdown. The following settings affect this:

- **Fill with Aspect:** This typically resizes the object and fonts to fit inside of the rectangle you create by resizing the object. It attempts to keep the content of the object proportional to the original aspect ratio of the object.
- **Fill:** Stretches the contents of the object to fill the space inside of the rectangle you create when resizing the object.
- **Clip:** This does not attempt to resize the object contents, but cuts out portions of the content if the rectangle you create while resizing is too small.

Many objects behave differently with respect to the stretch settings and you may find some objects do not do what you think they should. A little “fiddling” is necessary in many cases. Once you’ve created a report and added a few objects you can save it. The report will show in the report listing and you can continue working on it by editing it. You can also print or preview the report from the listing.

Editing an Existing Report

Editing an existing report is simply a matter of opening the report editor as you would to create a new report, selecting the report and then clicking the *Edit >>* button. Essentially, every time you create a new report you use the editing feature to alter it. If the report already exists you simply skip the process of adding a new report and select the existing report instead.

Previewing and Printing Reports

You can preview and print reports from two separate places. To access a report directly for printing or previewing you simply click on the report in the report listing that appears as part the *Reports* pull down menu in QlikView for Windows. This processes the report after presenting you with a print dialog. The print dialog allows you to preview or print the report. If you select *Print Preview,* the report appears in the preview window, which pops up over the dialog. The preview window allows you to page through the report, print the report and zoom in on a page. It also allows you to preview more than one page at a time by clicking the *Add Page* button, which shows two pages at a time side by side. To zoom in on a page you click on it. The mouse pointer will zoom in and out by clicking on the page. Another way to preview or print a report is to pull the report up in the report editor as though you are editing it. You will notice a print preview icon on the tool bar, which processes and launches the selected report in the print preview window. The print preview window is the same one used when directly accessing the report.

It is also possible to embed a button in the QlikView document that calls a report directly. To do this you must add a *Button* object to one of the tab sheets. When you bring up the properties of the button you can click on the *Actions* tab and add a new action. The action type you need is called *Printing* and the action name is called *Print Report*. Once you've added the action you will see an option on the right to enter the Report ID. This is the ID QlikView assigned to the report when you created it. You can see the report ID in the report listing after selecting *Edit Reports...* from the *Reports* pull down menu. It typically follows the format of RP01, RP02 etc. As you add reports the number increments. You can also enter the Windows or network printer name for the action if you don't want the report to print on the default printer. The printer name must be the name used by Windows to reference the printer. Note that there is a *Show Print Dialog* option when the *Print Report* action is assigned to a button. This is not checked by default, so you may wish to consider checking it to give the user the option of selecting a printer.

QlikView Report Best Practices

There are a few things worth considering when you begin creating and using reports. While some of these are not required, you will find that if you follow these recommendations, the report development, management and use will go better for you and your users.

Managing QlikView Objects for Reporting

Virtually any object in a QlikView document can be used in a report. However, this is often problematic because objects for reporting often require special settings and configurations to meet the needs of the report. This means that as a best practice you should consider duplicating objects, or creating new objects specifically for use in reports. These objects should not be available for use by the end user since they are often redundant and can clutter the application. You can duplicate objects by selecting them and copying them to the Windows clipboard. The most common way to do this is to select the object by clicking on it and pressing the *Ctrl+C* key combination. You can then paste the object on the same tab sheet or a different one by pressing the *Ctrl+V* key combination.

To address the challenge presented by having to create and maintain separate objects for QlikView reports consider creating separate tab sheets to house report objects. This allows you to organize your report objects without concern for how they might affect usability and clarity of the QlikView document. To do this you add a tab sheet, as you normally would, by using the *Layout* pull down menu. Name your tab sheet in a manner that indicates it will contain reporting objects (e.g. Report 1, Report 2 etc.). Create or copy objects to the tab sheet and edit them as needed for use in one or more reports. Once created and updated, the reporting tab sheets can be hidden to remove them from the user's view. It would not be wise to allow users to edit or use objects upon which reports depend since such interaction could alter the look and output of one or more reports.

To hide a tab sheet in QlikView, right click on it to access its properties dialog. On the *General* tab, change the *Show Sheet* option to *Conditional* and enter a zero into the expression field. This will make the sheet disappear from the document. If you want to make it reappear so you can edit the objects again, go to the *Settings* pull down menu and select *Document Properties*, then click on the *Sheets* tab in the document properties dialog. This will show all sheets, even if some of them are hidden. From here you can select a tab sheet and pull up its properties. Click *Always* in the *Show Sheet* settings and the tab will reappear.

Create Report Selections Tab Sheet

Because selections can be made across all of the tab sheets in a document, and such selections are often specific to the objects on a given sheet, it may be desirable to consolidate the selection objects associated with reports on a single tab sheet. This tab sheet can act as a report management console from which your users can clear all selections, make report specific selections and launch reports via buttons. A report selections tab sheet may include items such as a current selections box, a clear all selections button, various list boxes, and buttons to launch reports.

Report Development

Creating a simple report within a QlikView document is relatively easy. However, making a report produce more sophisticated results requires a deeper understanding of the features and options associated with QlikView reporting.

Adding Pages

QlikView reports can include any number of pages. It is possible to create several page sets in a report where a page set is represented either by a single page or several auto-generated pages based on data that will not fit on a single page. The two options for creating pages in a QlikView document include the following:

- **Single-Page**: This type of page only produces a single page in the report when it is processed. A single page is created even if an object with data rows that extend beyond the page size is used. Typically, this type of page is used to show charts, text objects and limited data.
- **Multi-Page:** The multi-page page type produces one or more pages in the processed report depending on the number of rows associated with the object you place on it. This type of page can only have one object in the main (center) area of the page. However, it includes *Introduction* and *Appendix* sections before and after the main (center) section. These sections print one or more objects before or after the multi-page portion processes. They act sort of like a report header and report footer.

When adding a multi-page page to your report, you are prompted for a setting that includes banding and looping options as part of the *Page Settings* dialog that appears. This is discussed later in this chapter. Figure 8-7 shows how single paper and multi-page pages appear. Notice that the multi-page page on the left navigation pane shows several stacked pages to indicate it is different. Note in earlier versions of QlikView these page types were sometimes referred to as "multi-paper" and "single-paper" pages.

FIGURE 8-7 PAGE TYPES

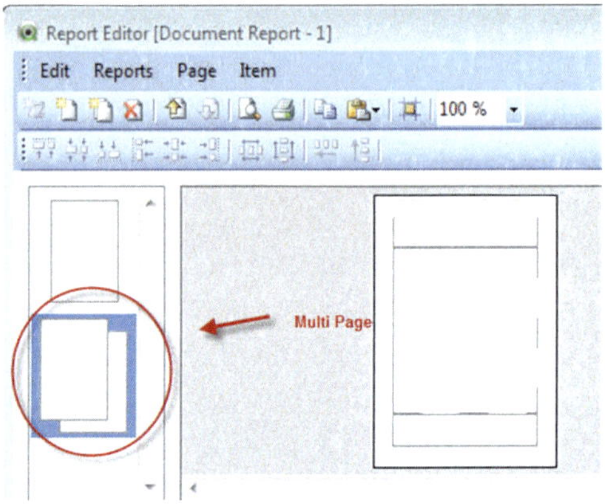

When you create a new report in a QlikView document, an initial page is created automatically. The initial page is a *single-paper* type of page.

Managing Report Data Selections

It is important to understand how user selections affect data that appears in a report. If you fail to review how selections are being applied, then the report may produce undesired results. By carefully considering how to manage user selections with respect to report processing you can ensure that reports produce the anticipated results and users will be confident in their use.

QlikView Possible Values

QlikView reports have several options associated with them for managing how data is filtered (selected) when they are processed. In QlikView the data items that are selected (showing in green) and the associated data items (showing in white) are referred to as "possible" values. By default a report ignores all selections in the QlikView document host and includes both possible and excluded values. As a result, if you create a new report it will include all data for the objects you use in the report. However, you can adjust this behavior so that the report behaves differently with respect to selections. There are three options to control report selections. They are found in the *Report Settings* which can be accessed from the *Reports* pull down menu in the report editor (not the Reports menu option at the top of QlikView for Windows). Once selected, the *Report Settings* option produces a dialog with various options. On the last tab, labeled *Selections,* there is an option for *Initial Selection* from which you can choose one of these settings:

- Current: Which honors the selections made in the QlikView document at the time the report is processed.
- Clear All: Which is the default setting and ignores all selections in the QlikView document.
- Bookmark: Which allows you to predefine any combination of selections and have them automatically applied each time the report is processed.

Showing Selections on the Report

If you have set up the report to honor current selections in the QlikView document, you should consider showing the document's selection criteria so recipients of the report understand what data was included in the report when it was processed. There are two ways to show document selections in a QlikView report. The first is to drag a *Current Selections box* object on to a page in the report. This is not ideal because the current selections box is a screen oriented object. It is designed to allow the user to interact with selections and it does not look proper on a report. It is also very difficult to get the current selections box to show the selection data and size in a manner that works well. In some cases, such as when there are numerous selection values, items may be truncated. In other cases the font size and scaling of the object may be very small or very large.

The better approach is to create a text object and write an expression that returns the current selections stamp. The function to do this allows you to control how selection information for different fields is separated. By doing this you can have nicely formatted text in a report that highlights what data the report includes. The following expression syntax can be used to produce such results in a text object:

```
='REGIONS: ' & CHR(13) & getFieldSelections(Region)
```

In this example, the selections for the field "Region" will be shown one line below a label the reads "REGIONS". The result of this would look like the following on the report assuming the user selected the four regions shown.

```
REGIONS:
AR, AZ, CA, CO
```

Headers and Footers

Most reporting solutions provide a capability to add reference data to the very beginning or top and very end or bottom of the report. Additionally, reference data such as page numbers may be added to the beginning or end of each page in a report. QlikView reporting includes a limited set of these capabilities.

Report Headers and Footers

To create header and footer information at the report level you must access the *Report Settings* dialog from the *Report* pull down menu in the report editor. The tab labeled *Header/Footer* provides options for adding text and reference data to the left, center and right sections of both the report header and footer.

In addition to typing in static text into the header and footer you can also add predefined reference data by either selecting the icons at the top of the tab or by typing the corresponding variable names. The common reference data includes the following variables:

`&[Page]`
the current page of the report (page number)

`&[Pages]`
the total number of pages in the report

`&[Date]`
the system date at the time the report is run

`&[Time]`
the system time at the time the report is run

`&[File]`
the .QVW file name and full path

`&[Picture= <file_name>]`
embeds a file that was imported into the QlikView document (usually done with a text object background image)

`&[Report]`
the name of the report in the QlikView document

Information placed in these sections appears at the top or bottom of each page in the report respectively. This is slightly different from other tools where the report header information only appears at the top of the first page, and report footer information appears at the bottom of the last page. To show information only once (at the very beginning or end of the report), you must place the desired object on the first page or last page. If either of these is a multi-paper page you need to use the *Introduction* and *Appendix* sections that appear at the top and bottom of the multi-paper page respectively. When editing a multi-paper page you can adjust the amount of vertical space these sections consume by dragging the splitter bar between them and the middle section (consider zooming in to do this) or by right clicking in the margin of the page and accessing the *Page Settings* dialog. There is also a wrench icon in the lower left corner that launches the *Page Settings* dialog. This dialog allows you to set the height of the *Introduction* and *Appendix* sections by percent of page. You will also notice that this dialog allows you to control where these sections appear with within the multi-page set. The default is *First Paper* for the *Introduction* and *Last Paper* for the *Appendix*. Keep in mind that if you want the footer information to appear at the very end of the report and you have multiple multi-page sets in the report, you will have to do this on the last multi-page set.

Listing, Grouping and Sub-Totaling Data in a Report with Table Objects

To produce conventional columnar reports in QlikView the best option is to use one of the two table objects. These are located under the *Charts* menu selection when you right click on a tab sheet to add a sheet object. They are selected and created in the same manner as a graphical chart. There are two types of tables in QlikView:

- **Straight Table**: This table type shows two or more columns of data in a standard table view that is similar to a spreadsheet.
- **Pivot Table**: A pivot table shows data hierarchically where columns and rows can be stacked on top of or next to each other.

To group data in a conventional fashion the best sheet object to use is the *pivot table*. Pivot tables allow you to stack several dimensions on top of each other and create subtotals for each. When used on a multi-paper page, a pivot table can create output that is similar to grouped reports produced in other reporting tools. This is because the multi-paper page set allows the dynamic creation of pages for data that won't fit on the first page, and the pivot table allows you to create a hierarchy and provide subtotaling at each level.

Pivot Table Formatting

Pivot tables have many of the same formatting options found in straight tables and other sheet objects, but they also include specific formatting challenges that require special attention. When using pivot tables there are some settings that allow you to make the report closely resemble conventional banded report groupings. Additionally, there are features in QlikView that provide significant control over formatting, but use of these features can be idiosyncratic and may require that you perform certain things in proper sequence. By combining pivot tables with specialized formatting you will find you can produce a reasonably high quality result that includes grouping and subtotaling.

Grouping

To group data in a pivot table you must create dimensions in the appropriate order. Dimensions can be created by selecting fields or by creating expressions to "calculate" a dimension from within the pivot table properties. This is standard pivot table functionality, but in the case of reporting you may wish to use the "Calculated Dimension" option more often because you may not want to modify the load script to accommodate reporting needs. The calculated dimension functionality is available on the "Dimensions" tab of the properties dialog and allows you do things such as concatenate text values. For example, if you wanted a dimension created on a combination of *last_name* and *first_name* fields you could do the following in an expression representing a calculated dimension:

```
=[Industry Category] & ' - ' & [Industry]
```

In this case no modification to the load script is needed since the dimension is only needed for satisfying reporting needs. If you added a field in the load script, which would also meet this need, you would be adding overhead to the data model and more memory would be consumed by the document. Additionally, a new field would become available to users who collaborate on this document. The new field, since it exists only to fulfill a reporting need, may not be desirable.

Stacking Dimensions and Expanding

When you add more than one dimension to a pivot table QlikView places it under the last existing dimension by default. You can drag the dimension up or down to stack it where you wish. The red arrow that appears while dragging a dimension helps to show where the dimension will appear when you let go of the mouse button. There's nothing different about this from what your user might do when using a pivot table, but in this case you are preparing to pivot table to meet the grouping and subtotaling needs of your report. Think about this from a report grouping perspective. Since your pivot table will be used only for reporting you will likely want to fully expand the dimensions from the start. You can do this by manually expanding it, but you may want to consider using the *Always Fully Expanded* checkbox on the *Presentation* tab of the pivot table properties.

By default pivot tables place stacked dimensions next to each other horizontally. This is not desirable for reporting because you have limited horizontal space on a printed page. You will want to make the stacked dimensions occur as a hierarchy on the first column and have the other columns represent values in most cases. To correct this you can use the *Indent* checkbox on the *Style* tab of the pivot table properties dialog. This forces lower-level dimensions to appear under higher-level dimensions. You can still adjust the column widths after doing this to ensure you have the full text of each level showing the way you wish.

Sub-Totaling

The default behavior for pivot tables is not to show subtotals. To change this check the *Show partial values* checkbox on the *Presentation* tab of the object properties dialog. Note that this option is disabled if indenting is activated on the *Style* tab, but you can simply disable indenting and then re-enable it after showing partial sums to address this problem.

Managing Borders

Table Borders

Table objects, by default, include a border that surrounds the entire table. For reporting, this may not be desirable because it makes the table look as though it is nothing more than a screen print of an object. The table border can be eliminated by setting its width to zero points (0 pt.). This is done on the *Layout* tab of the table properties dialog.

Cell Borders

Lines around borders within a table's cells can be controlled in QlikView, but often are not because when users interact with tables these border lines are helpful. However, when producing an object for use in a QlikView report it is best to turn some of these lines off to make the report appear less cluttered. Vertical lines are controlled by two checkboxes on the *Style* tab of the table object's properties dialog.

Formatting Tags for Dimensions and Expressions

Starting with the Built-in Styles

Managing the styling of various object elements in QlikView can be tricky. Before diving into custom tag and cell formatting you should begin by experimenting with the built-in styles that can be applied to most sheet objects. These are found in a drop down list on the *Style* tab of the object properties dialog. By starting with a style that is close to what you want for your report you can minimize the effort and time needed for formatting. Additionally, in some cases you will find that you simply cannot achieve what you want with custom tags and cell formatting. However sometimes the built-in styles can do things you cannot. By starting with a built-in style you may be able to get what you want. After selecting a style you can customize it if you want additional formatting done.

Using Formatting Tags on Dimensions and Expressions

Formatting tags are used to override the default or user property settings for certain attributes in a QlikView sheet object. *Appendix A* of this book provides more information about formatting tags and how to use them. Formatting tags allow you to customize the formatting of chart and dimension information in tables. They include the following:

- Text Color
- Text Format such as font weight and style
- Background Color
- Line Format including width and line style (dashes)
- Pie Slice Attribute for Pie Charts

Custom Formatting of Cell Attributes in Pivot and Straight Tables

Not only is it possible to override formatting at a dimension (or attribute) level, but also at an individual cell level within table objects. This means that when using a pivot or straight table, you can format the table's appearance at a more granular level. Many QlikView users are unaware of these advanced formatting features. These features are not necessarily important in cases where users are interacting with the tables. However, reporting often requires more attention to detail since reports are intended for use as printed materials. Many QlikView reports fail to meet high quality reporting standards because these advanced formatting features go unnoticed and unused.

How to Begin with Cell Formatting

As mentioned previously, it is a good idea to use the built in styles as a starting point. This is especially true when working with cell formatting. By selecting a style on the *Style* tab of the table's properties dialog, QlikView automatically sets a variety of cell attributes. To get started with a basic style, consider selecting the *Clean* style option. It appears to be the best way to remove borders around various cells. Even though the *Clean* style peforms some additional background and font formatting, it is the best option for getting the attributes to an unformatted starting point because other styles, including the default, tend to implement cell borders which can be difficult to remove manually in some cases.

Using the Custom Format Cell Feature

In both types of tables data is divided into cells. A cell not only shows the data, but also has certain formatting characteristics. QlikView provides a means for manipulating these characteristics so that you can override default formatting at a more granular level. The name of this feature is the *Custom Format Cell* option. It appears as a right-click popup menu on pivot and straight tables. This option is found when you hover over a specific area (cell) of the table and perform a right mouse click. It is very helpful when designing objects for reports because it allows you to format the look and feel of the data in a manner consistent with conventional reporting standards.

In order to custom format a cell in a pivot or straight table you must have one of the two following settings set correctly. Otherwise the option will not appear or be available to you.

1. **User Preferences:** On the *Design* tab of the table properties, check the *Always Show Design Menu Items* checkbox.
2. **Design Grid:** Alternately, this feature appears when you have the *Design Grid* option showing, which is activated from the *View* pull down menu at the top of QlikView for Windows.

Once the required settings are made, the *Custom Format Cell* option appears as a right-click menu item when you hover over various cells in a table object. When you select the *Custom Format Cell* menu item from the popup menu, a new dialog appears that gives you some control over cell attributes such as line style and color, background color and basic font attributes. A preview of the changes you make appears on the left side of the dialog. In most cases the changes occur instantaneously. The *Apply change to* drop down list allows you to make the change for all occurrences of a dimension or expression or only for the one on which you clicked.

FIGURE 8-8 CUSTOM FORMAT CELL DIALOG

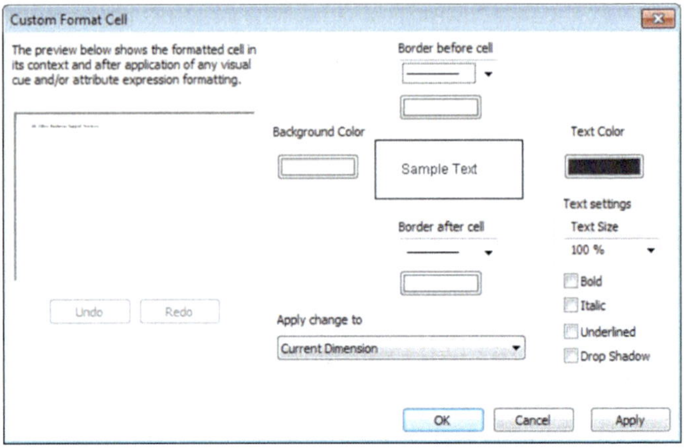

Straight Table Cell Formatting

Straight tables are reasonably simple because they only offer one level of dimensionality. Multiple dimensions in straight tables appear as columns. One important note is that you will not want to enable drilldown functionality on any straight table used in a report. This functionality won't work in the report and may create formatting challenges. The *Custom Format Cell* option is available for both pivot and straight tables.

Pivot Table Cell Formatting

Pivot table cell formatting can be tricky because dimensions in pivot tables can be stacked on top of each other, so an indenting feature is often used in reporting to make sub-dimensions appear below main dimensions vertically. A few important things to remember when using pivot tables include the following:

1. Turn off *Indent Mode* on the *Style* tab of the properties dialog before attempting to set cell format attributes. In some cases if indenting is active you will not be able to affect certain cells such at sub-total cells.
2. Pay close attention to the *Apply change to* option when formatting cells in a pivot table. Because dimensions can be stacked and indented it is more likely that you might only apply the formatting to one area of the table and not all areas at the selected level.

Report Banding and Looping

In some cases it is desirable to loop through a given set of field values and produce a page for each item in the field. In QlikView this is called *Banding,* which is an option associated with the page settings in a QlikView report. Banding can also be applied the report as a whole.

What does Banding do?

Banding forces replication of the report content for each item in a given field from the document's data set. Banding can be applied to the entire report or to a given page set in the report. It is important to understand that if you select a field for banding at the report level, you may prohibit page level banding from having any data values available for processing. Generally, it is not a good idea to use banding at both the report and page levels simultaneously. When using banding at the page level, the page set (single-paper or multi-paper) will be run for each instance of a field value. For example, if the banding field is "region" then the pages are processed once for each region as though the user had run the report separately by selecting a region first.

Activating Banding at the Page Level

To activate banding at the page level you need to access the *Page Settings* dialog by right clicking on the page or by selecting *Page Settings* from the *Page* pull down menu in the report editor.

By checking the *Loop page over possible values in field* checkbox, page level banding is enabled and you can select the field from the document data set on which the banding process is based. It is important to remember that if there are a high number of field values for the field you select it may take some time for the report to process.

Controlling Banding with Selections

By default, QlikView reports ignore document selection, which means that banding occurs across the entire data set even if your user has made selections in the document prior to running the report. To address this there is a report setting that forces the report to honor the selections made in the document. This is found in the *Report Settings* dialog. See the section that appeared earlier about *Managing Report Data Selections* for more information on this.

The reporting and printing features included in QlikView are more robust than most users realize. While the approach to creating and configuring reports is substantially different from that of other tools, the core features and capabilities are adequate to produce a reasonably high quality report output. If you know some of the tricks, such as those highlighted here, you can make QlikView reports closely resemble the output of other reporting tools. This, coupled with the QlikView document manager (Publisher) and PDF generator options, allows QlikView environments to send user specific reports via email in PDF format automatically. These features allow many organizations to standardize on QlikView since it can fulfill both analysis and reporting needs.

Chapter 9: Sharing and Securing QlikView Documents

After creating a QlikView document, you have a rich, interactive application that makes analyzing data and understanding information easy and interesting. The next step is to share your work with your user community who will benefit from the combination of your creative effort and QlikView's unique set of features. Sharing a QlikView document can be done in several ways. Part of the process for sharing a document should include consideration for how the document and the document's data need to be secured. This chapter will introduce you to several ways in which to share and secure your QlikView documents. This is one of the most important topics covered in this book because, unless you are using QlikView exclusively for personal needs, your work must be made available to others to have value. There are a number of considerations that affect how QlikView documents are used by both end users and fellow developers. Failure to understand the basics of QlikView architecture, editions and licensing usually results in problems.

Sharing QlikView documents can be accomplished in several ways. Each method of sharing has certain requirements, features and security issues associated with it. Each method also may present limitations and issues relative to the needs of your users. For these reasons you need to carefully consider all of the options. It is also critical that you begin to understand the direction that QlikTech is taking with the product line so you can consider how your deployment approach might be affected by future updates of the QlikView product. Finally, you will want to consider the balance between cost, capability and security when deciding how to make your QlikView content available to users.

Sharing a QlikView Document: Two Approaches

By now you should understand that a QlikView document resides with its data in a .QVW file. Each .QVW file represents a single QlikView document including a load script, tab sheets, sheet objects, reports and expressions. There are fundamentally two ways to make your QlikView document available to others. The simple way to share your document is to copy and send it to another user who has a licensed copy of QlikView for Windows installed. This can only be done if you and the other user have licensed copies of QlikView (more on this later). The second way you can share your QlikView document is to deploy it to a QlikView server. When using a QlikView server, users with whom you wish to share your document may access it using a variety of devices.

Each of the two approaches to how QlikView documents are shared has their own requirements, limitations and issues. You should spend a little time understanding each option so you can make the right decision about how to proceed. Many QlikView developers take the cheapest approach first due to limitation on budget. But, this isn't always in your organization's best interest as it drives up ownership costs by increasing the time, effort and resources needed to maintain and secure QlikView content. At a minimum, we recommend that you review how QlikView servers make document sharing better and easier.

QlikView Servers and Clients: An Introduction

A rapidly growing use of QlikView involves server deployments. QlikView servers make the sharing, securing, processing and managing of QlikView documents a practical and manageable proposition for organizations seeking to use QlikView for more than a few users. QlikView servers are also scalable. They include clustering and load balancing capabilities so that very large documents may be simultaneous accessed by a high number of users.

QlikView servers are computers that run the QlikView server software. They reside on your organization's network and allow users to access documents without requiring a copy of each document to be copied and distributed. QlikView servers run on Windows based server hardware and are relatively easy to install. However, understanding how to configure a QlikView server usually requires some assistance if you haven't been to one of the QlikView server classes. While it is beyond the scope of this book to provide details about QlikView server configurations, later in this chapter you will learn how to deploy your document to a QlikView server.

QlikView Server Features

QlikView servers provide an array of enterprise ready features that make QlikView more than an exceptional data analysis tool. These features include the following:

- Security Capabilities: These include such things as row/record level security management, Windows AD security integration and custom security features.
- Content Distribution: Through the use of the QlikView Publisher technology, documents can be processed and distributed with consideration for data security on an automated basis. This feature set also provides a mechanism to automatically email PDF versions of embedded reports to users outside of the system or local network.
- Auditing: QlikView servers can audit, at a remarkably detailed level, a wide variety of user activities and document access scenarios.
- License Management: Users and licenses are centrally managed in a QlikView Server, allowing for proactive license management and optimization.
- Clustering: Aside from load balancing for heavy user loads and documents with large amounts of data, QlikView servers can also be configured to provide fail-over

capabilities to ensure the platform remains highly available.

- Multi-Client Support: QlikView servers allow users of a variety of devices such as tablets, smartphones, Web browsers and Windows PC's to access and share QlikView documents.
- Collaboration Features: When deployed to a QlikView server, a QlikView document may incorporate a variety of collaboration features such as user created tab sheets and objects (even from a Web interface), threaded discussion groups about a document and (with Version 11) real time sharing interaction between multiple users.

In order for QlikView users to leverage these and other server features, they must use one of the QlikView clients. These clients are designed to interact with QlikView servers. It should be noted that some features, such as collaboration, are not available with all types of QlikView clients.

QlikView Clients

While the focus of this book has primarily focused on the use of the QlikView Windows client, you should know there are many other ways for users to access your server based QlikView documents. QlikView servers include support for a variety of interfaces that make documents available from a variety of devices. These interfaces are called "clients." QlikView clients exist for many popular devices such as PC's, smart phones and tablets. QlikView supports the following types of client interfaces:

- Windows Client: Also called QlikView Developer, this client is the main Windows application referenced in this book. It is installed when you download and install QlikView Personal Edition and has a variety of licensing options as previously described.
- Web AJAX Client: The main Web interface for QlikView is based on what is sometimes called an AJAX Zero Footprint Client (ZFC). This client is built into the QlikView server

and corresponding Web server platform. It allows anyone using a modern Web browser to access QlikView documents without additional software. This client is feature rich and is likely the area of the most focus by QlikTech in the future. Most users access server based QlikView content using this client.

- Mobile Client: In previous versions of QlikView there were separate mobile clients available for Apple iPhone, iPad, Google Android and Windows/Java enabled devices. However, beginning with QlikView version 10 a new multi-touch Web client has been provided to replace all other mobile clients. This new client allows touch screen users to perform the necessary operations to fully utilize a QlikView document without a mouse. In our experience this client is being well received by Apple iPad users and users of other mobile devices. It also makes it possible to create one application that can be used on both mobile devices and Web browsers. However, some consideration for the difference in screen size is important when developing documents. The QlikView mobile client has multi-touch functionality, which allows it to address issues on touch screen devices. These include such user activities as making multiple selections and scrolling large lists of data.

QlikView Editions and Licensing

While it is beyond the scope of this book to address all of the specifics concerning editions and licensing options, some basic information about these topics is important. QlikView editions and licensing will have profound effect on your decision for how you deploy and share QlikView documents with users. The information shared here applies to QlikView versions 9 through 11. However, within these versions are subtle differences not only in functionality, but in licensing options and costs, which change from time to time. It is a good idea to get consulting assistance from a certified QlikView partner before making a final decision about how you will deploy your QlikView documents to your users.

QlikView Editions

As of the release of this book there are two editions of the Windows based QlikView software (QlikView Developer). However, a little history may be helpful for those upgrading from versions earlier than version 9. In versions 8 and earlier, QlikView for Windows was divided into two editions that were eliminated later: QlikView Analyzer and QlikView Professional (or "Pro"). Each of these had different costs and features. Beginning with version 9 these two editions were combined into a single edition called QlikView Developer. Licensed users of the older editions became users of QlikView Developer when they upgraded to version 9 or later. Beginning with version 9 QlikView also became available in a Personal Edition (PE), which can be downloaded for free from the QlikView Website. Personal Edition is a full featured edition of QlikView Developer, not a trial edition. It does not time out nor does it require a purchase. However, Personal Edition does not allow sharing of QlikView documents. When you install QlikView Personal Edition on your computer, the QlikView documents you create with it cannot be opened on another computer using QlikView Personal Edition. If your documents are opened in a licensed edition of QlikView (QlikView Developer) then they will be converted for use only with other licensed editions and can no longer be used in Personal Edition. Personal Edition is also restricted from opening QlikView documents stored and shared on a QlikView server. Personal Edition is truly "personal," but it is also free and a good option for getting started with QlikView. In fact, Personal Edition is the same software as QlikView Developer. The only difference is a key code and/or license enablement file (LEF). This means you can begin using QlikView Personal Edition and then purchase a key code to upgrade so you can share your work. We see this as a very smart and generous move on QlikTech's part because it makes it easy to get started and helps individuals who have little or no budget realize value from QlikView. It also grows the base of QlikView users and QlikView content.

Regardless of the edition, QlikView Developer (QlikView for Windows) is a MS-Windows based software application that allows you to use and develop QlikView documents. In all of these cases QlikView, as its primary method, directly accesses a QlikView file located on local disk (i.e. your local C: drive) or a shared folder on a local area network (i.e. a mapped drive or file share). However, QlikView Developer (QlikView for Windows), depending on how it is licensed, can also open files shared on a QlikView server and it can allow multiple users to access the same QlikView document on a local area network without a QlikView server.

Since QlikView licensing, as with all software-licensing, changes from time to time, a detailed review does not make sense for this book. Additionally, it would be inappropriate and ultimately inaccurate for us to include anything about licensing cost. But, some basics about how QlikView licensing works may be helpful in getting you started in the right direction. Please keep in mind that the licensing specifics are subject to change and none of what we are sharing in this book is official or provided by QlikTech. We believe it is best for you to engage your local certified QlikView partner or sales representative about licensing and cost early in your experience with QlikView. Also, keep in mind that this information may not apply to your situation. With that understood there are few things about licensing that we feel everyone who develops QlikView content should understand.

QlikView Developer (QlikView for Windows), the Windows based client and authoring application, can be licensed in a few ways. For users who do not have a QlikView server available there is a Local Client license, which allows the locally installed QlikView software to open and share QlikView documents from disk and network file shares. The local client license, in our opinion, is a risky proposition for several reasons. First, it assumes that all computers on the network have similar memory and processing resources. If that is not the case, a QlikView document may work fine for one user and fail for another. Second, each user will be pulling all of the QlikView document data over the network each time it is accessed or reloaded. If the document uses a significant amount of data and/or there are many users, this may become a problem for the entire network affecting all users, not just QlikView users. This is especially true if the network spans geographies (i.e. is a WAN). Finally, using the QlikView Local Client licensing requires you to consider how the document and its data are secured. There is no central administration of such things with local clients. This means data security and important security policies can easily be overlooked and there is no way to know when such problems might occur. After a period there may be a number of security violations and there will be no practical way to audit or control them.

All other forms of QlikView licensing are made available from a licensed QlikView server. If a user of QlikView Developer does not have a local client license then by default a Personal Edition of QlikView (no sharing) is being used. In this case the user must acquire a license from a QlikView server. When a license is acquired from a QlikView server it is "leased." That means that the user's local QlikView Developer software has a license for a period of time, after which the license will expire. This expiration only occurs if the user does not access the server within a specified number of days. If a user's license lease expires, then that license may be reassigned to another user or it may be reissued to the same user again. QlikView server administrators may also revoke a user's server license and then reassign it to another user. However, if this is done the license will go into a quarantine state for one day. This prevents administrators from randomly reassigning licenses to avoid purchasing the appropriate volume of licensing.

To obtain a server based license lease a user must access the server by opening a shared QlikView document from the server. The first time this is done a license lease, assuming a license is reserved for the user or available automatically from the license pool, will be created for the user. A license lease results in conversion of the local copy of QlikView from Personal Edition to a licensed edition allowing for the sharing of content. This process also creates license lease information about the user and user's computer on the QlikView server. To lease a license from a Personal Edition of QlikView you must connect to the server using the QVP network protocol. QVP is a propriety network protocol that is built into the QlikView Developer and QlikView server software.

Connecting to a QlikView Server

There are several ways for users to access QlikView server documents, including access by Web browsers and mobile devices. These are covered in more detail later in this chapter. The method covered here involves using a local copy of QlikView for Windows to open a file from (and in) a QlikView server. Don't confuse this with opening a QlikView document (.QVW file) from a network share or local drive. In the case of using the QVP protocol, the server is opening the document on your (or the user's) behalf. This accomplishes two things. It creates or updates a license lease for your local copy of QlikView from the server, and it allows you to leverage the server's memory, rather than your local machine's memory. The document actually opens in the server and displays on your computer. When you open a QlikView document this way you cannot edit it. This is because it is shared and running on the server. Other users may also be accessing it at the same time. However, you can make selections, interact with sheet objects, run reports and analyze data. This can be helpful for users with local copies of QlikView who need access to documents with large amounts of data. Since the document is using the server's memory the user can interact with hundreds of millions or billions of rows of data without a local computer containing significant memory resources.

You connect to a QlikView server from your local copy of QlikView by using the *File>Open in Server* pull down menu item in QlikView. This results in a *Connect to Server* dialog from which you can use the QVP protocol to connect to a QlikView server and see a list of documents. On the right side of the dialog window you will see a group of options named *Authentication*. The options in this group help you build a connection string to the QlikView server with the correct user credentials for accessing server content. The types of authentication (the radio buttons) provide the following options:

- *Use NT Identity*: When selected, this option uses your local Windows login and password to authenticate you to the QlikView server. If you are in the same Windows domain as the QlikView server and the server is set up use Windows Authentication (it is by default), then you should be able to use this option. This presumes the QlikView administrator has assigned you a license or that the server allows automatic distribution of licenses.
- *Anonymous*: If the QlikView server allows anonymous access, this option will get you in without having to provide a user name and password. Most don't, so it is unlikely this will work for you.
- *Alternate Identity*: This option applies if you are on a computer that is not part of the QlikView server's Windows domain. You can put a fully qualified user name in the User ID box to authenticate as a different user (one that is in the QlikView server's Windows domain and is authorized by the QlikView administrator). You do this by selecting this option and typing in something similar to the following:
- *mywindowsdomain\mywindowsuserid.* If you need to use this option, chances are that there could be a firewall between you and the QlikView server, which means certain ports would also have to be open in order to allow you to authenticate.

Once you have selected an authentication option and, if necessary, entered the appropriate user ID you will notice that the text box at the top left of the dialog shows a partial URL string using the QVP protocol. It will read something like the following:

qvp://mywindowsdomain\mywindowsuserid@

Immediately following the at symbol (@) you must type in the name of the QlikView server. It should look similar to the following:

qvp://mywindowsdomain\mywindowsuserid@qvservername

Once you complete the server connection URL string, click on the *Connect* button and you will be connected to the server. Depending on the method of authentication you may also be prompted for a password. You should note that after a successful connection to a server, the server name and URL string are stored and you won't have to do this to connect to the same server again in the future. The URL string for each QlikView server to which you connect appears in the dropdown list associated with the text box for future use.

Once connected to a QlikView server, the server and its document folders appears in the list box below the server connection string. What is displayed in this list box is based on the way in which security and authorization is configured for your user credentials on the QlikView server. You will only see what the administrator has made available to you. When you click on a folder in the list, the grid at the bottom of the dialog populates with documents to which you have access rights. To access a document, click on it and then click *Open*. The document opens in the server and is displayed in your local copy of QlikView. The dialog will disappear.

QlikView Server Deployment

QlikView documents are, as previously discussed, nothing more than files (.QVW files) that are accessed by QlikView. A QlikView file may also contain data if a data reload has been performed. QlikView files are highly compressed. This means that the amount of space consumed on the computer's disk and in the computer's memory is not nearly as much as the data requires in its raw form. In order for your document to be shared with other users from a QlikView server it must be moved to the server. There are several steps involved in doing this, but it doesn't take long to do.

Deploying a Document to QlikView Server

To make QlikView files available on a QlikView server you must copy them to the server. This is done in a manner that is similar to the way you might copy a Windows based file to any computer or to a file server. A file copy can be performed in several ways including using *Windows Explorer*, a command line instruction or other methods such as FTP uploading. The location in which you place the QlikView file matters. QlikView server uses specified drive and folder locations (mounts) to manage QlikView document files. If your QlikView file is not in one of these locations, it will not be available to the server.

The default location for storing QlikView files on a QlikView server is a folder under the *ProgramData* folder on the system partition (usually the C: drive) of the server. The default path on a server is usually the following:

```
c:\ProgramData\QlikTech\Documents
```

You should note that the *ProgramData* folder is usually a hidden folder and does not appear in the folder list inside of *Windows Explorer*. You can change the settings in *Windows Explorer* to show hidden files to see and access this folder. Keep in mind that the default folder location is often changed when QlikView server is installed. You should ask your QlikView administrator how the server was configured and which folder or set of folders are used by the server to store user documents. Also, keep in mind that if your QlikView server is licensed with QlikView publisher (a separate distribution feature) the folder structures may be more complex. Finally, you must have the appropriate file system rights to copy files to the server and folders.

Once your QlikView file is copied to the server and placed in the proper folder, the server will be able to find and make it available. However, your QlikView administrator must do several things before the document is available for use by users. These include the following:

1. Users must be appropriated licenses in the QlikView server. A local client license will not allow access to server based documents.
2. The document must be authorized for use. This is done by the QlikView administrator who can control which users have access to the document (see the section below covering *Securing Documents on a QlikView Server*).
3. Any dependencies that your document has must be made available and have appropriate security rights set for the QlikView server account. These include such things as QlikView data files (.QVD files) and references to text or other files in the load script (*include* statements).

It is a very good idea to test your QlikView document on the server after it has been deployed. This requires you to have a server license. A local client license allows you to create, edit and deploy (copy) your documents to the QlikView server, but you will not be able to open them in the server without a server license. If you don't have a QlikView server licensed allocated, find someone who does and make sure they have rights to your document. Have them test your document in one of the QlikView clients (ideally the Web client). Also, make sure that your QlikView administrator has set up and tested your document for data reloading. The server can reload the data for your document based on a predetermined schedule. You should discuss this with your administrator and know that it is configured and working properly.

Securing Documents on a QlikView Server

There are two categories of security on a QlikView server. Each serves a different, but important purpose. Understanding these categories and their associated mechanisms is important. While much of this only pertains to QlikView administrators, it is helpful for you to know how security works on a QlikView server so that you can help address accessibility issues. The following definitions are important:

- Authentication: Authentication is the process of identifying who is accessing the QlikView server and determining if they are allowed to connect. It does not include controlling what they can see or do once they have access.
- Authorization: Authorization is the process of determining what an authenticated user is permitted to access and do on the server. It presumes the user has been authenticated and the user is known to the server.

Server Authentication

Your QlikView administrator can control which users may authenticate to the server and what documents they are authorized to access. This is done, in most cases, using Windows Security, which is the default mechanism for authentication and authorization on QlikView servers. This means for any user to have access to QlikView server documents, the user must first authenticate to the Windows server on which QlikView server is installed. In most cases this is accomplished using *Active Directory* (AD). However, if a QlikView server is not in an AD domain (an AD domain combines Windows users and servers into a single security context) or resides in a different AD domain than the users, Windows authentication may still be used. In some cases our customers have setup stand-alone servers (no AD domain). When this is done we set up local Windows user accounts on the server to allow authentication to the server. AD domains are not a prerequisite to using Windows authentication, but they are common in many organizations.

Server Authorization

Authorization represents the way in which the relationship between authenticated users and QlikView documents are created and maintained. Once a user is authenticated and known to QlikView server, access to QlikView documents for the user is controlled by the server. The server determines what documents the user is authorized to access. This is done in most QlikView servers using Windows file system permissions. There is no mechanism for securing documents in a QlikView server management console unless the server is configured to use advanced DMS authentication. The normal method for determining which users can access which document files is done with file system permissions in Windows. The most common way to achieve this is to use *Windows Explorer* and right click on the folder in which a document exists or the document file itself to access its properties. From the file properties dialog, security is managed in the same way your network administrator manages security for files on a file server. QlikView server is able to determine which document files a user can access by reading the Windows security information about the document.

Securing and Sharing Load Script Connection Strings

In many cases QlikView documents are created using integrated Windows security in the load script connection strings to authenticate to databases and other data sources. This is done because the developer (you) does not think about how the document will authenticate to the underlying data sources when it is deployed to a QlikView server. This creates problems because when the document is processed on the QlikView server the user credentials will be different than when tested by the developer. The user credentials on the server are derived from the account used by the QlikView services in Windows on the server. If these accounts don't have permission to the source databases, and they likely do not, the data reload will fail when QlikView server attempts to update the document data.

To address this you can have the database administrator give the QlikView Server services account permission to the source database, but this is not always desirable. Instead, consider using a known database account and moving the connection string information out of the QlikView document. The QlikView load script can reference external files. This is done by using an *include* statement in the load script. By removing the connection string (the entire *CONNECT* statement) from the load script, you can make it unavailable to users who deploy documents to the QlikView server and standardize how documents authenticate to data sources.

To update your load script syntax so it uses an external file to read in the *CONNECT* statement you must first copy the *CONNECT* statement to a text file and then delete the line from the script. Next you add an *include* statement in the load script where the *CONNECT* statement resided. Your load script syntax should now look similar to the following:

```
$(include=filename.txt)
```

In this example the dollar sign and open parenthesis tells the load script a special command is being used. The word *include* is a special variable known to QlikView. The *filename.txt* file will be read and used as though you typed its contents into the load script manually. The text file can be stored in a secure directory to which the QlikView service account has read access, but the developers who deploy documents to the server do not. The user password is still scrambled in the connect string within the text files if it was originally.

Under this scenario, one text file containing a connect statement can service many QlikView documents, making it easier to handle credential and database location changes down the road.

This strategy should also work for QlikView data files (QVD's). Developers, who create, maintain and deploy documents to the QlikView server, can have different versions of the text file to allow them to work on the documents and authenticate to the database without knowing what credentials are used on the server. This assumes the same paths to the text file are used on the developer's workstations and the QlikView server. For this reason, consider creating a secure directory for the text files under the document folder on the server. This will make the path relative and therefore the same on both the developer's workstation and the server. Here is an example:

```
foldername/filename.txt
```

rather than

~~`D:\foldername\filename.txt`~~

In the first example above, the folder named "foldername" would not be accessible by developers, but would be accessible by the QlikView service account on the server. These rights would be set up in Windows. The second example would be wrong because the path is not relative and may not work on both the server and developer's workstations.

Sharing QlikView Documents without a QlikView Server

If no QlikView server is available, and if you have local client licenses for two or more local copies of QlikView, then you can share QlikView documents (.QVW files) on the network. You can also send these files to other licensed users for them to use locally.

How to Share Documents

There is no magic to sharing a QlikView document file (.QVW). The only real requirement is that the file is available to all users on the local area network. However, there are several things to consider when doing this. To make a QlikView document file sharable, you need two things:

1. Two or more licensed copies of QlikView installed on two or more computers.

2. A shared folder on the network (file share) in which the QlikView document (.QVW file) can be stored.

Alternately, you can send .QVW files back and forth without sharing them on the network. However, keep in mind that if the files include data, the size of the file transfer may be too big for email attachments and Web downloads depending on your IT infrastructure restrictions.

Important Considerations when Sharing Documents

As previously mentioned there are several issues with this approach that warrant careful consideration. Review the following before deciding to approach sharing this way:

1. Computer Resources: When using QlikView this way, each user opens the QlikView document in a local copy of QlikView. That means the user's computer memory and processor are responsible for managing the document and data. If the user's computer has limited available memory, the document may not open or may perform poorly. Keep in mind that even if your users have significant memory in their computers, the available memory and processing resources may be low depending on what other applications they are running.
2. File Sharing Problems: Another issue to keep in mind is that since more than one user may be accessing the same file at the same time, sharing violations may occur if a user wants to change the document structure and save the changes. We know this has happened in a number of situations.
3. Document Security: When a QlikView document file (.QVD) is shared between users with the QlikView for Windows software, each user may be able to change the document, reload the data and modify the load script. This can be controlled to some degree using file system security on the machine where the document resides. However, this issue can result in severe problems and may

degrade from the benefit you hope to enjoy from using QlikView. Don't let this situation result in poor acceptance of QlikView.

4. Data Security: Since QlikView documents materialize (store) data after each reload, it is possible for data security policies to be violated. While there are features in QlikView that can help mitigate this, the steps necessary to secure document data when documents are shared or copied may be prohibitive or, in some cases, impossible.

All of these problems are addressed with the implementation of a QlikView server. However, in some cases server implementations may be cost prohibitive or impossible for other reasons. One of the nice things about QlikView is that in spite of all of the advantages of having a QlikView server, it isn't required to get up and running. Nor is it necessary to make QlikView content sharable on a small scale. Many other BI tools fail to offer this level of flexibility and, as result, often cannot be considered. QlikView file sharing opens the door for establishing a basic implementation and scaling up as needed.

Securing QlikView Documents for Distribution

All of the elements of a QlikView document are, by default, exposed to anyone with a licensed version of QlikView for Windows. Documents that are deployed to a QlikView server can be locked down so that users cannot edit them. However, documents that are manually distributed or shared on a network file server remain vulnerable to editing by users accessing them from their workstations in most cases. There are some obvious things that can be done to prevent users from editing a document stored on a network file server. For example, the network administrator can set file security for a QlikView document to read-only. But, users will still be able see the document internals such as the load script and sheet object properties. In some cases you may want to share your QlikView document with licensed users for evaluation purposes while restricting them from accessing your work. Situations such as this are difficult to control because QlikView documents are limited in terms of security when they are not deployed to a QlikView server. Yet, there are things you can do to lock down a QlikView document when sharing it with others. These options are not comprehensive and some of your work may be exposed to users with QlikView on their workstations, but you can limit access to much of the document structure.

There are a several security features in the document properties (*Settings>Document Properties...>Security*) of your document. However, these settings can be changed (re-enabled) by other developers unless you also implement section access (see the section of this chapter covering *Securing Data*). Section access is a feature that allows you to restrict access to document features and data based on the user name. The user's name can be identified by how the user logs on to Windows, logs on to a QlikView server or answers a document prompt for a user name and password. If you do not include section access functionality in your document you can't lock down your work when it is distributed to users with full versions of QlikView. Even without using section access there are some options that lock down portions of your document for anyone who accesses it after you save and distribute it (even you, so be careful). However, if you do implement section access, the settings on the security tab of the *Document Properties* dialog offer a reasonable level of restriction to key document features. These include:

- The ability to save the document. You should note that if you uncheck this option the save icon disables. To save the document just close and confirm you want to save changes when prompted.
- The ability to access *Document Properties*, which will restrict users from overriding other security settings.
- The ability to edit the load script.
- The ability to perform a reload.
- The ability to export and print (separate options).

- Several other options pertaining to how the document may be used.

Even if you set up section access and disable all of the security options in *Document Properties*, users will still have access to some of your work. They will be able to see sheet object properties and expressions. While you can prevent them from saving changes they make, you cannot prevent them from seeing the expression editor and properties dialog.

Protecting the Load Script

You can control access to the load script in your QlikView document. This can be helpful if you want ensure other QlikView developers cannot modify the load script. There are two primary reasons for why you might want this. First, you may wish to prohibit changes to how the data is organized, associated and calculated. This is especially important if the load script performs complex linking or summarizations of data since such load script syntax can be confusing and vulnerable to the slightest change. Second, you may want to prohibit the use of your document with other data sources, or you may wish to prevent it from being reloaded. By hiding the load script syntax you can accomplish these goals. This may be important to you if you are sharing your document for evaluation purposes.

To restrict access to your document's load script you must create a hidden script. This is done in the load script editor. NOTE: Before performing any of the steps below, save a copy of your QlikView document. If you forget your password to the hidden script, portions of your QlikView document's load script will no longer be useable. You can do this by following these steps:

1. Choose *File>Create Hidden Script...* from the pull down menu item in the load script editor.
2. A dialog appears asking you to create and confirm a password. Enter and confirm a password and click OK. This will be needed to edit the hidden script in the future.

3. A new tab appears in the script editor named Hidden Script. Cut and paste your entire load script from the other tabs in your document into this tab.
4. Save your document and test it by reloading data. The script should execute the same as before.

The next time you open the document, the hidden script tab will not appear. To access it you need to use the file pull down menu (*File>Edit Hidden Script...*) at which time you will be prompted for the password. The data model is still viewable and other developers will be able to add to the script by entering statements into a visible tab. However, your syntax and logic will not be available to them.

If you combine the hidden script feature with other features such as the ability to reference external files in the load script (*include* variable), you can devise a mechanism that uses a file to control if the load script can run. Other uses of the hidden script feature might include forcing data to be limited to a predefined number of rows or data that meets certain criteria. The chapter on *Advanced Data Loading Techniques* covers several options for managing data in the load script. These techniques can be used in a hidden script.

Securing Data (Section Access)

In many cases it is necessary to ensure that certain users only see certain data. This is commonly referred to as data security, which can include both row level security (record level) and column level (field level) security. There are several ways to impose data security on a QlikView document. The most basic, and least supportable, way is to create two copies of your document with different load scripts and different sheet objects so that each document only contains the appropriate data for a given group of users. You then secure access to the document files on the network or on the QlikView server. This approach, however, creates a number of problems and is difficult, if not impossible, to maintain in most cases. Under this scenario you might find that you have dozens or even hundreds of copies of your document. Each of these would have to be updated when changes are required.

Another option involves using QlikView server functionality known as *QlikView Publisher*. QlikView Publisher is an add-on product to QlikView server. Among other things it allows QlikView document security to be processed on the server. This process is commonly referred to as "loop and reduce," because the publisher system loops through the original document and reduces the data based on rules your QlikView administrator creates. Each document copy is then made available to a select set of users. QlikView Publisher automates this process so you only have to maintain changes in the source document. However, QlikView Publisher isn't always available because it is not included with QlikView server. If your organization chooses not to purchase and implement QlikView Publisher, this option is not viable for you.

The final option for controlling data security in QlikView is implemented from within a QlikView document. It is commonly referred to as called *Section Access*. This term can be a little misleading in that Section Access is not a process, but rather a portion of the QlikView load script. QlikView manages all data in the load script. This is where data sources are accessed, data is loaded and the QlikView in-memory data model is assembled. There are fundamentally two sections to a QlikView load script. Unless both are used, there is nothing in the load script syntax to indicate the separation of these sections. One of these sections is called *Section Access*. The other is called *Section Application*. Section application is the section that is always present and it is where you place load script syntax. It isn't necessary for this section of the load script to be identified formally unless section access is also used.

Section access is an area at the beginning of the load script that allows you to create rules for how data in the load script relates to users who access your QlikView document. It must precede the other load script syntax because the statements you create in section access affect how data is made available in the document. Section access and section application are identified in the load script with simple statements ending with a semicolon. Here is an example:

```
SECTION Access;

SECTION Application;
```

The only script syntax that is typically found before the section access statement is the declaration of global variables and their settings (SET statements) that are created by default. However, section access can appear at the very beginning of the load script. All other standard syntax follows the section application statement, which follows the section access statement. Between these two statements lies syntax (not yet created in the example above) that defines data security for the document.

The most important thing to understand when creating section access syntax is that it is very similar to other statements used in the load script. The key difference is that section access knows to relate user names to the users who access your document automatically. In essence, section access is nothing more than a mapping of user names to values found elsewhere in the load script. Section access is able to identify users by how each user authenticates to a QlikView server. If your document is not deployed to a QlikView server or if the user information provided by the server's authentication process doesn't match the credentials found in the document, the user will be prompted for a document level user name and password. Section access can also be configured to identify the user by the Windows user name. This allows you to deploy the document any way you like and know that data and other elements of the document will require either appropriate Windows credentials or a valid user name and password combination. The method used by your document is determined by you when you create syntax in section access.

Securing Row Data with Section Access

Section access uses an entitlement table to control access. The entitlement table is created in the load script and adheres to a specific set of rules. When this table exists within the section access portion of the load script, QlikView uses it to compare the user's credentials to the data in the table and applies security accordingly. Most examples of section access that you will find in *QlikCommunity* and other resources assume you are creating an in-line table for use in section access. This can be confusing because it leads developers to believe that an in-line table is required for use with section access. It is not. The entitlement table you create in section access can be sourced from any supported data source. For example, you can create an entitlement table in Excel or MS-SQL Server that fulfills the requirements for section access. However, there are some requirements for how the table is structured and how the fields are named. If you don't adhere to these requirements, sections access won't work.

The rules below must be followed exactly to create a section access entitlement table:

1. Field Names: The fields for the entitlement table must include the following at a minimum. There are other features and fields that may be used for various scenarios, but these are the basic requirements to get started with section access:
    a. *ACCESS*
    b. *USERID or NTNAME*
    c. *PASSWORD (if not using NTNAME)*
    d. The table must include a field name that matches a field in your data model. This field controls row level access for the user. It must be in UPPERCASE and the corresponding field in the data model must be in UPPERCASE.
2. All filed names in the entitlement table must be in UPPERCASE.

3. All data values in the entitlement table and all corresponding values in the data model table must be in UPPERCASE. This does not include user names or passwords. It is directed at the field used to match values to the data model. This can be a problem since the data model values may not be in uppercase. You can use the *UPPER* function to force them to uppercase, but you may not want them displayed that way in the document. See the section in this chapter covering *Creating a Summary Entitlement Table* for help on how to get around this problem.
4. When using NTNAME as the user name, the values in the table must include the fully qualified user Windows user name. For example:

   ```
   mymachinename\username
   ```

   OR

   ```
   mywindowsdomain\username
   ```

5. Document Properties: You must set document properties as follows in order for section access to work. Open *Document Properties* from the file pull down menu and review and set the following document properties. Shown with the tab they are on:
   a. *Opening* tab: Check the *Initial Data Reduction Based on Section Access* check box. This allows the section access syntax to be recognized and used during data reloads.
   b. *Opening* tab: Check the *Strict Exclusion* check box. This forces the restriction of all data if no match is found in the entitlement table. If it is not checked all data will be shown when a match isn't found.
   c. *Opening* tab: Check the *Prohibit Binary Load* checkbox. This prevents the user from being able to load data from another QlikView document. It's generally a good idea to prevent this.

d. *Server* tab: Check the *Filter AccessPoint Document List Based on Section Access* check box. This prevents the document from being displayed in the AccessPoint server portal if the user is not allowed to access it.

When using section access the document is in one of two security modes. The first is *ADMIN* mode and the second is *USER* mode. These modes are controlled by the *ACCESS* field in the entitlement table. When in *ADMIN* mode, the user has access to all features of the document (depending on security settings in document properties) and may still be restricted to certain rows of data. However, *ADMIN* mode users may be able to edit the load script and therefore may be able to override row level security. It is important to have at least one user set up in *ADMIN* mode, especially if your entitlement table is an in-line table, because otherwise you may not be able to access and maintain the document. *USER* mode users may have a variety of document features restricted and typically have row-level security values that limit their data. Most of the users in your entitlement table will likely be setup in *USER* mode.

The following example shows an in-line table being used as an entitlement table for section access. In this case, all field values are hard coded in to the load script.

```
Section Access;

LOAD * INLINE [
ACCESS, USERID, PASSWORD, CITY
ADMIN, ADMIN, Passw0rd,
USER, user1, Passw0rd, ATLANTA
USER, user2, Passw0rd, NEW YORK CITY
];

Section Application;
```

In the example above, the script syntax that appears after the section access statement represents how the entitlement table is created and what it contains. The section application statement determines where section access ends and where the normal load script syntax begins. In this example, the first three fields (ACCESS, USERID and PASSWORD) are special fields used by section access and must appear as shown in uppercase names. The fourth field is a field name found in the data model (from the customer table). The table for this field is loaded in the section application part of the script. This field is what allows section access to filter data for specific users. This field name and its values must be in uppercase. The corresponding values in the customer table found in the section application part of the load script must also be in upper case. The following shows how the customer table is loaded to ensure that the city values and field name are in upper case:

```
Section Application;

OLEDB CONNECT TO [...

customer:
LOAD upper(city) as CITY,
SQL SELECT city,
FROM customer;
```

The section access entitlement table does not need to be an in-line table. It can be loaded from an Excel file, flat file, or database. The same load and SQL SELECT syntax common to other parts of the QlikView load script may be used. The only requirement is that the table format (field names, structure and data) follow the rules for section access functionality. The following is an example of the same entitlement table being loaded from an Excel file.

```
Section Access;

LOAD ACCESS,
     USER,
     PASSWORD,
     CITY
FROM
[entitlement.xlsx]
(ooxml, embedded labels, table is Sheet1);
```

Note that in this example the field names are in uppercase and the Excel file is located in the same folder as the QlikView document (relative pathing). The Excel data on the first worksheet looks like the following:

ACCESS	USER	PASSWORD	CITY
ADMIN	admin	Passw0rd	
USER	user1	Passw0rd	ATLANTA

Securing Data based on Multiple Values

Most examples that we've found for how to set up section access are based on the assumption that a given user should be restricted to data for a single value match. For example, *user1* should only be able to see data for Atlanta. However, in our experience this is rarely the case. Most organizations need to allow specific users to see data based on multiple value matches. For example, *user1* should be able to see data for Atlanta and New York City. You address this in the section access entitlement table by including multiple rows of data for the same user. While not ideal from a data maintenance perspective, this approach works well and is not difficult to implement. The following is an example of an in-line table with multiple values for a user.

```
Section Access;

LOAD * INLINE [
ACCESS, USERID, PASSWORD, CITY
ADMIN, ADMIN, Passw0rd,
USER, user1, Passw0rd, ATLANTA
USER, user1, Passw0rd, NEW YORK CITY
USER, user2, Passw0rd, COLUMBUS
];
```

In the example above, *user1* is granted access to data for both Atlanta and New York City. The second user, *user2*, only has access to Columbus data.

Creating a Summary Entitlement Table

Section access offers an important capability. However, due to the formality and rules upon which it is based, section access can also result in an undesirable effect on your document. The most significant issue is the result of the requirement for uppercase fields names and field values. Because section access must associate with data in the regular data model, the requirement for both field names and data to be in uppercase has a direct effect on how data looks and works inside of the document. For example, if you use city names to restrict access, all city names must be in uppercase (all characters). This is a problem, since users will likely not want to see all city names, or any value for that matter, in uppercase. Yet, if you don't force this, then section access fails and you won't have any data security in your document.

To address this situation you can create a second entitlement table that performs the translation of field names and values to uppercase without affecting how the normal tables look and work inside of the document. Our team refers to this second table as an entitlement summary table. It can be created in the section access portion of the load script, which means it won't appear as part of the regular data model. This table must load all of the values used to filter data for users in the primary entitlement table used by section access. For example, if you use the city field from a table named customer, the entitlement summary table would load all city values from the customer data source. It would also include a second field that forced the city values to uppercase. The second field must have an uppercase name. It is used in the primary entitlement table. Below is an example of the syntax for both primary and summary entitlement tables:

```
Section Access;

LOAD * INLINE [
ACCESS, USERID, PASSWORD, ECITY
ADMIN, ADMIN, Passw0rd,
USER, user1, Passw0rd, ATLANTA
USER, user2, Passw0rd, NEW YORK CITY
];

OLEDB CONNECT TO [Provider= …

LOAD upper(city) as ECITY,
    city;
SQL SELECT city
```

```
FROM CRMSample.dbo.customer;
Section Application;
...
```

In this example, the first table (the primary entitlement table) is an in-line table. Notice that all field names are in upper case and the values for the ACCESS and ECITY fields are in uppercase as required. The ECITY field is the field used to associate the entitlement table to the summary entitlement table (the next table in the script). The field name could have been "CITY" since associations between tables are case sensitive, but naming it "ECITY" makes it a little clearer that it is used only for entitlement value matching. The second table (the summary entitlement table) requires a CONNECT statement because it retrieves data from the underlying database. Since the customer table hasn't been loaded yet, a RESIDENT load is not possible. This adds overhead to the reload process and uses more memory, but may be worth the cost in many cases.

Securing Fields with Section Access

Data security involves restricting access to rows and columns of data. In some cases you may need to allow all rows (records) of data to be shared with a user, but you may need to restrict one or more columns (fields). For example, certain users might be prohibited from seeing salary amounts, but can access all other employee data. Section access facilitates the need to restrict field access to certain users by using the same entitlement table that restricts row level access. However, if field restrictions are needed then an addition field must be added to the entitlement table. This additional field is named *OMIT*. For each row in the entitlement table, the *OMIT* column (field) must have the name of the field to be restricted. Unlike the field used in the entitlement table to enforce row restrictions, the *OMIT* field values may be in lower case. The following is an example:

```
Section Access;

LOAD * INLINE [
ACCESS, USERID, PASSWORD, OMIT, CITY
```

```
ADMIN, ADMIN, Passw0rd,
USER, user1, Passw0rd, , ATLANTA
USER, user2, Passw0rd, quantity, *
];
```

In this example, *user1* has a row restriction that limits the data to include only rows for the city Atlanta. But, *user1* can access all fields. This means that if *user1* wanted to create an expression for a chart using the quantity field, she could. However, *user2* could not. The restriction for *user2* is for the field named quantity. Notice it is in lower case. The field name in the data model is also in lowercase. Since that field name appears in the OMIT column of the entitlement table, *user2* is not able to see or use it. However, *user2* has access to all rows, as indicated by the wildcard (*) in the CITY column.

NOTE that the wildcard (*) in section access behaves differently than you might expect. If a user is assigned a wildcard value (*) in a section access field, it means that user has access to all values for that field that exists in the section access table, but not necessarily all data values that may exist otherwise. For example, if the section access field is region, but only 4 distinct regions are listed in the section access table, a user with a wildcard assigned (*) only has access to those 4 regions, not all possible regions.

Securing Section Access Syntax

It may be desirable to secure the section access portion of your load script even if you choose not to secure the entire load script. This is easily done by using the *Hidden Script* tab in the load script editor. Click on the *File* pull down menu and select the *Hidden Script...* item. This is covered in more detail earlier in this chapter as a means for securing the entire load script. However, copying just the section access portion into the hidden script is a common approach.

Section Access Considerations

Using section access can be difficult if you are not aware of some idiosyncrasies which may cause your document to behave in unexpected ways. You should know that section access works well. It is commonly used in many environments. However, when setting it up and testing it, you can easily become confused and begin to question how it works. The following key points are very important to consider:

1. Always backup (make a copy) of your document (.QVW file) before adding section access syntax. It is possible to lock yourself out of your own document and there's no way to recover from such a mistake.
2. When testing section access, you must reload the data, save the document and close QlikView for Windows. Then reopen it. Closing the document (leaving QlikView running) and reopening it will not invoke changes you made to section access in every case. If you do not see the anticipated behavior, you likely have not reloaded the data, saved the document or closed and reopened QlikView. Make this a habit when testing your section access syntax.

If you have an error in your section access syntax, no security is enforced. Testing section access is critical because if it fails then your security will be breached. Do not confuse this with getting the entitlements wrong. In other words, if your section access entitlement table maps a user to the wrong data, section access will still work properly even though your users may have access to data they should not (or *vice versa*). Improper values relating users to data are not considered errors in the section access syntax. In such cases section access may be working fine, you just have the wrong data (values). If your section access syntax is wrong, for example if you have the wrong field names, field case or table format, the section access as a whole fails. This means all data will be displayed to all users of the document. When a syntax error occurs in section access it is not reported during a data reload. You will not know unless you review the data and features based on the rules you set up.

Chapter 10: Best Practices

Establishing a working set of standards and applying best practices, especially early in the development cycle, can significantly speed up development, optimize processing, and ultimately result in a better user experience. While certain standards may differ from one environment and user community to the next, there is a basic set of best practices that will enable you to achieve better results when they are applied on a consistent basis to your QlikView development effort. Failing to consider these, and similar practices, has often led to dissatisfaction with the resulting QlikView content for some organizations. The dissatisfaction often is the result of either poorly performing data loads, poorly performing QlikView documents or documents that are difficult to update. In at least one situation, we found that a complex QlikView document was created that would not function on a QlikView server, making it impossible to deploy and share. The following recommendations, while not the only things you might consider, will help to mitigate these problems and ensure that your QlikView content, users and platform work well.

A QlikView document can be divided into two parts: The load script, which directly affects the amount of memory needed as well as the efficiency of the loading process and data associations, and the user interface. The user interface obviously determines how well the user can interact with and understand the data, but its design also affects how easy it will be to maintain key aspects of the QlikView document after it has been created. In the following sections of this chapter, you will be presented with practices that pertain to each of these two document components. By establishing a set of guidelines for each, it will become clear how to best approach QlikView document development. Other important considerations include a review of general settings that affect both parts of the document as well as specific standards to use when designing for mobile devices.

Load Script Best Practices

The size and performance of a QlikView document is fundamentally dependent on the number of rows and columns it loads into memory. The in-memory associative data model for a document affects not only the amount of memory used by the document, but also how the user interface performs when executing such operations as selecting, summing and counting (expressions processing). It should not come as any surprise that limiting the data set to only the rows needed, along with removing any references to columns in the load script that are not used in the user interface, is the best way to improve the overall performance of a QlikView document. However, there are many other best practices that you should consider when creating your QlikView load script:

- **Organize your load script**: Organizing your script has no effect on performance, but it may reduce the effort and time needed to make changes to the script. It will also make the script easier to navigate and understand which is helpful if more than one person is responsible for maintaining the document. To better organize your load script you can create tabs, which divide the script syntax into separate areas. The script still executes sequentially beginning with the first line of the first tab, but it will be easier to find specific segments of the script. A few ideas worth considering include: Creating a different tab for each of the following; each data source, each dimension, a master calendar or other calendar, a breakdown of large data sources where there are many columns and/or complex multiline preload syntax, other logically divisible representations of data sources and script concepts. Ideally, you will develop a standard for how our organization commonly organizes load scripts through the use of tabs to assist other people designing and maintaining QlikView in your organization and to ensure consistency.

- **Comment your load script**: Commenting the load script syntax in your QlikView document is important for a variety of reasons and is easily done. It involves nothing more than beginning a line or part of a line with two forward slashes. A primary reason for using comments is to break the syntax of your load script into manageable segments that have descriptions about them. This makes it easier to find where in the script something might need to be changed. For example, you might have a number of lines of script code for a master calendar which creates and drops tables. At some point, one or more fields in the calendar table will have to be associated with a field from the rest of your data model. If you wish to reuse this calendar scripting or change its association, it would helpful to highlight the part of the syntax where the field name that associates the calendar table to the rest of the data model exists. Another use of comments pertains to keeping track of the load script processing flow when multiple passes are made at the same data, which can be a daunting task. Unless clear commenting is used to enumerate and explain each step as it is occurring, it may be very difficult to update the load script later. This is because tables can be loaded into memory, referenced later in the script and loaded into other tables (resident loads), joined into other tables, or ultimately dropped. While this data management capability is one of the things that makes QlikView so versatile, without appropriate notation such syntax in the load script can be confusing and hard to support. By adding comments that explain what is being done and why, the QlikView document is more supportable and your ability to leverage the effort to solve certain data problems will be easier to reuse in other documents.
- **Keep your document lean**: It's obvious to more seasoned QlikView developers that removing unnecessary rows and

columns of data from the document helps improve both load time and runtime performance of the document. The best way to decide if a row or column of data is necessary is to identify its use in the user interface. This is especially true with columns of data (fields). If there are fields that are not exposed in screen objects and are not needed for collaboration on the QlikView server, remove them. Additionally, if there is data that users don't need to see or aggregate (rows), then exclude them where possible. For example, it is not unusual to see a QlikView document load ten or twenty years of data when users only analyze the current and previous year. Even if such a document works fine on the server, the unnecessary memory use may be restricting how many other documents can be loaded and used at the same time. Over time such problems become significant issues, so it is a best practice to optimize from the start. Because QlikView makes it so easy to update document design, you can add columns and rows as your users discover needs for them. It is a good idea to remember that when analyzing data everything is equivalent to nothing.

- **Name tables and columns consistently**: Establish standards within your development community for naming fields and tables created in your script. You need to make some careful considerations here, as your decisions made for this set of standards will affect your standards for design of the user interface. For example, if you decide to reference all of the columns in lowercase and use underscores (_) for spaces, you may find yourself generating labels for those same fields in the user interface in order to make them more business friendly and visually appealing. On the other hand, if you opt to alias every column so that it appears exactly as you would like it to look in the user interface you may spend considerably more time working in your load script. We are inclined to opt for the second choice, since it minimizes the possibility that misleading labels will be applied in the user interface. If you alias your column names and wish to use multiword names, you will need to place the names inside of square brackets or double quotes, which is a little extra work. However, by aliasing the names of columns and using business friendly aliases such as [Order Date] or [Order Number], users who participate in online collaboration will have a better experience. Likewise, some sheet objects do not allow you to provide a label for fields, such as the *Current Selections* sheet object. This is yet another reason to alias your fields in the load script.

User Interface Design Best Practices

The best way to get the most out of your investment in QlikView is to do what is necessary to encourage users to access and interact with your QlikView documents. Providing your users with a simple yet elegant, responsive and attractive user interface is critical to engaging users. Consider the following when creating user interfaces in QlikView:

- **Use a consistent color scheme**: This best practice is easy to apply if your organization has official colors for their logo or standard corporate colors used in collateral materials. However, there are certain colors and color combinations that you want to avoid in most circumstances. First, try to stay away from dark colors if possible, as they do not draw the eye as effectively as brighter colors and can make your QlikView document appear overly formal. However, bold colors should not necessarily represent your standard palate; since more muted tones require less work for the brain to interpret and can significantly reduce eye fatigue. Secondly, be careful with the use of red and green. These two colors are ineffective for users who are color-blind. They also tend to have a connotation of bad and good, which can be misleading if such indication is not intended. Reserve the use of these colors for indicating a positive or negative quality in a measure's value. Once you have developed a palette of colors, make sure that it is shared with other QlikView designers in the organization. Maintaining consistency across documents can be tricky, but it has a desirable impact on the user community and improves the effectiveness of your QlikView documents.

- **Place your objects consistently across sheets**: There are some elements that you may wish to appear on all sheets within a document. Some of these may include navigation arrows, calendar or date objects, current selection boxes, and list boxes. Make sure that these are located in the exact same position across all sheets. It can be distracting when navigating from sheet to sheet if the same element is even slightly offset from the previous sheet. This is easily done by copying a "master" sheet once you have all of those elements in place, or even copying each individual sheet object and pasting it as needed. QlikView 10 provides the ability to use linked objects to more easily maintain consistency across sheet objects, which is something worth exploring. It is worth noting that common Windows key combinations such as *Ctrl+C* for "copy" and *Ctrl+V* for "paste" will work with any QlikView sheet object. When you copy and then paste an object onto a new tab sheet, the location and size properties remain the same. Additionally, you can set these properties manually by accessing the caption tab of the properties dialog.
- **Design for a standard resolution**: The rule of thumb when designing QlikView documents that will be deployed to the web is to aim for a resolution of 1024x768. While there is no screen resolution that will please everyone, this is a good option for most monitors in use today. However, ideally you will size your document so that is uses slightly less than the desired resolution (especially vertically). This helps to account for browser toolbars and padding when the document is deployed to a QlikView server for delivery to Web clients. QlikView offers the

ability to resize your canvas so that it appears at a predetermined resolution, making it easier to design a document with screen resolution in mind. Simply navigate to the menu bar and select *View > Resize > 1024x768*.

- **Facilitate the analytical process with layout**: You can help guide your users through their analytical processes by maintaining a logical flow in the layout of your QlikView document. This is done by determining the best location for where sheet objects appear on a sheet. The typical approach to analysis tends to be "top-down." In other words, users start with high-level summarized information such as a grand total or total for a dimension that indicates a problem by showing a comparison or performance indicator. The indicator prompts users to investigate at a lower level of detail and the layout of the tab sheet objects provide well placed and sized objects such as charts or list boxes as appropriate at convenient locations to facilitate the next level of analysis and exploration. Keep the most important information toward the top half of the tab sheet. The upper left-hand quadrant tends to be where most western European and North American users like to begin their review. The flow then should be from left-to-right and then top-to-bottom. Understanding this helps to ensure that your QlikView document is easy to understand and use. Another consideration is to consolidate most, but not necessarily all, of the selection objects such as list boxes and current selections boxes along the left side from top-to-bottom, and place the content items such as charts and tables on the right. This approach mimics what many users experience in common software applications such as Microsoft Outlook or in popular Web sites such as Facebook. Also, keep in mind that when using multiple tab sheets the ideal scenario is usually to make the first tab sheets contain the most common and highest level analysis. If possible avoid having multiple tab rows, which can overwhelm users. Keep in mind that by using buttons and variables, both of which work well in server deployments, you can hide and show tab sheets and sheet objects on a given tab sheet. This approach can reduce the number of tabs needed and simplify the user interface.

- **Provide a button to navigate back to AccessPoint**: If you are designing QlikView documents to be deployed to a QlikView server chances are that users will access it via the QlikView AccessPoint Web portal and they will use a Web client. It can be confusing to users when they access a document from AccessPoint because when the document is presented there is nothing in the browser content frame that indicates how to navigate back to the main screen of AccessPoint. Due to the preponderance of web applications on the internet and the various ways in which they function, users have become wary of using the browser's back arrow to return to the previous Web page. When viewing a QlikView document in the Web client, the browser's back arrow returns the user to the main view of AccessPoint. To mitigate any confusion, we recommend placing a button with an action associated with the URL of AccessPoint on the first tab sheet (or elsewhere as appropriate) in order to make it clear to users how to exit the document and return to AccessPoint.
- **Optimize your expressions:** Expressions are very common in QlikView documents and can add significant overhead to how the document performs. In some cases complex expressions can cause simple user actions such as navigation from one tab sheet to another to take minutes to complete. While these problems are rare and tend to only happen when there is a large amount of data in memory and where the load script is not well engineered, you should try to design all QlikView documents in a way that optimizes end user performance. To address this, wherever possible you want to create expressions in the load script. The benefits of doing so are two-fold: You reduce the need for designers to interpret business logic into logical expressions across the UI, and it increases

performance since the expressions have already been calculated and the results can simply be displayed within the UI. In cases where expressions must be written within the user interface try not to combine fields from multiple tables into a single expression. When a single expression references columns from multiple tables, logical "hops" are required to make associations during the calculation of those values. These hops take time and tax the processor because they require many rows of data across multiple tables to be scanned. When there is limited data, that is - a small number of rows per table, this isn't a problem. But, when the data volume grows it becomes a significant issue. To address this, when loading data in the document's load script use join syntax to combine those fields into a single table or follow the recommended approach of structuring your in-memory data model as a "star schema." There is more on this below and in the chapter covering *Advanced Data Loading Techniques*.

Data Model Best Practices

Loading your data into your QlikView document and UI layout are two areas where standards can and should be applied. However, the specifics of how you structure the in-memory data in the QlikView data model are absolutely critical. The structure of your data model influences how well QlikView can compress the data in memory and as a result directly affects how much memory the document consumes and how well it performs. The following practices will help you optimize your data model design.

- **Reduce uniqueness in your data**: QlikView compresses in-memory data by eliminating redundancy. For example, if you have customer order data that contains the city where the order was shipped, QlikView stores each city name only once rather than repeating it for each order. By doing this the amount of memory needed to load a QlikView document is much lower than you might expect. The more unique each value in a column is, the less effective the compression algorithms built into QlikView become at optimizing your data for analysis. The quintessential example is with columns that contain date-timestamps. If you store dates at the second or millisecond level, chances are every record will be unique making it impossible for QlikView to optimize the column of data. However, if there is no need to analyze data at the second, minute or even hour level, then removing the timestamp reduces the uniqueness of your data substantially. Another alternative is to parse out the date components in the load script and re-assemble them if needed using expressions. This is done by deriving year, month and day columns from a date-time field rather than allowing the date-time field to exist in your data model.

- **Avoid synthetic keys and tables**: Synthetic tables and keys are created automatically when multiple column names are identical between two or more tables. While some people will argue that synthetic keys are not necessarily bad, we contest this for several reasons. First, they are confusing and unintentional, which means that chances are the person who created the QlikView document doesn't understand why they exist or how to better engineer the data model. Second, it is very important to understand that the automatic creation of synthetic tables consumes processing power unnecessarily. As data volumes grow, this unnecessary overhead not only affects the time it takes to load the data, but also the performance of the user interface. To avoid synthetic keys you must ensure that that there is only one key field in common between any two tables. There are several different methods you can use to solve synthetic key/synthetic table problems. This information is covered in more detail in the chapter on *Advanced Data Loading Techniques*.
- **Try to maintain a star-schema data model:** Star-schema data models are the most efficient way to ensure minimal use of memory and good performance within a QlikView

document. By creating a QlikView data model with a single, centralized "fact table" surrounded by dimension tables, you ensure that for each fact (numeric value used in expressions) you are storing associated dimensional data only one time. This allows for greater compression within the QlikView document. Star-schema data models also optimize performance from a user's perspective. When a user selects a value in a list box, QlikView finds all related (associated) data through the associations in the data model. Each time QlikView traverses a table in the data model, it is considered a "hop." The fewer hops that have to be made across the data model, the better the performance. This process occurs every time a user makes a selection and corresponding expressions must be calculated. This does not mean that a single flat table would be better than a star-schema. A flat table with all of the data may be fewer hops, but will substantially increase the amount of memory needed for the document. The compression algorithms are more effective when the dimensions are separated from each other and from the fact table. As a result, the star schema model is the best overall option because it minimizes hops while reducing uniqueness in the data, allowing QlikView to minimize the document's memory footprint.

- **Check your data's statistics:** If you have been using QlikView, even for a short period of time, you have likely come to appreciate the concept of "data discovery." Working with QlikView typically results in a new and more complete understanding of your data. It allows you to see both the good and bad attributes of your data clearly since all data is available in memory at the same time.
- The *Table Viewer* provides several features which help in identifying potential problems that commonly arise in data. You can open the *Table Viewer* by either pressing *Ctrl+T* or selecting it from the *File* menu. It is also on the toolbar in the script editor. When using the *Table Viewer* you can hover the mouse pointer over a key field in a table

(the field that forms the association to another table) and see a small informational box with statistics about that field. The two most important statistics are *Information Density* and *Subset Ratio*.

- *Information Density*, a percentage, describes the percent of the rows in the column that have data. An *Information Density* of 100% means that all rows contain data for that field, while an *Information Density* of 50% indicates that only half of the rows contain values in the field. Key fields should always have an *Information Density* of 100%. If they don't, the document will likely show erroneous results.
- The *Subset Ratio* value indicates the percentage of all unique values in the entire data model that are represented by the selected field in this table. For example, if you have a key field named *product_id* in both the *product* and *order* tables, and the *Subset Ratio* for the *product_id* in the product table is less than 100%, you have orphaned records in your data model. In other words, there are product records with no association to orders. You know this because there are *product_id* values somewhere in your data model that are not represented by the values in your product table.
- **Use a master calendar:** Master calendars are segments of code found in the load script that manage calendar ranges and make it easier to produce user interface components that help with selecting dates. Additionally, a master calendar allows you to control which dates exist in the data. Using a master calendar to generate dates for your data model allows you to accomplish two major objectives: Frist, it reduces uniqueness across dates in your data model, which lowers the memory footprint. Second, it allows you to fill in holes in your calendar data created by missing dates. That is, dates for which there are no records in the data. For example: if no orders were placed on 2/11/2009, that date will not appear in your

data. This creates a hole in your calendar if you base it on the *order_date* field. When presenting the user with a calendar selector (i.e., a year-month list box or combination of list boxes for year, month and day) 2/11/2009 would not appear. This can be confusing to the user and make the document seem incorrect even though it doesn't cause a problem in most situations. By creating a master calendar this issue can be addressed and you can further optimize memory use.

FIGURE 10-1 DATA MODEL FEATURES: DATA DENSITY

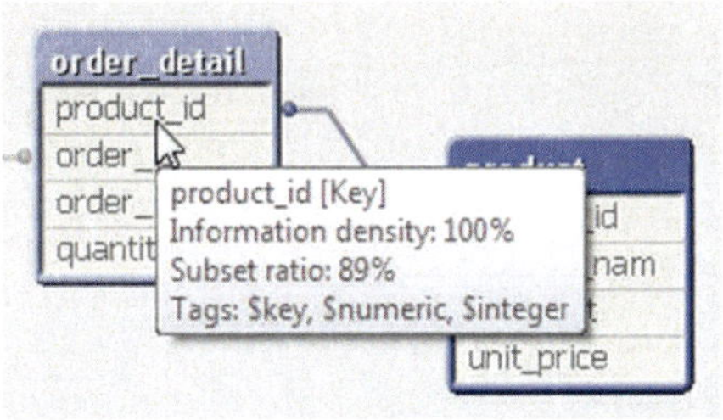

General Settings

There are some settings that override the load script and user interface defaults. Other settings provide you with more options for managing your QlikView development environment. These settings can be found on the menu bar under *Settings* and several of them are worth some review.

User Preferences

The settings under *User Preferences* apply to your specific installation of QlikView for Windows. They affect any documents you build with it. The following user preferences are helpful and important. You should review them and consider changes to the default settings.

- **[General Tab] Keep Progress Open after Reload:** If you check the box next to this setting, the window that appears after you click the *Reload* button (when loading data) will remain open after the data has finished loading into memory. This can be helpful in determining how circular references or synthetic keys are being created. It also provides information about how the data is loading and how long the data load has taken to process. The default is to close the dialog after the reload is complete. This can be disconcerting if you have a small amount of data, because the dialog will seem to blink and disappear.

- **[Save Tab] Save before Reload:** We recommend that you check this checkbox. It preserves any changes you made to the load script prior to reloading data by saving the QlikView document (QVW) back to disk. In the event that you made significant changes and encounter a problem during data loading, your document may close; causing you to lose the time and effort that went into your last set of modifications to the document.

Document Properties

The settings under *Document Properties* apply only to the current document you have open. Each QlikView document can have different settings. There are several document properties worth reviewing. They include:

- **[General Tab] Generate Logfile:** This property is particularly useful if you need to contact support for help with a problem regarding a given QlikView document. It is worth noting that QlikView support is only offered to customers who purchase ongoing maintenance and support agreements. Such support is also limited to issues with the software and does not cover questions or problems concerning the document design (development) or load script. However, this logging feature also helps when engaging a QlikView consultant and can reduce the time and cost of solving development problems. Checking this box generates a log file in the same file location as your QlikView document with information about how the data is loaded into the document.

- **[Tables Tab]:** While not specifically a setting, you should review this tab to look at the number of unique values you are loading for each field versus how many total values there are in memory for that field. This can indicate ways to optimize the in-memory data structure (data model).
- **[Number Tab]:** This tab allows you to set the default formatting for all of the fields in the document. It eliminates the need to independently set number formatting on each object you create in the user interface. For example, if you have an *order_amount* field that you would like formatted as "money," setting it here ensures that every time the field is used in a chart or table it is formatted accordingly.

Designing for Mobile Best Practices

One of the advantages that QlikView has over many other Business Intelligence tools is that it allows you to create content once and deploy that same content to several different types of clients (users). Consumption of a QlikView document can be done using the QlikView for Windows local client, a web browser based viewer known as the zero footprint AJAX client, or a mobile device such as a smart phone or tablet. Accessing and using a QlikView document from each of these clients can be done without the need to alter the document's design for use on each device. However, there are some guidelines you should consider if the same document will be deployed to mobile devices as well as desktop web browsers.

iPad

There are two main areas of consideration for a QlikView document consumed on an iPad vs. a QlikView document consumed via a standard web browser. They are screen real estate and interaction. Screen real estate represents the amount of screen space available on different devices. Obviously, a tablet such as an iPad has less horizontal and vertical space than a computer monitor. A smartphone such as an iPhone or Droid phone have even less space. This challenge is compounded by the respective screen resolution of various devices. Interaction, that is the way in which the user interacts with the QlikView document, is also an area of concern. Computers offer input devices not found on tablets and phones. The primary example of this is the mouse, which is more than a pointing device. Mice provide users with hovering, double clicking, right clicking, click and drag and wheel scrolling.

- **Resolution:** Generally speaking, you should aim for a screen resolution of 980x590 when designing a QlikView document to be used on an iPad (first generation) or similar tablet. This is slightly less than the standard mentioned above for web browsers, but will work well on both. Keep in mind that if your document has so many tabs that additional tab rows are needed, your document will start to scroll off the bottom of the screen, in which case you should reduce the vertical size even more.
- **Use Container Objects:** Container objects are new to QlikView v10 and allow for many chart and table objects to occupy the same real estate on the screen. In prior versions, you can achieve similar results by utilizing the "Auto Minimize" feature located on the Layout tab of each object's Properties. Another option is to use variables to show and hide objects via buttons. All of these approaches are viable options for ensuring that you get the most out of screen real estate for each device.
- **Fonts:** Not all fonts are supported in the iPad Safari web browser (or any other web browser on the iPad and similar tablets). Stick to standard fonts such as Arial, and avoid reducing the font size below 11 point.
- **Use Buttons:** Because your mobile users interact with the document using their fingers rather than a mouse on an iPad, you want to provide *Buttons* that have *Actions* associated with them for common tasks. Using buttons for tasks such as navigation and applying filters based bookmarks makes your QlikView document much easier

to use on mobile devices and work just as well in other QlikView clients. This can also eliminate the need for the tabrow altogether, which provides more screen real estate with which to work.

- **Avoid Multi Boxes:** While this may seem counter-intuitive since *Multi Boxes* generally save real estate, interacting with them using your finger can be challenging. Instead, make sure that you only use *List Boxes* when user selection is needed. You can also use *Search* objects to duplicate some of the functionality found in Multi Boxes.

There are many other things that may, given your situation, be advisable. We strongly encourage you to keep an eye on QlikCommunity and consider joining the QlikView social media groups such as the one found on LinkedIn. New documentation and ideas are frequently made available.

Appendix A: Formatting Tips, Keyboard Shortcuts and Command Line Options

Using Formatting Attributes on Dimensions and Expressions

Formatting attributes, which are sometimes referred to as "formatting tags," are used to override the document default or user property settings for a dimension or expression in a chart. In some cases these attributes are the only option for controlling the look and feel of certain chart characteristics, so they are important for making your QlikView document look the way you want. Using them expands what you can do with QlikView charts and provides conditional formatting capability for special chart features. These options are also very useful when creating charts and tables specifically for reporting use, but are applicable to any chart type.

You access the formatting attributes by drilling down on the dimension or expression names in the object properties dialog. For dimensions, you click on the plus sign next to the dimension name in the *Used Dimensions* listing and various attribute categories appear under the dimension name. You can right click on these attributes and create an expression to control the associated attribute's formatting characteristics. Figure A-1 illustrates the formatting attributes for a dimension in a bar chart.

Figure A-1: Access Formatting Attributes for Chart Dimension

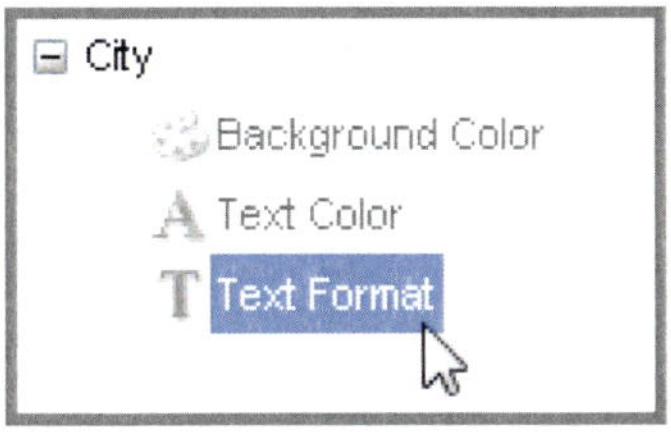

You can follow the same process for chart expressions on the *Expressions* tab of the chart's properties dialog.

The expressions you create to control these formatting attributes must, in some cases, include special tag syntax that is dissimilar to common expression syntax. For this reason we have included a variety of examples for each of the tags. Each example appears on one line; if you see two lines of examples there are two separate examples. It is important to note that, in some versions of QlikView, if you create expressions to set formatting attributes, you may not be able to clear them later by simply deleting the expression syntax. This appears to have been addressed in service releases for version 10 and later, but your version of QlikView may have this problem. If your version has this problem QlikView leaves remnants of the original tag expression associated with the attribute. You can get around this problem if you *right-click* on the tag attribute and select *Clear Expression* from the popup menu.

There are a variety of formatting attributes that appear for dimensions and expressions in chart objects. Chart Expressions include formatting attributes not available for dimensions because chart expressions affect how values are illustrated in a chart. For example, a *pie* chart might be better formatted with the pie slices separated. For this reason a *Pie Popout* attribute appears for chart expressions. In a line chart it might be helpful to adjust the thickness or style of the line so a *Line Style* attribute is available. It is important to note that even though such attributes are not relevant for a *bar* chart they still appear in the list. When you expand a dimension or expression in a chart, the formatting attributes appear as though they are grayed out or unavailable. This grayed out appearance occurs as a default for attributes because they don't have expressions created to activate them. Once you create a formatting expression for a given attribute it appears in color to indicate the attribute is in use.

Edit a formatting attribute can be done by double clicking on it, or by right clicking and selecting *Edit Expression* from the popup menu. Other right click options include a *Clear Expression* option, which deletes any expression syntax created for the attribute, and a *Copy* attribute, which copies the expression syntax to the Windows clipboard.

Text Color

Use one of the chart color functions to set the color. Examples of text color formatting expressions:

```
=RGB(200,200,200)

=blue()

=syscolor(COLOR_MENU)
```

Possible color functions include a variety of predetermined RGB values for basic colors and system colors. Here is a short list:

black()	darkgray()
lightgray()	white()
blue()	lightblue()
green()	lightgreen()
cyan()	lightcyan()
red()	lightred()
magenta()	lightmagenta()
brown()	yellow()
qliktechblue()	qliktechgray()

The *syscolor(value)* function allows use of predefined system colors where *"**value**"* corresponds to the parameter in the Windows API function *GetSysColor(value)*. This means you can use commonly known Windows values when formatting color attributes. Some of the common values are shown below. These names represent numeric values.

COLOR_SCROLLBAR	COLOR_BACKGROUND
COLOR_ACTIVECAPTION	COLOR_INACTIVECAPTION
COLOR_MENU	COLOR_WINDOW
COLOR_WINDOWFRAME	COLOR_MENUTEXT
COLOR_WINDOWTEXT	COLOR_CAPTIONTEXT
COLOR_ACTIVEBORDER	COLOR_INACTIVEBORDER
COLOR_APPWORKSPACE	COLOR_HIGHLIGHT
COLOR_HIGHLIGHTTEXT	COLOR_BTNFACE
COLOR_BTNSHADOW	COLOR_GRAYTEXT
COLOR_BTNTEXT	

Text Format

Use one of the tags listed below to format the text value of a dimension. These tags must be enclosed in single quotes and it is not case sensitive. You can combine tags within the single quotes to set multiple attributes.

```
<B> Bold
<I> Italic
<U> Underline
<>  Remove Formatting (no formatting)
```

Examples of these tags as they would appear in the expression editor:

```
=’<B>’
=’<B><I>’
```

Background Color

This allows you to override the background color of an object element in the same manner as that for text color. See the text color examples for how to do this. The only difference is that you are selecting a different attribute.

Line Format

For some objects, such as line charts, you will see a line format option. In these cases you can add tags that affect how lines appear. There are two types of tags, one for the style of the line and one for the width of the line:

`<Wn>` Width of the line where *“n”* is a numeric value that can include decimals.
`<Sn>` Style of the line where *“n”* is a numeric value. The following table shows which numbers relate to various line styles.

1 = Solid Line
2 = Dashed Line
3 = Dotted Line
4 = Dash-Dot-Dash

Also, note that you can make the various settings conditional based on the results of an expression. This allows you to show different types of lines for different conditions and states in a multi-lined line chart. The following example illustrates how to use these values in the expression editor:

```
=’<W2>’
='<W1.5><S2>'
=’<W1.5><S1>’
=’<W3>’
=if (Region=’OH’,’<S2>’,’<S1>’)
=if (count(Region) > 1,’<S2>’,’<S1>’)
```

The *Pie Slice* Attribute for Pie Charts

This attribute allows you to separate a slice of a pie chart to make the chart more readable and visually appealing. This is done by setting the attribute to a numeric value that is greater than zero. It can be done conditionally on a dimension value, making it possible to separate a given slice from the rest of the pie, or by simply passing a single value to separate all slices from each other (exploded view). By setting the value to zero, no separation of the slices will occur in the chart. The following examples illustrate the proper expression syntax to use:

```
=if ([Product Category]='Office Equipment',1,0)
=1
=0
```

The *Show Value* Attribute

Set this expression attribute by adding an expression of either =1 for true or =0 for false to force the respective values on the bars of a *bar* chart. This overrides the Expression property *Values on Data Points*, which also forces the display of values on the bars. However, it only overrides for the "true" or "1" setting. Setting the attribute to zero won't hide the values on the bars if you have checked the *Values on Data Points* checkbox. This attribute doesn't seem to work for some charts such as *pie* charts. Because this attribute will override the default behavior of not showing values on bars, it can conditionally show values based on expression logic. The following examples illustrate the proper expression syntax to use:

```
=if ([Order Count]>=3,1,0)
=1
```

Formatting Masks (numbers, dates etc.)

QlikView provides a variety of data formatting features. In some cases, the mechanisms for controlling how data is formatted are built into the dialogs such as with *Numbers* for chart expressions. In other cases you may need to apply formatting in the expression or script syntax. This section provides some examples and overview.

Chart Numbers (Format Pattern)

Charts must include at least one expression to determine the values shown in the chart. There is a *Numbers* tab that controls number formatting on the properties dialog for each chart. The dialog allows for quick and easy selections, but you can also create custom format patterns and enter them directly in to the *Format Pattern* text box. This format pattern affects how the data is presented and not necessarily how the numbers in the legend or along the Y axis appear. Here are some examples:

```
###,###.##0 K        12,034.100 K
```

General Keyboard Shortcuts

The following key combinations can be used to bypass the mouse and perform the corresponding functions from the keyboard in QlikView for Windows. If you right click on the toolbar in QlikView for Windows and select *Customize,* and then click the tab named *Options,* you can enable an option named *"Show shortcut keys in ScreenTips."* This will allow you to see the corresponding shortcuts when you point your mouse at the icons in the toolbars. Here are few of the more common shortcuts:

- **Ctrl+Shift+Q: Document Support Information:** This launches a dialog that provides information about the document and other information related to the QlikView version installed on the local workstation. It also includes the License Key, Client Build Number, and Operating System information. It allows you to copy this information as text to the Windows clipboard.
- **Ctrl+Shift+O: Connect to Server dialog box:** Launches the dialog that allows you to connect to a QlikView server and open a document on the server.

- **Ctrl+Q: Current Selections Box:** Launches a dialog box that shows the current selections. This is not the same as the sheet object and does not become part of the document.
- **Ctrl+E: Edit Script:** Launches the script editor dialog, which allows you to review and edit the document's connections and load script.
- **Ctrl+R: Reload Script:** This performs a reload of the document data.
- **Ctrl+T: Table Viewer:** Launches the table viewer, which shows the in-memory data model for your QlikView document.
- **Ctrl+O: Open:** Launches the QlikView file-open dialog for opening a QlikView document (.QVW).
- **Ctrl+S: Save:** Performs a save of the current QlikView document.
- **Ctrl+G: Turn Grid on/off:** Shows or hides the alignment-grid on the tab sheets.
- **Ctrl+M: Edit Module:** Launches the dialog that allows you to edit the code module for macro functionality in the document.
- **Ctrl+N: New:** Creates a new QlikView document and makes it the active document.
- **Ctrl+B: Add Bookmark:** Launches the dialog that allows you to create a new bookmark based on the current user selections.
- **Ctrl+Shift+L** and **Ctrl+Shift+U: Lock/Unlock:** Performs a lock/unlock of the current user selections respectively.
- **Ctrl+Shift+Z** and **Ctrl+Shift+Y: Undo/Redo Layout:** Performs undo or redo respectively of the last change you made to the layout of the document.
- **Alt+Enter: Object Properties:** Launches the properties dialog for the currently selected sheet object.
- **Ctrl+Q+Q**

- Used in the load script to produce standard syntax for generating different types of data. This is useful when you need to derive and augment data with system generated values.

Using Keyboard Shortcuts and the Mouse to Manipulate Charts

It is not commonly known that QlikView allows you to manipulate chart layout in a semi-free form manner. Holding down the *Ctrl* and *Sift* keys (**Ctrl+Shift**) simultaneously allows you to adjust the size and position of chart's plot area. Other areas of the chart, such as the legend area in a pie chart, may also become adjustable in some cases. Each movable part of the chart will appear in a red rectangle. You can then hover over an edge of the rectangle and click and drag to resize it. For example, you can move the chart title and resize the bar or pie area. You can also move and resize the legend. To move an item, position the mouse over the center of the desired red rectangle and click and drag. Keep in mind that you can *undo* your changes using the undo/redo options or keyboard shortcuts. Not all chart parts are movable and sizable.

QlikView Command Line Options

It is possible to control how QlikView for Windows behaves by passing a variety of command line options when launching it in Windows. To do this you must run the QlikView executable file (qv.exe), which is commonly found in the QlikView directory under the appropriate "Program Files" directory in Windows. This directory location varies depending on the version of Windows and if you are running a 64 bit or 32 bit version of QlikView. A command line should follow this pattern:

```
qv.exe [options] doc_path_and_name.qvw
```

These options are well documented in the QlikView reference guide, but here are the common options:

/r **Reload Switch:** This opens the document and reloads the data. When the data load completes, QlikView closes the document and closes itself.

/rp **Partial Reload:** This performs a partial reload and then closes the document and QlikView.

/l **Open and Load Data:** This opens the document and performs a reload of the data, but leaves the document open in QlikView. The document is not saved.

/lp **Open and Partially Load Data:** This opens the document and performs a partial reload of the data, but leaves the document open in QlikView. The document is not saved.

/v **Set a Variable:** This options is immediately followed by a variable name and assignment value. The variable is set to the value before the load script executes. Here's an example: `/vname_of_var=variable_value`

/nodata **Open with NoData:** This opens the document without allowing any data values for variables, table or field data.

/nosecurity **Security Override:** This option deactivates built in security features designed to guard against hostile code. This feature is targeted at macros and scripts embedded in the document. It also deactivates warning dialogs.

Made in United States
Orlando, FL
04 November 2026

90137916R00205